pp 35-36 missing

JOHN WILLIS'

SCREEN WORLD

1975

Volume 26

CROWN PUBLISHERS, INC.

419 PARK AVENUE SOUTH

NEW YORK, N.Y. 10016

T O

M A E W E S T

who, after more than six decades as an entertainer, remains
the archetypal sex symbol—a devilishly insinuating, sultry,
curvaceous, endearing legend. John Mason Brown aptly
wrote: "Sex is for her a cartoon which she delights in
animating. If she is a high priestess of desire, she is also its
most unabashed and hilarious parodist."

JACK NICHOLSON and FAYE DUNAWAY
in "Chinatown"

CONTENTS

EDITOR: JOHN WILLIS

Assistant Editor: Stanley Reeves

STAFF: Joe Baltake, Mark Cohen, Frances Crampon, Miles
Kreuger, Robert Maldonado, Don Nute, Evan Romero

ACKNOWLEDGMENTS: We wish to express our gratitude to the following who
helped make this volume possible: Karen Augusta, Stephanie Austin, Mike Berman,
Susan Bloch, Bernis Block, Kent Carroll, Philip Castanza, Ed Connor, Gary Crowdus,
Yvonne Cumberbatch, Alberta D'Angelo, Gary Dartnall, Roy Eisenberg, Caryl Feld-
man, Barry Fishel, Dawn Hanrahan, Sam Helfman, Hillary James, Mike Jusko, Sey-
mour Krawitz, Ely Landau, John Lee, Marvin Levey, Ruth Pologe Levinson, Arlene
Ludwig, Leonard Maltin, Ginny Martin, Tom Miller, Eric Naumann, Alexandria
Nikitas, Nancy O'Rourke, Ron Perkins, Alvin Player, Karen Raiman, Adam Reilly,
Arthur Rubine, William Shelble, Eve Segal, Sol Shiffrin, Hortense Shorr, Ted Spiegel,
John Springer, Larry Steinfeld, John Sutherland, Dan Talbot, Jerry Ticman, Jana Tran,
John Wiencko

1. Robert Redford

2. Clint Eastwood

3. Paul Newman

4. Barbra Streisand

5. Steve McQueen

6. Burt Reynolds

7. Charles Bronson

8. Jack Nicholson

9. Al Pacino

10. John Wayne

11. Dustin Hoffman

12. Woody Allen

13. James Caan

14. Liza Minnelli

15. Charlton Heston

16. Gene Hackman

TOP 25 BOX OFFICE STARS OF 1974

17. Jack Lemmon

18. Faye Dunaway

19. George C. Scott

20. Walter Matthau

1974 RELEASES

January 1 through December 31, 1974

21. Marlon Brando

22. George Segal

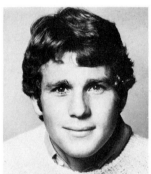

23. Ryan O'Neal

24. Roger Moore

25. Elliott Gould

Glenda Jackson

Jon Voight

Liv Ullmann

7

WILLIE DYNAMITE

(UNIVERSAL) Producers, Richard D. Zanuck, David Brown; Director, Gilbert Moses, III; Screenplay, Ron Cutler; Story, Joe Keyes, Jr., Ron Cutler; Photography, Frank Stanley; Art Director, John T. McCormack; Editor, Aaron Stell; Music, J. J. Johnson, Gilbert Moses, III; Sung by Martha Reeves and The Sweet Things; Costumes, Bernard Johnson; Assistant Directors, James Hogan, William Holbrook; Produced in association with Generation 70; In Technicolor; Rated R; 102 minutes; January release.

CAST

Willie	Roscoe Orman
Cora	Diana Sands
Robert Daniels	Thalmus Rasulala
Pashen	Joyce Walker
Bell	Roger Robinson
Celli	George Murdock
Pointer	Albert Hall
Honey	Norma Donaldson
Sola	Juanita Brown
Willie's Mother	Royce Wallace
Georgia	Judy Brown
Connie	Marilyn Coleman
Scatback	Mary Wilcox
Pearl	Marcia McBroom
Willie's Lawyer	Jack Bernardi
Sergeant	Ted Gehring
Cyrus	Ron Henriquez
Bailiff	Wynn Irwin
Sugar	Richard Lawson
Judge #1	Ken Lynch
Judge #2	Davis Roberts

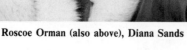

Roscoe Orman (also above), Diana Sands

Juanita Brown, Roger Robinson Above: Joyce Walker, Roscoe Orman Top: Diana Sands

RHINOCEROS

(AMERICAN FILM THEATRE) Executive Producer, Edward Lewis; Producer, Ely A. Landau; Director, Tom O'Horgan; Screenplay, Julian Barry; Adapted from play by Eugene Ionesco; Production Manager, Irving Temaner; Production Associate, Les Landau; Photography, Jim Crabe; Music, Galt MacDermot; Editor, Bud Smith; Design, Jack Martin Smith; Costumes, Noel Taylor; In color; Rated PG; 101 minutes; January release.

CAST

John	Zero Mostel
Stanley	Gene Wilder
Daisy	Karen Black
Carl	Robert Weil
Norman	Joe Silver
Mrs. Bingham	Marilyn Chris
Logician	Robert Fields
Young Woman	Melody Santangelo
Cashier	Lou Cutell
Waiter	Don Calfa
Lady with cat	Kathryn Harkin
Restaurant Owner	Lorna Thayer
Doctor	Howard Morton
Mr. Nicholson	Percy Rodrigues

Right: Zero Mostel, Gene Wilder

Karen Black, Gene Wilder Above: Robert Weil, Gene Wilder, Marilyn Chris, Joe Silver

Gene Wilder, Zero Mostel Above: Percy Rodrigues, Karen Black, Joe Silver, Robert Weil

9

BUSTING

(UNITED ARTISTS) Producers, Irwin Winkler, Robert Chartoff; Direction and Screenplay, Peter Hyams; Music, Billy Goldenberg; Photography, Earl Rath; Editor, James Mitchell; In color; Rated R; 92 minutes; February release.

CAST

Michael Keneely	Elliott Gould
Patrick Farrel	Robert Blake
Carl Rizzo	Allen Garfield
Stephen	Antonio Fargas
Marvin	Michael Lerner
Rizzo's Bouncer	Sid Haig
Judge Simpson	Ivor Francis
Sgt. Kenfick	John Lawrence
Jackie	Cornelia Sharp
Weldman	William Sylvester
Dr. Berman	Logan Ramsey
Desk Sergeant	Richard X. Slattery

Right: Elliott Gould, Robert Blake

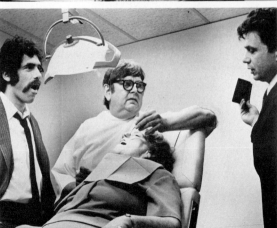

Elliott Gould, Cornelia Sharp

Elliott Gould, Logan Ramsey, Robert Blake
Above: Michael Lerner, Elliott Gould

10

McQ

(WARNER BROS.) Producers, Jules Levy, Arthur Gardner; Written and Co-Produced by Lawrence Roman; Director, John Sturges; Photography, Harry Stradling, Jr.; Designer, Walter Simonds; Editor, William Ziegler; Executive Producer, Michael A. Wayne; Music, Elmer Bernstein; Assistant Directors, Ron R. Rondell, Ric Rondell; In Panavision and Technicolor; A Batjac and Levy-Gardner Production; Rated PG; 116 minutes; February release.

CAST

McQ	John Wayne
Kosterman	Eddie Albert
Myra	Colleen Dewhurst
Toms	Clu Gulager
Pinky	David Huddleston
J. C.	Jim Watkins
Santiago	Al Lettieri
Elaine Forrester	Julie Adams
Rosey	Robert E. Mosley
Stan Boyle	William Bryant
LaSalle	Joe Tornatore
Radical	Richard Kelton
Walter Forrester	Richard Eastham
Bob Mahoney	Dick Friel
Bodyguard	Fred Waugh

Right: John Wayne

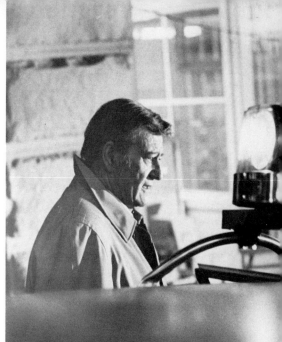

**John Wayne, and above with
Diana Muldaur**

**John Wayne, Diana Muldaur
Above: Al Lettieri, John Wayne**

THIEVES LIKE US

(UNITED ARTISTS) Executive Producer, George Litto; Producer, Jerry Bick; Associate Producers, Robert Eggenweiler, Thomas Hal Philips; Director, Robert Altman; Assistant Director, Tommy Thompson; Photography, Jean Boffety; Editor, Lou Lombardo; Screenplay, Calder Willingham, Joan Tewkesbury, Robert Altman; Based on novel by Edward Anderson; In color; Rated R; 123 minutes; February release.

CAST

Bowie	Keith Carradine
Keechie	Shelly Duvall
Chicamaw	John Schuck
T-Dub	Bert Remsen
Mattie	Louise Fletcher
Lula	Ann Latham
Dee Mobley	Tom Skerritt
Capt. Stammers	Al Scott
Jasbo	John Roper
Noel	Mary Waits
James Mattingly	Rodney Lee, Jr.
Alvin	William Watters
Lady in train station	Joan Tewkesbury
Bank Hostages	Edward Fisher, Josephine Bennett, Howard Warner
Mrs. Stammers	Eleanor Matthews
Woman in accident	Pam Warner
Coco-Cola Girl	Suzanne Majure
Sheriffs	Walter Cooper, Lloyd Jones

Left: Shelley Duvall, Keith Carradine

Ann Latham, Bert Remsen

Shelley Duvall

Ann Latham, Bert Remsen
Top: Louise Fletcher, Shelley Duvall

Keith Carradine, Shelley Duvall
Top: Al Scott, John Schuck, Keith Carradine

13

WHERE THE LILLIES BLOOM

(UNITED ARTISTS) Producer, Robert B. Radnitz; Director, William A. Graham; Screenplay, Earl Hamner, Jr.; Based on book by Vera and Bill Cleaver; Photography, Urs Furrer; Music, Earl Scruggs; Performed by the Earl Scruggs Revue; Editor, Nick Brown; Title song composed and sung by Barbara Mauritz; In color; Rated G; 97 minutes; February release.

CAST

Mary Call	Julie Gholson
Devola	Jan Smithers
Romey	Matthew Burrill
Ima Dean	Helen Harmon
Miss Fleetie	Sudie Bond
Roy Luther	Rance Howard
Connell	Tom Spratley
Goldie Pease	Alice Beardsley
Mrs. Connell	Helen Bragdon
Kiser Pease	Harry Dean Stanton

**Right: Julie Gholson, Matthew Burrill
Top: Jan Smithers, Harry Dean Stanton**

Julie Gholson, Harry Dean Stanton, Jan Smithers, Matthew Burrill Above: Helen Harmon

Matthew Burrill, Helen Harmon, Jan Smithers, Julie Gholson

MAN ON A SWING

(PARAMOUNT) Producer, Howard B. Jaffe; Director, Frank Perry; Screenplay, David Zelag Goodman; Photography, Adam Holender; Music, Lalo Schifrin; Designer, Joel Schiller; Editor, Sidney Katz; Assistant Directors, Louis A. Stroller, Bill Eustace; Costumes, Ruth Morley; In color; Rated PG; 110 minutes; February release.

CAST

Lee Tucker	Cliff Robertson
Franklin Wills	Joel Grey
Janet Tucker	Dorothy Tristan
Dr. Anna Willson	Elizabeth Wilson
Dr. Nicholas Holmar	George Voskovec
Dr. Philip Fusco	Ron Weyand
Willie Younger	Peter Masterson
Ted Ronan	Lane Smith
Dan Lloyd	Joe Ponazecki
Richie Tom Keating	Christopher Allport
Diana Spenser	Patricia Hawkins
Man in motel	Richard Venture
Maggie Dawson	Dianne Hull
Donald Forbes	Gil Gerard
Mr. Dawson	Richard Dryden
Mrs. Dawson	Alice Drummond
Sam Gallagher	Richard McKenzie
Father Connally	Brendan Fay
Mrs. Brennan	Clarice Blackburn
Paul Kearney	Nicholas Pryor
Peter Russell	Josef Sommer
Steve Barron	Shawn Campbell
Ronnie	Benjamin Slack
Coach	Clarence Felder
Evelyn Moore	Penelope Milford
Check-out Man	Bruce French
Mrs. Segretta	Loretta Fury
Plant Manager	Roy Mason
Man in plant	James Galvin

Cliff Robertson, Joel Grey (also above)
Top: Robertson, Richard McKenzie, Peter Masterson

Top: George Voskovec, Cliff Robertson, Joel Grey, Peter Masterson Below: Grey, Robertson

BLAZING SADDLES

(WARNER BROS) Producer, Michael Hertzberg; Director, Mel Brooks; Screenplay, Mel Brooks, Norman Steinberg, Andrew Bergman, Richard Pryor, Alan Uger; Story, Andrew Bergman; Photography, Joseph Biroc; Designer, Peter Wooley; Editors, John C. Howard, Danford Greene; Music, John Morris; Title song (John Morris, Mel Brooks) sung by Frankie Laine; Choreography, Alan Johnson; Costumes, N. Novarese; Assistant Director, John C. Chulay; A Crossbow Production; In Panavision and Technicolor; Rated R; 93 minutes; February release.

CAST

Bart	Cleavon Little
Jim	Gene Wilder
Taggart	Slim Pickens
Olson Johnson	David Huddleston
Rev. Johnson	Liam Dunn
Mongo	Alex Karras
Howard Johnson	John Hillerman
Van Johnson	George Furth
Gabby Johnson	Claude E. Starrett, Jr.
Gov. Lepetomane/Indian Chief	Mel Brooks
Hedley Lamarr	Harvey Korman
Lili Von Shtupp	Madeline Kahn
Harriett Johnson	Carol Arthur
Charlie	Charles McGregor
Miss Stein	Robyn Hilton
Buddy Bizarre	Dom DeLuise
Dr. Sam Johnson	Richard Collier
Gum Chewer	Don Megowan
Cut Throat #1	Karl Lukas
Lyle	Burton Gilliam
Count Basie	Himself

Left: Cleavon Little (on horse), also Top Right with Gene Wilder

Gene Wilder, Cleavon Little

Harvey Korman, Madeline Kahn

Madeline Kahn Above: Harvey Korman,
Mel Brooks Top: Kahn, Cleavon Little

Top: Cleavon Little, Alex Karras

MAME

(WARNER BROS) Producers, Robert Fryer, James Cresson; Director, Gene Saks; Screenplay, Paul Zindel; Based on musical by Jerome Lawrence, Robert E. Lee, Jerry Herman; Art Director, Harold Michelson; Music and Lyrics, Jerry Herman; Choreography, Onna White; Costumes, Theodora van Runkle; Assistant Directors, Jack Aldworth, Jim Benjamin, Jerry Lee Ballew; In Panavision and Technicolor; Rated PG; 132 minutes; March release.

CAST

Mame	Lucille Ball
Beauregard	Robert Preston
Vera	Beatrice Arthur
Older Patrick	Bruce Davison
Sally Cato	Joyce Van Patten
Mr. Upson	Don Porter
Mrs. Upson	Audrey Christie
Agnes Gooch	Jane Connell
Young Patrick	Kirby Furlong
Mr. Babcock	John McGiver
Gloria Upson	Doria Cook
Pegeen	Bobbi Jordan
Ito	George Chiang

Top Right: Lucille Ball

Lucille Ball, Jane Connell Above:
Lucille Ball (on moon)

Lucille Ball Above: Lucille Ball,
Robert Preston

LOVIN' MOLLY

(COLUMBIA) Producer, Stephen Friedman; Based on novel "Leaving Cheyenne" by Larry McMurtry; Director, Sidney Lumet; Photography, Edward Brown; Editor, Joanne Burke; Music, Fred Hellerman; In color; Rated R; 98 minutes; March release.

CAST

Gid	Anthony Perkins
Johnny	Beau Bridges
Molly	Blythe Danner
Mr. Fry	Edward Binns
Sarah	Susan Sarandon
Eddie	Conard Fowkes
Mr. Taylor	Claude Traverse
Mr. Grinsom	John Henry Faulk

Right: Anthony Perkins, Blythe Danner

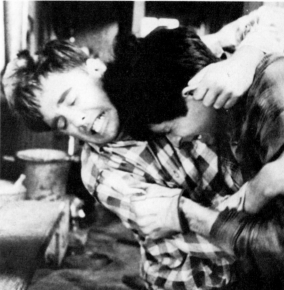

Beau Bridges, Anthony Perkins
Above: Blythe Danner, Anthony Perkins

Beau Bridges, Blythe Danner
Above: Bridges, Anthony Perkins

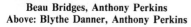

19

THE GREAT GATSBY

(PARAMOUNT) Producer, David Merrick; Director, Jack Clayton; Associate Producer, Hank Moonjean; Photography, Douglas Slocombe; Designer, John Box; Music, Nelson Riddle; Costumes, Theoni V. Aldredge; Screenplay, Francis Ford Coppola; Based on novel by F. Scott Fitzgerald; Editor, Tom Priestley; Art Directors, Eugene Rudolf, Robert Laing; Assistant Director, David Tringham; In Eastmancolor; Rated PG; 144 minutes; March release.

CAST

Jay Gatsby	Robert Redford
Daisy Buchanan	Mia Farrow
Tom Buchanan	Bruce Dern
Myrtle Wilson	Karen Black
George Wilson	Scott Wilson
Nick Carraway	Sam Waterston
Jordan Baker	Lois Chiles
Meyer Wolfsheim	Howard DaSilva
Mr. Gatz	Roberts Blossom
Klipspringer	Edward Herrmann
Wilson's Friend	Elliot Sullivan
Gatsby's Bodyguard	John Devlin
Mourner	Tom Ewell
Twins	Janet and Louise Arters

1974 Academy Awards for Best Costume Design, Best Scoring

Left: Robert Redford

Mia Farrow, Robert Redford

Sam Waterston, Mia Farrow **Above:** Bruce Dern, Lois Chiles, Farrow, Waterston, Robert Redford

Robert Redford, Mia Farrow Above: Scott Wilson,
Sam Waterston, Lois Chiles Top: Karen Black

Mia Farrow, Robert Redford
Top: Bruce Dern

THE SUGARLAND EXPRESS

(UNIVERSAL) Producers, Richard D. Zanuck, David Brown; Director, Steven Spielberg; Screenplay, Hal Barwood, Matthew Robbins; Story, Steven Spielberg, Hal Barwood, Matthew Robbins; Production Executive, William S. Gilmore, Jr.; Photography, Vilmos Zsigmond; Art Director, Joseph Alves, Jr.; Editors, Edward M. Abroms, Verna Fields; Music, John Williams; Assistant Directors, James Fargo, Thomas Joyner; In Technicolor and Panavision; Rated PG; 108 minutes; March release.

CAST

Lou Jean .... Goldie Hawn
Capt. Tanner .... Ben Johnson
Slide .... Michael Sacks
Clovis .... William Atherton
Mashburn .... Gregory Walcott
Jessup .... Steve Kanaly
Mrs. Looby .... Louise Latham
Baby Langston .... Harrison Zanuck
Mr. Nocker .... A. L. Camp
Mrs. Nocker .... Jessie Lee Fulton
Russ Berry .... Dean Smith
Dietz .... Ted Grossman
Hunter .... Bill Thurman
Standby .... Kenneth Hudgins
Drunk .... Buster Danials
Mark Fenno .... Jim Harrell
Logan Waters .... Frank Steggall
Hot Jock #1 .... Roger Ernest
Hot Jock #2 .... Guich Koock
Looby .... Merrill L. Connally
Gas Jockey .... Gene Rader
Hubie Nocker .... Gordon Hurst
Sparrow .... George Hagy
Big John .... Big John Hamilton
Deputy .... Kenneth Crone
Judge .... Judge Peter Michael Curry
Attorney.. Charles Conaway
and Robert Golden, Rudy Robbins (Mechanic), Charlie Dobbs (Cop), Gene Lively (Reporter), John L. Quinlan III (Bailiff), Bill Scott (Station Man), Ralph E. Horwedel (Dispatcher), Edwin "Frog" Isbell (Jelly Bowl)

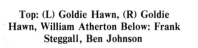

Top: (L) Goldie Hawn, (R) Goldie Hawn, William Atherton Below: Frank Steggall, Ben Johnson

Goldie Hawn Above: William Atherton, Goldie Hawn, Michael Sacks

CONRACK

(20th CENTURY-FOX) Producers, Martin Ritt, Harriet Frank, Jr.; Director, Martin Ritt; Screenplay, Irving Ravetch, Harriet Frank, Jr.; Based on "The Water Is Wide" by Pat Conroy; Photography, John Alonzo; Music, John Williams; Designer, Walter Scott Herndon; Associate Producer, Richard Kobritz; Assistant Directors, Irby Smith, Anthony Brand; Editor, Frank Bracht; In Panavision and DeLuxe Color; Rated PG; 107 minutes; March release.

CAST

Pat Conroy	Jon Voight
Mad Billy	Paul Winfield
Skeffington	Hume Cronyn
Mrs. Scott	Madge Sinclair
Mary	Tina Andrews
Quickfellow	Antonio Fargas
Edna	Ruth Attaway
Little Man	James O'Reare

The Class:

Mac	MacArthur Nelson
William	William Hunter III
Kathy	Kathy Turner
LaCrisia	LaCrisia Hardee
Freida	Freida Williams
Johnny	Johnny Bell
Margaret	Margaret Perry
Cathy	Cathy Wilson
Rosemary	Rosemary Miller
Ronnie	Ronnie Leggett
Veola	Veola Clements
Ronny	Ronny Harris
Rickey	Rickey Walker
Rebecca	Rebecca Cobbs
Anthony	Anthony Demery
Dennis	Dennis Williams
Kevin	Kevin Perry
Top Cat	Ellis Lamar Cash
Deborah	Deborah Jones
Carlos	Carlos Chambliss
John	John Kennedy

**Right: Hume Cronyn, Jon Voight
Top: MacArthur Nelson, Jon Voight**

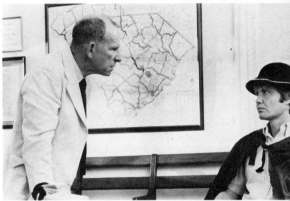

**Jon Voight, also above
with Madge Sinclair**

Jon Voight, Paul Winfield

23

BADLANDS

(WARNER BROS.) Produced, Directed, and Written by Terrence Malick; Executive Producer, Edward R. Pressman; Photography Brian Probyn, Tak Fujimoto, Stevan Larner; Art Director, Jack Fisk; Editor, Robert Estrin; Music, George Tipton; Associate Producer, Lou Stroller; Assistant Directors, John Broderick, Carl Olsen; A Jill Jakes Production; In color; Rated PG; 95 minutes. March release.

CAST

Kit	Martin Sheen
Holly	Sissy Spacek
Father	Warren Oates
Cato	Ramon Bieri
Deputy	Alan Vint
Sheriff	Gary Littlejohn
Rich Man	John Carter
Boy	Bryan Montgomery
Girl	Gail Threlkeld
Clerk	Charles Fitzpatrick
Boss	Howard Ragsdale
Trooper on plane	John Womack, Jr.
Maid	Dona Baldwin
Gas Station Attendant	Ben Bravo

Left: Martin Sheen

Martin Sheen, Sissy Spacek

Sissy Spacek, Martin Sheen
Top: (L) Warren Oates, (R) Sissy Spacek

THE CONVERSATION

(PARAMOUNT) Produced, Directed, and Written by Francis Ford Coppola; Co-Producer, Fred Roos; Associate Producer, Mona Skager; Music, David Shire; Photography, Bill Butler; Designer, Dean Tavoularis; Editors, Walter Murch, Richard Chew; Assistant Director, Chuck Myers; In Technicolor; Rated PG; 113 minutes; April release

CAST

Harry Caul	Gene Hackman
Stan	John Cazale
Bernie Moran	Allen Garfield
Mark	Frederick Forrest
Ann	Cindy Williams
Paul	Michael Higgins
Meredith	Elizabeth MacRae
Amy	Teri Garr
Martin Stett	Harrison Ford
Receptionist	Mark Wheeler
The Mime	Robert Shields
Lurleen	Phoebe Alexander

Left: Gene Hackman

Teri Garr, Gene Hackman

Gene Hackman, Cindy Williams, Frederic Forrest

Elizabeth MacRae, Gene Hackman
Top: Michael Higgins, Gene Hackman

Gene Hackman, also top with
Mark Wheeler

CLAUDINE

(20th CENTURY-FOX) Executive Producer, J. Lloyd Grant; Producer, Hannah Weinstein; Director, John Berry; Screenplay, Tina and Lester Pine; Associate Producer, Dick Di Bona; Music, Curtis Mayfield; Performed by Gladys Knight and The Pips; Photography, Gayne Rescher; Designer, Ted Haworth; Art Director, Ben Kasazkow; Editor, Luis San Andres; Assistant Director, Burt Bluestein; Costumes, Bernard Johnson; A Third World Cinema Production; In DeLuxe Color; Rated PG; 92 minutes; April release.

CAST

Claudine	Diahann Carroll
Roop	James Earl Jones
Charles	Lawrence Hington-Jacobs
Charlene	Tamu
Paul	David Kruger
Patrice	Yvette Curtis
Francis	Eric Jones
Lurlene	Socorro Stephens
Owen	Adam Wade
Minister	Harrison Avery
Process Server	Mordecai Lawner
Teddy	Terry Alexander
Dance Teacher	Carolyn Adams
Cops	Bob Scarantino, Bill Bressant
Miss Kabak	Elisa Loti
Mrs. Winston	Roxie Roker
Delivery Boy	David Blackwell
Bar Woman	Jay Van Leer
Bus Women	Judy Mills, Alyce Webb, Lil Henderson, Yvonne Sutherland
Mr. Winograd	Bernie Barrow
Mrs. Winograd	Joan Kaye
Sanitation Foreman	Stefan Gierasch
Cool Cat	Tim Pelt
Dice Man	Charles Cleveland
Prostitute	Sandi Franklin
Gospel Leader	Rev. Carlton Coleman
Young Brothers	Lee Dupree, Ralph Wilcox, Arthur Evans
Stunt Cops	Alex Steven, Harry Madsen

**Left: Diahann Carroll, Socorro Stephens
Top: Diahann Carroll, James Earl Jones**

James Earl Jones, Diahann Carroll

James Earl Jones

Diahann Carroll

THE SUPER COPS

(MGM) Producer, William Belasco; Director, Gordon Parks; Screenplay, Lorenzo Semple, Jr.; Based on book by L. H. Whittmore; Music, Jerry Fielding; Photography, Dick Kratina; Art Director, Stephen Hendrickson; Assistant Director, Kurt Baker; Editor, Harry Howard; In Metrocolor; Rated R; 94 minutes; March release.

CAST

Greenberg	Ron Leibman
Hantz	David Selby
Sara	Sheila E. Frazier
Lt. Novick	Pat Hingle
Krasna	Dan Frazier
Lt. O'Shaughnessy	Joseph Sirola
Judge Kellner	Arny Freeman
D. A. Heller	Bernard Kates
Carlos	Alex Colon
Joe Hayes	Charles Turner
John Hayes	Ralph Wilcox
Frank Hayes	Al Fann
Detective Basoff	David Greenberg
Detective Neel	Robert Hantz
Billy	Norman Bush
Victor	Arthur French
Girl	Tamu
Angel	Hector Troy
Old Sarge	Charles White
Instructor	Ralph Strait
Lt.-Gym Instructor	Joseph P. McCartney
Capt. Busch	Pat Corley
Capt. Arbow	Albert Henderson
Lt. Stratton	Barton Heyman

**Right: Robert Hantz, David Greenberg
Top: Ron Leibman, Sheila Frazier**

Ron Leibman, David Selby

David Selby, Ron Leibman

THUNDERBOLT AND LIGHTFOOT

(UNITED ARTISTS) Producer, Robert Daley; Direction and Screenplay, Michael Cimino; Photography, Frank Stanley; Art Director, Tambi Larsen; Editor, Ferris Webster; Music, Dee Barton; A Malpaso Company Film; In Panavision and Color; Rated R; 115 minutes; May release.

CAST

Thunderbolt	Clint Eastwood
Lightfoot	Jeff Bridges
Goody	Geoffrey Lewis
Melody	Catherine Bach
Curly	Garey Busey
Red Leary	George Kennedy
Vault Manager	Jack Dodson
Tourist	Gene Elman
Welder	Burton Gilliam
Dunlop	Roy Jenson
Secretary	Claudia Lennear
Crazy Driver	Bill McKinney
Mario	Vic Tayback

Right: Jeff Bridges, George Kennedy, Clint Eastwood, Geoffrey Lewis

Clint Eastwood, Jeff Bridges, also above with Catherine Bach

George Kennedy Above: Jeff Bridges, George Kennedy, Clint Eastwood

NEWMAN'S LAW

(UNIVERSAL) Producer, Richard Irving; Director, Richard Heffron; Associate Producer, Herb Wright; Screenplay, Anthony Wilson; Photography, Vilis Lapenieks; Art Director, Alexander A. Mayer; Editor, John Dumas; Assistant Directors, John Gaudioso, William Holbrook; An MCA Presentation; In Technicolor; Rated PG; 98 minutes; May release.

CAST

Vince Newman	George Peppard
Garry	Roger Robinson
Reardon	Eugene Roche
Eastman	Gordon Pinsent
Dellanzia	Abe Vigoda
Falcone	Louis Zorich
Frank Acker	Michael Lerner
Jimenez	Victor Campos
Quist	Mel Stewart
Beutel	Jack Murdock
Hinney	David Spielberg
Jaycee	Theodore Wilson
Sharon	Pat Anderson
Clement	Regis J. Cordic
Edie	Marlene Clark
Assistant Coroner	Kip Niven
Immigration Man	Richard Bull
Spink	Howard Platt
Conrad	Dick Balduzzi
Matron	Penelope Gillette
First Assistant	Kirk Mee
Real Estate Agent	Don Hanmer
Gino	Antony Carbone
Cop #1	Jude Farese
Baines	Stack Pierce
Dashiki	Jac Emel
Ginger	Donald Newsome
Grainie	Titos Vandis
7 year old black boy	Wilbert Gowdy
Pants	Louis J. DiFonzo
Hooker on stairwell	Dea St. Lamont

George Peppard, Pat Anderson
Above: George Peppard (C)

Top: (L) Stack Pierce, George Peppard
(R) Roger Robinson, George Peppard

LOST IN THE STARS

(AMERICAN FILM THEATRE) Producer, Ely A. Landau; Director, Daniel Mann; Screenplay, Alfred Hayes; Based on novel "Cry the Beloved Country" by Alan Paton; Book and Lyrics, Maxwell Anderson; Music, Kurt Weill; Executive Producer, Edward Lewis; Assistant Directors, Reggie Callow, Les Landau; Photography, Robert Hauser; Editor, Walt Hannemann; Art Director, Jack Martin Smith; In color; Rated G; 114 minutes; May release.

CAST

Stephen Kumalo	Brock Peters
Irina	Melba Moore
John Kumalo	Raymond St. Jacques
Absalom	Clifton Davis
Rose	Paula Kelly
James Jarvis	Paul Rogers
Judge	John Williams
Carmichael	Ivor Barry
Arthur Jarvis	Harvey Jason
Matthew	Alan Weeks
Alex	H. B. Barnum III
Grace	Pauline Myers
Johannes	Ji-Tu Cumbuka
Van Jarsdale	John Holland
Paulus	John Hawker
Linda	Myrna White
Edward Jarvis	Michael-James Wixted
Eland	William Glover

Right: Clifton Davis, Melba Moore

Brock Peters, Raymond St. Jacques
Above: Pauline Myers, Brock Peters

Melba Moore, Brock Peters
Above: Brock Peters, Paul Rogers

DAISY MILLER

(PARAMOUNT) Producer-Director, Peter Bogdanovich; Screenplay, Frederic Raphael; Based on story by Henry James; Associate Producer, Frank Marshall; Photography, Albert Spagnoli; Art Director, Ferdinando Scarfiotti; Costumes, John Furness; Editor, Verna Fields; Assistant Director, Tony Brandt; A Copa de Oror Production; A Directors Company Presentation; In color; Rated G; 91 minutes; May release.

CAST

Annie P. "Daisy" Miller	Cybill Shepherd
Frederick Winterbourne	Barry Brown
Mrs. Ezra B. Miller	Cloris Leachman
Mrs. Costello	Mildred Natwick
Mrs. Walker	Eileen Brennan
Giovanelli	Dulio Del Prete
Randolph C. Miller	James McMurtry
Charles	Nicholas Jones
Eugenio	George Morfogen
Hotel Receptionist in Vevey	Jean Pascal Bongard
Tutor	Albert Messmer
Polish Boys	Jacques Guhl, Hubert Geoldin
Man at Chillon	David Bush
Chillon Guide	Henry Hubinet
Miniaturist	Maurizio Lucci
Mrs. Walker's Butler	Tom Felleghy
Punch and Judy	Luigi Gabellone
Hotel Receptionists in Rome	John Bartha, Salamon Amedeo
Pianist	Renato Talvacchia
Opera Singer	Salvatore Lisitano
Doctor	Bondi Esterhazy
Mrs. Walker's Guests	Rodolfo Lodi, Elaine Olcott, Cesare Rotondi

Left: Cybill Shepherd

Cybill Shepherd, Barry Brown

Eileen Brennan, Nicholas Jones, Duilio Del Prete, Cybill Shepherd Above: Barry Brown, James McMurtry, Cloris Leachman

ZANDY'S BRIDE

(WARNER BROS.) Producer, Harvey Matofsky; Director, Jan Troell; Screenplay, Marc Norman; Based on "The Stranger" by Lillian Bos Ross; Photography, Jordan Cronenweth; Designer, Al Brenner; Editor, Gordon Scott; Music, Fred Karlin; Assistant Directors, Miles Middough, Barry Stern; Costumes, Pat Norris; In Panavision and Technicolor; Rated PG; 116 minutes; May release.

CAST

Zandy Allan	Gene Hackman
Hannah Lund	Liv Ullmann
Ma Allan	Eileen Heckart
Songer	Harry Dean Stanton
Frank Gallo	Joe Santos
Pa Allan	Frank Cady
Mel Allan	Sam Bottoms
Maria Cordova	Susan Tyrrell
Bill Pincus	Bob Simpson
Paco	Fabian Gregory Cordova
Farraday	Don Wilbanks
Street Girl	Vivian Gordon

Right: Liv Ullmann, Gene Hackman

Liv Ullmann, Susan Tyrrell
Above: Liv Ullmann, Gene Hackman

Liv Ullmann, Gene Hackman
Above: Eileen Heckart, Liv Ullmann

DIRTY MARY CRAZY LARRY

(20th CENTURY-FOX) Producer, Norman T. Herman; Associate Producer, Mickey Zide; Director, John Hough; Screenplay, Leigh Chapman, Antonio Santean; Based on novel "The Chase" by Richard Unekis; Music, Jimmy Haskell; Assistant Director, Ronald Schwary; Editor, Chris Holmes; Photography, Mike Marguleis; An Academy Pictures Production; In DeLuxe Color; Rated PG; 93 minutes; May release.

CAST

Larry	Peter Fonda
Mary	Susan George
Deke	Adam Roarke
Franklin	Vic Morrow
Hank	Fred Daniels
Stanton	Roddy McDowall
Evelyn	Lynn Borden
Cindy	Adrian Herman
Millie	Janear Hines
Dispatcher	Elizabeth James
Sur	William Campbell
Steve	John Castranova

Left: Susan George, Peter Fonda

Lyn Borden, Adam Roarke

Roddy McDowall
Top: Peter Fonda, Susan George, Adam Roarke

Vic Morrow, Ken Tobey

UPTOWN SATURDAY NIGHT

(WARNER BROS.) Producer, Melville Tucker; Director, Sidney Poitier; Screenplay, Richard Wesley; Photography, Fred J. Koenekamp; Designer, Alfred Sweeney; Associate Producer-Editor, Pembroke J. Herring; Music, Tom Scott; Title Song, Tom Scott, Morgan Ames; Sung by Dobie Gray; Assistant Directors, Bruce Chevillat, Charles C. Washburn; A Fine Artists Presentation; In Technicolor; Rated PG; 104 minutes; June release.

CAST

Steve Jackson	Sidney Poitier
Wardell Franklin	Bill Cosby
Geechie Dan Beauford	Harry Belafonte
Silky Slim	Calvin Lockhart
The Reverend	Flip Wilson
Sharp Eye Washington	Richard Pryor
Sarah Jackson	Rosalind Cash
Congressman Lincoln	Roscoe Lee Browne
Leggy Peggy	Paula Kelly
Madame Zenobia	Lee Chamberlin
Geechie's Henchman	Johnny Sekka
Slim's Henchman #1	Lincoln Kilpatrick
Irma Franklin	Ketty Lester
Slim's Henchman #2	Don Marshall
Little Seymour	Harold Nicholas

**Right: Sidney Poitier, Rosalind Cash
Top: Harry Belafonte, Calvin Lockhart**

Bill Cosby, Sidney Poitier Above: Johnny Sekka, Harry Belafonte, Poitier, Cosby

Bill Cosby, Sidney Poitier, and above with Harry Belafonte (C)

THE PARALLAX VIEW

(PARAMOUNT) Executive Producer, Gabriel Katzka; Producer-Director, Alan J. Pakula; Associate Producer, Charles Maguire; Screenplay, David Giler, Lorenzo Semple, Jr.; Based on novel by Loren Singer; Photography, Gordon Willis; Music, Michael Small; Editor, Jack Wheeler, Art Director, George Jenkins; Costumes, Frank Thompson; Assistant Directors, Howard W. Koch, Jr., John Poer; In Panavision and Technicolor; Rated R; 100 minutes; June release.

CAST

Frady	Warren Beatty
Lee Carter	Paula Prentiss
Austin	William Daniels
Jack	Walter McGinn
Rintels	Hume Cronyn
L. D.	Kelly Thordsen
Assassin (Busboy)	Chuck Waters
Red	Earl Hindman
Senator Carroll	Bill Joyce
Mrs. Carroll	Bettie Johnson
Art	Bill McKinney
Chrissy	Joanne Harris
Schecter	Ted Gehring
Shirley	Lee Pulford
Gale	Doria Cook
Hammond	Jim Davis
Organist	Joan Lemmo
Schwartzkopf	Anthony Zerbe
Turner	Kenneth Mars

Right: Warren Beatty, Hume Cronyn, Robert Lieb
Top: Warren Beatty, Paula Prentiss

Walter McGinn, Warren Beatty
Above: Warren Beatty, Doria Cook

Paula Prentiss, William Daniels
Above: Warren Beatty, Earl Hindman

HERBIE RIDES AGAIN

(BUENA VISTA) Producer, Bill Walsh; Director, Robert Stevenson; Screenplay, Bill Walsh; Based on story by Gordon Buford; Photography, Frank Phillips; Music, George Bruns; Art Directors, John B. Mansbridge, Walter Tyler, Editor, Cotton Warburton; Second Unit Director, Arthur J. Vitarelli; Set Decorator, Hal Gausman; Assistant Directors, Ronald R. Grow, Dorothy Kieffer; Costumes, Chuck Keehne, Emily Sundby; A Walt Disney Production; In Technicolor; Rated G; 88 minutes; June release.

CAST

Mrs. Steinmetz	Helen Hayes
Willoughby Whitfield	Ken Berry
Nicole	Stefanie Powers
Mr. Judson	John McIntire
Alonzo Hawk	Keenan Wynn
Judge	Huntz Hall
Chauffeur	Ivor Barry
Lawyer	Dan Tobin
Taxi Driver	Vito Scotti
Lawyer	Raymond Bailey
Doctor	Liam Dunn
Secretary	Elaine Devry
Loostgarten	Chuck McCann
Traffic Commissioner	Richard X. Slattery
Sir Lancelot	Hank Jones
Red Knight	Rod McCary

Left: Helen Hayes

Ken Berry, Helen Hayes in Herbie

Ken Berry, Helen Hayes Top: Stefanie
Powers, Helen Hayes, Ken Berry

Helen Hayes, John McIntire
Top: Keenan Wynn

43

THE GROOVE TUBE

(LEVITT-PICKMAN) Producer-Director, Ken Shapiro; Screenplay, Ken Shapiro, Lane Sarasohn; Photography, Bob Bailin; Associate Producer, Dale Bell; Animation, Linda Taylor, Pat O'Neill; A K-S Production; A Syn-Frank Enterprises Presentation; In color; Rated R; 75 minutes; June release.

CAST
Ken Shapiro
Richard Belzer
Buzzy Linhart
Chevy Chase
Christine Nazareth

and Richmond Baier, Paul Norman, Victoria Medlin, Jennifer Wells, Peter William Blaxill, Dennis Helfand, Frederick Stuthman, Lincoln Harrice, Berkeley Harris, William Paxton, Bill Kemmill, Alex Stephens, Bill Bailey, Lane Sarasohn, Mary Mendham

Right: Ken Shapiro

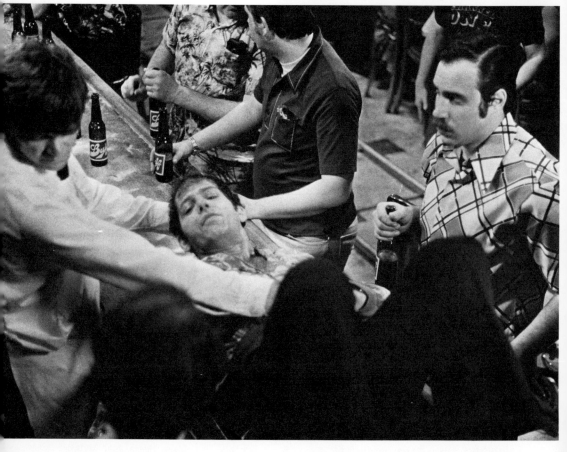

THE TERMINAL MAN

(WARNER BROS.) Produced, Directed, and Written by Mike Hodges; Based on novel by Michael Crichton; Photography, Richard H. Kline; Art Director, Fred Harpman; Editor, Robert Wolfe; Associate Producer, Michael Dryhurst; Costumes, Nino Novarese; Assistant Directors, Leonard S. Smith, Jr., Robert Dijoux, Dick Moder; In Technicolor; Rated PG; 104 minutes; June release.

CAST

Harry Benson	George Segal
Dr. Janet Ross	Joan Hackett
Dr. John Ellis	Richard A. Dysart
Angela Black	Jill Clayburgh
Dr. Arthur McPherson	Donald Moffat
Gerhard	Matt Clark
Dr. Robert Morris	Michael C. Gwynne
Detective Capt. Anders	Normann Burton
Dr. Ezra Manon	William Hansen
Ralph Friedman	James Sikking
The Priest	Ian Wolfe
Benson's Guards	Gene Borkan, Burke Byrnes
Richards	Jim Antonio
Questioner #1	Jordan Rhodes
Night Nurse	Dee Carroll
Instructor	Jason Wingreen
Edmonds	Steve Kanaly
Police Doctor	Fred Sadoff
Anesthetist	Robert Ito
Orderly	Victor Argo
Reporter	Lee DeBroux

Right: George Segal

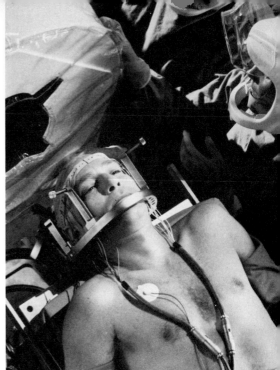

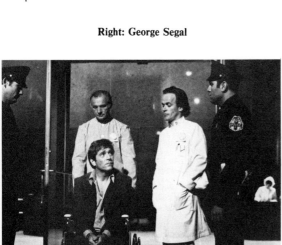

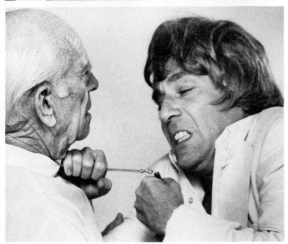

Ian Wolfe, George Segal
Above: George Segal, Michael Gwynne

Joan Hackett, George Segal

FOR PETE'S SAKE

(COLUMBIA) Co-Producers, Martin Erlichman, Stanley Shapiro; Executive Producer, Phil Feldman; Director, Peter Yates; Screenplay, Stanley Shapiro, Maurice Richlin; Photography, Laszlo Kovacs; Art Director, Gene Callaghan; Editor, Frank Keller; Costumes, Frank Thompson; Assistant Director, Harry Caplan; A Rastar Production; In color; Rated PG; 90 minutes; June release.

CAST

Henry	Barbra Streisand
Peter	Michael Sarrazin
Helen	Estelle Parsons
Fred	William Redfield
Mrs. Cherry	Molly Picon
Nick	Louis Zorich
Loretta	Vivian Bonnell
Bernie	Richard Ward
Judge Hiller	Heywood Hale Broun
Mr. Coates	Joe Maher
Check-out Man	Vincent Schiavelli
Loan Officer	Fred Stuthman
Angelo	Ed Bakey
Dominic	Peter Mamakos
First Worker	Norman Marshall
Second Cop	Joseph Hardy
Cop as woman	Wil Albert
Loanshark	Jack Hollander
Assistant Bank Manager	Gary Pagett
Insurance Man	Herb Armstrong
Lady in Supermarket	Bella Bruck
Telephone Lady	Anne Ramsey
Rocky	Bill McKinney
Drunk Driver	Sid Miller
Dog Trainer	Lew Burke
Man in theatre	Martin Erlichman

Left: Michael Sarrazin, Barbra Streisand

Barbra Streisand

Barbra Streisand
Top: Estelle Parsons, Barbra Streisand

Michael Sarrazin, Barbra Streisand
Above: John Hollander, Barbra Streisand

BUSTER AND BILLIE

(COLUMBIA) Producer, Ron Silverman; Executive Producer, Ted Mann; Screenplay, Ron Turbeville; Story, Ron Turbeville, Ron Baron; Director, Daniel Petrie; Photography, Mario Tosi; Editor, Michael Kahn; Music, Al DeLory; Songs, Hoyt Axton, Herbert "Happy" Lawson, Claude Casey, Troy L. Martin; Assistant Director, Lynn Guthrie; In color; Rated R; 100 minutes; June release.

CAST

Buster Lane	Jan-Michael Vincent
Billie	Joan Goodfellow
Margie Hooks	Pamela Sue Martin
Jake	Clifton James
Whitey	Robert Englund
Mrs. Lane	Jessie Lee Fulton
Mr. Lane	J. B. Joiner
Warren	Dell C. Payne

Left: Jan-Michael Vincent

Joan Goodfellow, Jan-Michael Vincent

Joan Goodfellow, Jan-Michael Vincent
Top: Robert Englund, Jan-Michael Vincent

THAT'S ENTERTAINMENT

(UNITED ARTISTS) Produced, Directed, and Written by Jack Haley, Jr.; Executive Producer, Daniel Melnick; Additional Music, Henry Mancini; Editors, Bud Friedgen, David E. Blewitt; Assistant Directors, Richard Bremerkamp, David Silver, Claude Binyon, Jr.; In Metrocolor; An MGM Presentation; Rated G; 132 minutes; June release.

Scenes from almost 100 MGM films made between 1929 and 1958, and narrated by Fred Astaire, Bing Crosby, Gene Kelly, Peter Lawford, Liza Minnelli, Donald O'Connor, Debbie Reynolds, Mickey Rooney, Frank Sinatra, James Stewart, Elizabeth Taylor

Right: Clark Gable in "Idiot's Delight"
Below: Louis Jourdan, Leslie Caron,
Maurice Chevalier in "Gigi"

"The Great Ziegfeld" Above: Ginger Rogers,
Fred Astaire in "Barkleys of Broadway"

Kathryn Grayson, Mario Lanza in "Toast of New
Orleans" Above: Gene Kelly, Leslie Caron in
"An American in Paris"

Jane Powell, Vic Damone, Ann Miller, Tony Martin,
Debbie Reynolds, Russ Tamblyn in "Hit the Deck"
Top: Ray Bolger, Jack Haley, Judy Garland, Bert Lahr
in "The Wizard of Oz"

Mickey Rooney, Judy Garland in "Babes on Broadway"
Above: June Allyson, Peter Lawford in "Good News"
Top: Nelson Eddy, Jeanette MacDonald in "Rose Marie"
Below: Cary Grant, Jean Harlow in "Suzy"

Frank Sinatra, Bing Crosby in "High Society"

CHINATOWN

(PARAMOUNT) Producer, Robert Evans; Director, Roman Polanski; Screenplay, Robert Towne; Photography, John A. Alonzo; Associate Producer, C. O. Erickson; Erickson; Music, Jerry Goldsmith; Costumes, Anthea Sylbert; Editor, Sam O'Steen; Designer, Richard Sylbert; Assistant Directors, Howard W. Koch, Jr., Michele Ader; Art Director, W. Stewart Campbell; Designers, Gage Resh, Robert Resh; In Panavision and Technicolor; Rated R; 131 minutes; June release.

CAST

J. J. Gittes	Jack Nicholson
Evelyn Mulwray	Faye Dunaway
Noah Cross	John Huston
Escobar	Perry Lopez
Yelburton	John Hillerman
Hollis Mulwray	Darrell Zwerling
Ida Sessions	Diane Ladd
Mulvihill	Roy Jenson
Man with knife	Roman Polanski
Loach	Dick Bakalyan
Walsh	Joe Mantell
Duffy	Bruce Glover
Sophie	Nandu Hinds
Lawyer	James O'Reare
Evelyn's Butler	James Hong
Maid	Beulah Quo
Gardener	Jerry Fujikawa
Katherine	Belinda Palmer
Mayor Bagby	Roy Roberts
Councilmen	Noble Willingham, Elliott Montgomery
Irate Farmer	Rance Howard
Barber	George Justin
Customer	Doc Erickson
Mulwray's Secretary	Fritzi Burr
Mortician	Charles Knapp
Boy on horseback	Claudio Martiniz
Cross' Butler	Frederico Roberto
Clerk	Allan Warnick
Curly	Burt Young
Curly's Wife	Elizabeth Harding
Mr. Palmer	John Rogers
Emma Dill	Cecil Elliott
Policemen	Paul Jenkins, Lee DeBroux, Bob Golden
Farmers in the valley	John Holland, Jesse Vint, Jim Burke, Denny Arnold

1974 Academy Award for Best Story and Screenplay

**Left: Jack Nicholson, Faye Dunaway
Top: Jack Nicholson**

**Jack Nicholson, Dick Bakalyan, Faye
Dunaway, Perry Lopez**

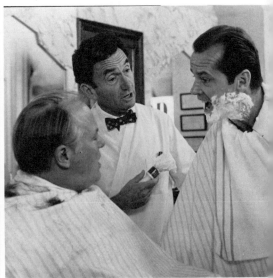

Doc Erickson, George Justin, Jack Nicholson

John Huston, Jack Nicholson Above: Roman Polanski, Nicholson, Roy Jenson Top: Nicholson

Faye Dunaway Above: Jack Nicholson, Perry Lopez (R) Top: Nicholson, Dunaway

53

MACON COUNTY LINE

(AMERICAN INTERNATIONAL) Executive Producer, Roger Camras; Producer, Max Baer; Director, Richard Compton; Story, Max Baer; Screenplay, Max Baer, Richard Compton; Editor, Tina Hirsch; Photography, Daniel Lacambre; Art Director, Roger Pancake; Costumes, Francis Dennis; Music, Stu Phillips; Theme Song Composed and Sung by Bobbie Gentry; Presented by Samuel Z. Arkoff; In Consolidated Film Industries Color; Rated R; 89 minutes; June release.

CAST

Chris Dixon	Alan Vint
Jenny	Cheryl Waters
Deputy Reed Morgan	Max Baer
Hamp	Geoffrey Lewis
Carol Morgan	Joan Blackman
Wayne Dixon	Jesse Vint
Deputy Bill	Sam Gilman
Lon	Timothy Scott
Elisha	James Gammon
Luke	Leif Garrett
Gurney	Emile Meyer
Augie	Doodles Weaver

Right: Alan Vint, Jesse Vint

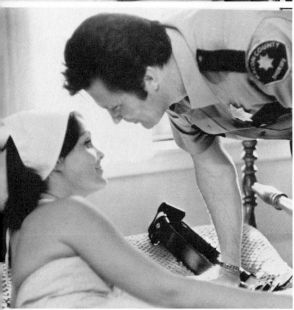

Joan Blackman, Max Baer Above: Cheryl Waters, Alan Vint, Jesse Vint

Max Baer Above: Geoffrey Lewis, Alan Vint, Jesse Vint

MR. MAJESTYK

(UNITED ARTISTS) Producer, Walter Mirisch; Director, Richard Fleischer; Screenplay, Elmore Leonard, Music, Charles Bernstein; Photography, Richard H. Kline; Editor, Ralph E. Winters; In DeLuxe Color; Rated PG; 103 minutes; July release.

CAST

Vince Majestyk	Charles Bronson
Frank Renda	Al Lettieri
Nancy Chavez	Linda Cristal
Wiley	Lee Purcell
Bobby Kopas	Paul Koslo
Gene Lundy	Taylor Lacher
Detective McAllen	Frank Maxwell
Larry Mendoza	Alejandro Rey
Sheriff Harold Ritchie	Jordon Rhodes
Julio Tomaz	Bert Santos
Gas Station Attendant	Vern Porter

Right: Charles Bronson

Al Lettieri, Lee Purcell Above: Frank Maxwell, Paul Koslo, Charles Bronson (R)

Linda Cristal, Charles Bronson Above: Taylor Lacher, Paul Koslo, Lee Purcell, Al Lettieri

BANK SHOT

(UNITED ARTISTS) Producers, Hal Landers, Bobby Roberts; Director, Gower Champion; Screenplay, Wendell Mayes; From novel by Donald E. Westlake; Photography, Harry Stradling, Jr.; Music, John Morris; Editor, David Bretherton; Art Director, Albert Brenner; Assistant Directors, Tom Shaw, Charles Bonniwell; In color; Rated PG; 100 minutes; July release.

CAST

Walter Ballantine	George C. Scott
El	Joanna Cassidy
Al. G. Karp	Sorrell Booke
FBI Agent Constable	G. Wood
Frank "Bulldog" Streiger	Clifton James
Victor Karp	Robert Balaban
Mums	Bibi Osterwald
Herman X	Frank McRae
Stosh Gornik	Don Calfa
Irving	Harvey Evans
Johnson	Hank Stohl
Painter	Liam Dunn
Jackson	Jack Riley
Man in privy	Pat Zurica
Policemen	Harvey J. Goldenberg, Jamie Reidy

Right: George C. Scott

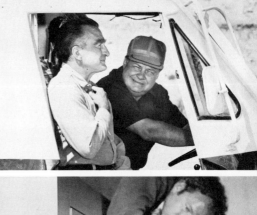

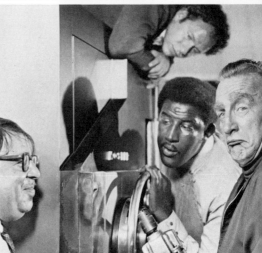

Joanna Cassidy, George C. Scott Above: Scott, Cassidy, Robert Balaban

Sorrell Booke, Robert Balaban, Frank McRae, George C. Scott Above: Scott, Clifton James

THE WHITE DAWN

(PARAMOUNT) Producer, Martin Ransohoff; Director, Philip Kaufman; Screenplay, James Houston, Tom Rickman; Adaptation, Martin Ransohoff; Based on novel by James Houston; Photography, Michael Chapman; Music, Henry Mancini; Editor, Douglas Stewart; Associate Producers, Don Guest, James Houston; Assistant Directors, Jon Andersen, Tony Lucibello; In Movielab Color; Rated R; 109 minutes; July release.

CAST

Billy	Warren Oates
Daggett	Timothy Bottoms
Portagee	Lou Gossett
Sarkak	Simonie Kopapik
Kangiak	Joanasie Salomonie
Neevee	Pilitak
Shaman	Sagiaktok
Sowniapik	Munamee Sako
Sowniapik's Wife	Pitseolala Kili
Ikuma	Meetook Mallee
Avinga	Seemee Nookiguak
Dirty Boy	Sakkeassie
Old Mother	Akshooyooliak
Panee	Neelak
Mia	Oolipika Joamie
Evaloo	Higa Ipeelie
Archer	Jacob Partridge
Shartok	Ashoona Kilabuck
Nowya	Namonai Ashoona
Hunters	Aupalotak Simonee, Atcheelak

Right: Timothy Bottoms, Warren Oates, Lou Gossett

Timothy Bottoms, Lou Gossett, Warren Oates Above: Joanasie Salomonie, Bottoms

Simonie Kopapik, Timothy Bottoms Above: Timothy Bottoms, Lou Gossett

DEATH WISH

(PARAMOUNT) Producers, Hal Landers, Bobby Roberts; Director-Co-Producer, Michael Winner; Screenplay, Wendell Mayes; From novel by Brian Garfield; Music, Herbie Hancock; Photography, Arthur J. Ornitz; Editor, Bernard Gribble; Assistant Directors, Charles Okun, Larry Albucher, Ralph Singleton; Designer, Robert Gundlach; Costumes, Joseph G. Aulisi; In Technicolor; Rated R; 93 minutes; July release.

CAST

Paul Kersey	Charles Bronson
Joanna Kersey	Hope Lange
Frank Ochoa	Vincent Gardenia
Jack Toby	Steven Keats
Sam Kreutzer	William Redfield
Aimes Jainchill	Stuart Margolin
Police Commissioner	Stephen Elliott
Carol Toby	Kathleen Tolan
Hank	Jack Wallace
District Attorney	Fred Scollay
Ives	Chris Gampel
Joe Charles	Robert Kya-Hill
Lt. Briggs	Ed Grover
Freak 1	Jeff Goldberg
Freak 2	Christopher Logan
Spraycan	Gregory Rozakis
Desk Sergeant	Floyd Levine
Alma Lee Brown	Helen Martin
Andrew McCabe	Hank Garrett
Patrolman Reilly	Christopher Guest

Left: Charles Bronson

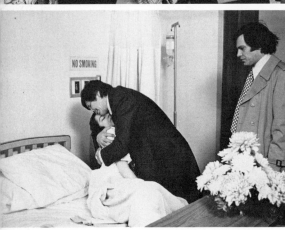

Charles Bronson, Kathleen Tolan, Steven Keats
Above: Christopher Logan, Tolan, Gregory Rozakis

Charles Bronson

Charles Bronson, also above with William Redfield

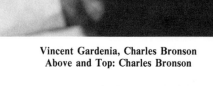

Vincent Gardenia, Charles Bronson
Above and Top: Charles Bronson

THE EDUCATION OF SONNY CARSON

(PARAMOUNT) Producer, Irwin Yablans; Director, Michael Campus; Screenplay, Fred Hudson; Based on book by Sonny Carson; Photography, Ed Brown; Vocals, Leon Ware; Music, Coleridge-Taylor Perkinson; Editors, Edward Warschilka, Harry Noward; Associate Producer, David Golden; Art Director, Manny Gerard; Costumes, Gene Coffin, Gregory Lecakin; Assistant Directors, Stephen Barnett, Frank Simpson; In Panavision and Movielab Color; Rated R; 104 minutes; July release.

CAST

Sonny Carson	Rony Clanton
Pigliani	Don Gordon
Virginia	Joyce Walker
Pops	Paul Benjamin
Young Sonny	Thomas Hicks
Moms	Mary Alice
Preacher	Ram John Holder
Lil' Boy	Jerry Bell
Benny	Ray Rainbow Johnson
Wolfe	Derrick Champ Ford
Lil' John	Roger Hill
Donovan	Chris Forster
Uncle Cal	George Miles
Cousin Red	Jess Bolero
Crazy	B. T. Taylor
Willie	Roger (D.A.) Davis
Sally Jean	Eleanora Douglas
Psychiatrist	Clifton Steere
Western Union Boy	Dennis Keir
Lil' Boy's Mother	Linda Hopkins
Parole Board Chairman	Mervyn Nelson
Supermarket Kids	Prince Olafami, Ronnie Cole, Steve Sellers
Judge	David Kerman
Funeral Singer	Ellerine Harding

Benny Diggs and the New York Community Choir, The Jolly Stompers, Tomahawks, Black Spades, Pure Hell, Morningside High School students

Top: Ray Rainbow Johnson (C), Jerry Bell (R)
Below: Rony Clanton, Joyce Walker, Jerry Bell

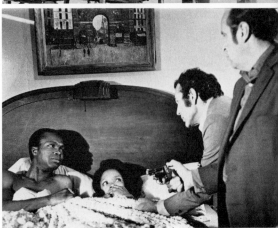

Joyce Walker, Rony Clanton

Rony Clanton, Joyce Walker, Don Gordon, Chris Forster

THE GIRL FROM PETROVKA

(UNIVERSAL) Producers, Richard D. Zanuck, David Brown; Director, Robert Ellis Miller; Screenplay, Allan Scott, Chris Bryant; Based on book by George Feifer; Photography, Vilmos Zsigmond; Art Director, George C. Webb; Editor, John F. Burnett; Music, Henry Mancini; Song, Roy Budd, Jack Fishman; Costumes, Deidre Clancy; Assistant Directors, Howard Kazanjian, Gary Daigler, Victor Tourjansky; An MCA Presentation; In Panavision and Technicolor; Rated PG; 104 minutes; August release.

CAST

Oktyabrina	Goldie Hawn
Joe	Hal Holbrook
Kostya	Anthony Hopkins
Minister	Gregoire Aslan
Ignatievitch	Anton Dolin
Alexander	Bruno Wintzell
Leonid	Zoran Andric
Judge	Hanna Hertelendy
Old Crone	Maria Sokolov
Passport Black Marketeer	Zitto Kazann
Helga Van Dam	Inger Jensen
Minister's Driver	Raymond O'Keefe
Kremlin Press Official	Richard Marner
Police Chief Valinikov	Michael Janisch
American Reporter	Harry Towb
Jogging Companion	Ted Grossman
Minister's Wife	Elisa Georgiadis
Cafe Waiter	Heinz Marecek
Shipyard Caretaker	Anatol Winogradoff

Right: Goldie Hawn, Hal Holbrook
Above: Holbrook, Hawn, Anthony Hopkins

Goldie Hawn, Gregoire Aslan, Hal Holbrook
Above: Bruno Wintzell, Hal Holbrook

Hal Holbrook, Goldie Hawn Above: Hawn, Zoran Andric (C)

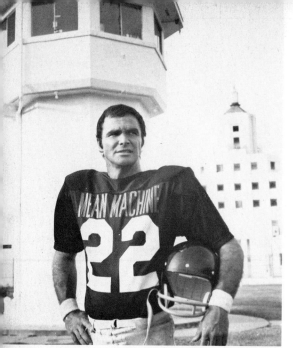

THE LONGEST YARD

(PARAMOUNT) Producer, Albert S. Ruddy; Director, Robert Aldrich; Screenplay, Tracy Keenan Wynn; Based on story by Albert S. Ruddy; Photography, Joseph Biroc; Associate Producer, Alan P. Horowitz; Music, Frank DeVol; Designer, James S. Vance; Editor, Michael Luciano; Assistant Directors, Clifford Coleman, Ron Wright; In Technicolor; Rated R; 120 minutes; August release.

CAST

Paul Crewe	Burt Reynolds
Warden Hazen	Eddie Albert
Captain Knauer	Ed Lauter
Nate Scarboro	Michael Conrad
Caretaker	Jim Hampton
Granville	Harry Caesar
Pop	John Steadman
Unger	Charles Tyner
Rassmeusen	Mike Henry
Warden's Secretary	Bernadette Peters
Mawabe	Pervis Arkins
Rotka	Tony Cacciotti
Melissa	Anitra Ford
Announcer	Michael Ford
Walking Boss	Joe Kapp
Samson	Dick Kiel
Shop Steward	Pepper Martin
Assistant Warden	Mort Marshall
Bogdanski	Ray Nitschke
Indian	Sonny Sixkiller
Mason	Dino Washington
Spooner	Ernie Wheelwright
Bartender	Joseph Dorsey
Team Doctor	Dr. Gus Carlucci
Trainer	Jack Rockwell
Tannen	Sonny Shroyer
Schmidt	Ray Ogden
Referee	Don Ferguson
Troopers	Chuck Hayward, Alfie Wise
Shokner	Bob Tessier
Levitt	Tony Reese
J. J.	Steve Wilder
Big George	George Jones
Big Wilbur	Wilbur Gillan
Buttercup	Wilson Warren
Little Joe	Joe Jackson
Howie	Howard Silverstein
Donny	Donald Hixon
Ice Man	Jim Nicholson

**Left: Burt Reynolds, Joe Kapp, Harry Caesar
Top: Burt Reynolds**

Burt Reynolds

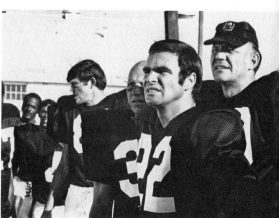

**Burt Reynolds, Michael Conrad,
John Steadman**

Burt Reynolds, Eddie Albert (also at top)
Above: John Steadman, Burt Reynolds

Anitra Ford, Burt Reynolds Above: Mort Marshall,
Eddie Albert Top: Reynolds, James Hampton

CALIFORNIA SPLIT

(PARAMOUNT) Producers, Robert Altman, Joseph Walsh; Director, Robert Altman; Screenplay, Joseph Walsh; Executive Producers, Aaron Spelling, Leonard Goldberg; Photography, Paul Lohmann; Editor, Lou Lombardo; Art Director, Leon Ericksen; A Won World Production; In color; Rated R; 108 minutes; August release.

CAST

Bill Denny	George Segal
Charlie Waters	Elliott Gould
Barbara Miller	Ann Prentiss
Susan Peters	Gwen Welles
Lew	Edward Walsh
Sparkle	Joseph Walsh
Helen Brown	Bert Remsen
Irate Lady at track	Barbara London
Barkeeper	Barbara Ruick

Left: Gwen Welles, George Segal

George Segal, Elliott Gould

**Gwen Welles, Elliott Gould
Above: Elliott Gould, Jay Fletcher**

**George Segal, also at top
with Joseph Walsh**

HARRY AND TONTO

(20th CENTURY-FOX) Producer-Director, Paul Mazursky; Screenplay, Paul Mazursky, Josh Greenfield; Photography, Michael Butler; Associate Producer-Assistant Director, Tony Ray; Assistant Directors, Jon Sanger, Dodie Fawley; Designer, Ted Haworth; Editor, Richard Halsey; Costumes, Albert Wolsky; In DeLuxe color; Rated R; 115 minutes. August release.

CAST

Harry	Art Carney
Shirley	Ellen Burstyn
Old Indian	Chief Dan George
Jessie	Geraldine Fitzgerald
Eddie	Larry Hagman
Wade	Arthur Hunnicutt
Burt	Phil Bruns
Norman	Joshua Mostel
Ginger	Melanie Mayron
Elaine	Dolly Jonah
Rivetowski	Herbert Berghof
Leroy	Avon Long
Happy Hooker	Barbara Rhoades
Junior	Cliff DeYoung

1974 Academy Award to Art Carney for
Best Performance by an actor

Left: Tonto, Art Carney

Art Carney (C) and above

Art Carney, Ellen Burstyn

Art Carney, Chief Dan George Above: Art
Carney, Barbara Rhodes Top: Carney

Art Carney (C), also above and top

THE DOVE

(PARAMOUNT) Producer, Gregory Peck; Director, Charles Jarrott; Screenplay, Peter Beagle, Adam Kennedy; Based on book "Dove" by Robin Lee Graham with Derek Gill; Photography, Sven Nykvist; Music, John Barry; Associate Producer, Milton Forman; Editor, John Jympson; Art Director, Peter Lamont; Assistant Directors, Paul Ibbetson, David Bracknell, Howard Grigsby, Gary Spero; In Panavision and Technicolor; Rated PG; 105 minutes; September release.

CAST

Robin Lee Graham	Joseph Bottoms
Patti Ratterree	Deborah Raffin
Lyle Graham	John McLiam
Charles Huntley	Dabney Coleman
Mike Turk	John Anderson
Tom Barkley	Colby Chester
Kenniston	Ivor Barry
Young Fijian	Setoki Ceinaturoga
Minister	Rev. Nikula
Cruise Ship Captain	Apenisa Naigulevu
Tim	John Meillon
Darwin Harbor Master	Gordon Glenwright
South African Customs Official	Garth Mead
Fred C. Pearson	Peter Gwynne
Mrs. Castaldi	Cecily Polson
License Bureau Clerk	Anthony Fridjohn
Reporter	Dale Cutts
Chief Pilot	Jose Augusto de Lima, Sampaio e Silva

Left and Top: Deborah Raffin, Joseph Bottoms

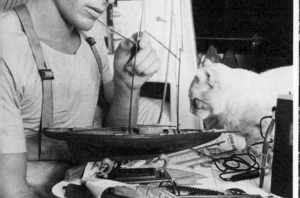

Joseph Bottoms, Joliette

Deborah Raffin, Joseph Bottoms

Antonia Brico

Antonia Brico in her thirties

ANTONIA: A PORTRAIT OF THE
WOMAN

(ROCKY MOUNTAIN) Producer, Judy Collins; Directors, Judy Collins, Jill Godmilow; Photography, Coulter Watt; Editor, Jill Godmilow; In color; 58 minutes; September release. A documentary in the life of Antonia Brico, conductor, teacher, pioneer in the concert halls of the world.

THE GAMBLER

(PARAMOUNT) Producers, Irwin Winkler, Robert Chartoff; Director, Karel Reisz; Screenplay, James Toback; Photography, Victor J. Kemper; Music, Jerry Fielding; Based on Symphony No. 1 by Gustav Mahler; Designer, Philip Rosenberg; Editor, Roger Spottiswoods; Costumes, Albert Wolsky; Assistant Directors, Ted Zachary, Tom Lofaro; In color; Rated R; October release.

CAST

Axel	James Caan
Hips	Paul Sorvino
Billie	Lauren Hutton
A. R. Lowenthal	Morris Carnovsky
Naomi	Jacqueline Brookes
Carmine	Burt Young
Jimmy	Carmine Caridi
One	Vic Tayback
Howie	Steven Keats
Monkey	London Lee
Las Vegas Gambler	M. Emmet Walsh
Bank Officer	James Woods
Spencer	Carl W. Crudup
Bernie	Allan Rich
Cowboy	Stuart Margolin
Sal	Ric Mancini
Moe	Joel Wolfe
Benny	Raymond Serra
Basketball Coach	William Andrews
Singer in the park	Joseph Attles
Pimp	Antonio Fargas
Vernon	Ernest Butler
Uncle Hy	Sully Boyar
Joe	Gregory Rozakis
Monique	Starletta De Paur
Ricky's Wife	Lucille Patton
Ricky	Ed Kovens
Basketball Janitor	Baron Wilson
Donny	Richard Foronjy
Donny's Driver	Frank Sivero
Man in park with Donny	Frank Scioscia
Sidney	Philip Sterling
Receptionist	Beatrice Winde

and Patricia Fay (Teller), Leon Pinkney (Street Basketball Boy), Alisha Fontaine (Howie's Girl), Presley Caton (Monkey's Girl) Mitch Stein, Jonathan Koshner (College Announcers), Charles Polk (Bartender), Dick Schaap (TV Announcer), Chick Hearn (Radio Announcer)

Left: James Caan, Morris Carnovsky
Top: James Caan, Paul Sorvino

Jacqueline Brookes, James Caan

James Caan, Lauren Hutton

Lauren Hutton, James Caan Above: Carmine
Caridi, Caan (also top)

James Caan (C), also above, and top
with Steven Keats

71

THE TAKING OF PELHAM ONE TWO THREE

(UNITED ARTISTS) Producers, Gabriel Katzka, Edgar J. Scherick; Director, Joseph Sargent; Screenplay, Peter Stone; Based on novel by John Godey; Music, David Shire; Associate Producer, Stephen F. Kesten; Photography, Owen Roizman; Costumes, Anna Hill Johnstone; Art Director, Gene Rudolf; Editors, Gerald Greenberg, Robert Q. Lovett; In color; Rated R; 104 minutes; October release.

CAST

Lt. Garber	Walter Matthau
Blue	Robert Shaw
Green	Martin Balsam
Grey	Hector Elizondo
Brown	Earl Hindman
Warren LaSalle	Tony Roberts
Denny Doyle	James Broderick
Correll	Dick O'Neill
The Mayor	Lee Wallace
Caz Dolowicz	Tom Pedi
Mrs. Jenkins	Beatrice Winde
Lt. Rico Patrone	Jerry Stiller
Patrolman James	Nathan George
Police Commissioner	Rudy Bond
Borough Commander	Kenneth McMillan
Mayor's Wife	Doris Roberts
Inspector Daniels	Julius Harris
The Maid	Cynthia Belgrave
The Mother	Anna Berger
The Homosexual	Gary Bolling
The Secretary	Carol Cole
The Delivery Boy	Alex Colon
The Salesman	Joe Fields
The Hooker	Mari Gorman
The Old Man	Michael Gorrin
The Older Son	Thomas LaFleur
The Spanish Woman	Maria Landa
The Alcoholic	Louise Larabee

Left: Earl Hindman, Robert Shaw, Martin Balsam, Hector Elizondo Top: Dick O'Neill, Carmine Forresta, Walter Matthau

Robert Shaw, James Broderick

Mari Gorman, Eric O'Hanian, Anna Berger, Thomas La Fleur, Jerry Holland, Hector Elizondo

Earl Hindman, Simon Deckard, Sal Viscuso
Above: Lee Wallis, Tony Roberts Top: Eric O'Hanian,
Anna Berger, Thomas LaFleur, Lucy Saroyan

Julius Harris, Walter Matthau Above: William
Snickowski, Gary Bolling, Earl Hindman
Top: Martin Balsam, Robert Shaw

73

AIRPORT 1975

(UNIVERSAL) Producer, William Frye; Executive Producer, Jennings Lang; Director, Jack Smight; Screenplay, Don Ingalls; Inspired by the film "Airport" and based on the novel by Arthur Hailey; Photography, Philip Lathrop; Art Director, George C. Webb; Editor, J. Terry Williams; Costumes, Edith Head; Music, John Cacavas; Song, Helen Reddy, R. Burton; Sung by Helen Reddy; Assistant Directors, Alan Crosland, Wayne Farlow; In Panavision and Technicolor; Rated PG; 107 minutes; October release.

CAST

Murdock	Charlton Heston
Nancy	Karen Black
Patroni	George Kennedy
Stacy	Efrem Zimbalist, Jr.
Gloria Swanson	Gloria Swanson
Mrs. Patroni	Susan Clark
Sister Ruth	Helen Reddy
Janice	Linda Blair
Scott Freeman	Dana Andrews
Urias	Roy Thinnes
Barney	Sid Caesar
Mrs. Devaney	Myrna Loy
Major Alexander	Ed Nelson
Mrs. Abbott	Nancy Olson
Purcell	Larry Storch
Sister Beatrice	Martha Scott
Sam	Jerry Stiller
Bill	Norman Fell
Arnie	Conrad Janis
Mrs. Scott Freeman	Beverly Garland
Winnie	Augusta Summerland
Colonel Moss	Guy Stockwell
Julio	Erik Estrada
Lt. Thatcher	Kip Niven
Fat Man	Charles White
Joseph	Biran Morrison
Amy	Amy Farrell
Carol	Irene Tsu
Gary	Ken Sansom
Danton	Alan Fudge
Bette	Christopher Norris
Air Force Sergeant	Austin Stoker
Oringer	John Lupton
First Friend	Gene Dynarski
Aldine	Aldine King
Sharon	Sharon Gless
Arlene	Laurette Spang

Left: Efrem Zimbalist, Roy Thinnes
Top: Charlton Heston, Karen Black

George Kennedy

Helen Reddy

Jim Plunkett, Linda Blair, George Kennedy
Above: Susan Clark Top: Augusta Summerland,
Gloria Swanson

Myrna Loy (foreground)
Above: Karen Black

LAW AND DISORDER

(COLUMBIA) Executive Producers, Michael Medwin, Edgar J. Scherick; Producer, William Rickert; Director, Ivan Passer; Screenplay, Ivan Passer, William Richert, Kenneth Harris Fishman; Music, Andy Badale; Associate Producers, Fred C. Caruso, Michael Zivian; Photography, Arthur J. Ornitz; Art Director, Gene Rudolf; Costumes, Ann Roth; Editor, Anthony Protenza; Assistant Directors, Alan Hopkins, Walter Skotchdopole, Robert Haralla; A Memorial/Leroy Street/Ugo/Fadsin Cinema Production; A Palomar Presentation; In color; Rated R; 103 minutes; October release.

CAST

Willie	Carroll O'Connor
Cy	Ernest Borgnine
Sally	Ann Wedgeworth
Irene	Anita Dangler
Karen	Leslie Ackerman
Gloria	Karen Black
Elliott	Jack Kehoe
Bobby	David Spielberg
Peter	Joe Ragno
Ken	Pat Corley
Flasher	J. Frank Lucas
Capt. Malloy	Ed Grover
Yablonsky	Pepper Wormser
Chico	Lionel Pina
F. U. Kid	Gary Springer
Jogger	Jay Fletcher
Desk Sergeant	Bill Richert
Morris	Jack Stamberger
Frank	Ed Madsen
Eddie	Adam Lessuck
Ralph	Sydney Sherrif
Dr. Richter	Alan Arbus
Chico's Mother	Theodorina Bello
Chico's Father	Peter Lago
Woman in cab	Rita Gam
Man in cab	Michael Medwin

Left: Ernest Borgnine
Top: Carroll O'Connor, Leslie Ackerman

Ernest Borgnine, Carroll O'Connor

Carroll O'Connor, Ernest Borgnine (also at top)

THE SAVAGE IS LOOSE

(CAMPBELL DEVON) Executive Producer, Robert E. Relyea; Producer-Director, George C. Scott; Screenplay, Max Ehrlich, Frank De Felitta; Photography, Alex Phillips, Jr.; Editor, Michael Kahn; Music, Gil Melle; In color; Rated R; 114 minutes; November release.

CAST

John .... George C. Scott
Maida .... Trish Van Devere
David .... John David Carson
Young David .... Lee H. Montgomery

Right: George C. Scott, Trish Van Devere

George C. Scott, Trish Van Devere
Above: Lee H. Montgomery, George C. Scott

John David Carson
Above: Trish Van Devere

THE KLANSMEN

(PARAMOUNT) Producer, William Alexander; Director, Terence Young; Screenplay, Millard Kaufman, Samuel Fuller; Based on novel by William Bradford Huie; Executive Producer, Bill Shiffrin; Editor, Gene Milford; Designer, John S. Poplin; Associate Producers, Joe Ingber, Michael Marcovsky, Rosemary Christenson, Peter A. Rodis, Alvin Bojar, Jerry Levy, Daniel K. Sobol; Photography, Lloyd Ahern; Music, Dale O. Warren, Stu Gardner; Additional Music, Mack Rice, Bettye Crutcher; Assistant Directors, Ridgeway Callow, Joseph Nayfack, Gene Anderson; In Technicolor; Rated R; 112 minutes; November release.

CAST

Sheriff Bascomb	Lee Marvin
Breck Stancill	Richard Burton
Butt Cut Cates	Cameron Mitchell
Garth	O. J. Simpson
Loretta Sykes	Lola Falana
Mayor Hardy	David Huddleston
Trixie	Luciana Paluzzi
Nancy Poteet	Linda Evans
Shaneyfelt	Ed Call
Vernon Hodo	John Alderson
Taggart	John Pearce
Flagg	David Ladd
Hector	Vic Perrin
Willy Washington	Spence Wil-Dee
Alan Bascomb	Wendell Wellman
Bobby Poteet	Hoke Howel
Johnson	Virgil Fry
Rev. Josh Franklin	Robert Porter
Rev. Alverson	Lee DeBroux
A. P. Reporter	Charles Briggs
N.Y. Times Reporter	Morgan Upton
Mrs. Shaneyfelt	Eve Christopher
Maybelle Bascomb	Susan Brown
Charles Peck	Gary Catus
Mary Anne	Jeanie Bell
Annie	Jo Ann Cowell
Jim Hodo	Scott E. Lane
Doctor	Bert Williams
Lightning Rod	Larry Williams

Right: Lola Falana, O. J. Simpson, Richard Burton Top: O. J. Simpson, Lee Marvin

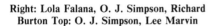

Lee Marvin, Cameron Mitchell

Lee Marvin, Linda Evans

THE TRIAL OF BILLY JACK

(TAYLOR-LAUGHLIN) Producer, Joe Cramer; Director, Frank Laughlin; Screenplay, Frank and Teresa Christina; Photography, Jack A. Marta; Music, Elmer Bernstein; Art Director, George W. Troast; Editors, Tom Rolf, Michael Economou, George Grenville, Michael Karr, Jules Nayfack; Associate Producers, Beverly Walker, Robert Schultz; Costumes, Moss Mabry; Assistant Directors, Jack Reddish, Thomas J. Connors III; In Panavision and Metrocolor; Rated PG; 170 minutes; November release.

CAST

Billy Jack	Tom Laughlin
Jean Roberts	Delores Taylor
Doc	Victor Izay
Carol	Teresa Laughlin
National Guardsman	William Wellman, Jr.
Russell	Russell Lane
Michelle	Michelle Wilson
Joanne	Geo Anne Sosa
Lynn	Lynn Baker
Posner	Riley Hill
Sheriff Cole	Sparky Watt
Blue Elk	Gus Greymountain
Patsy Littlejohn	Sacheen Littlefeather
Danny	Michael Bolland
Grandfather	Jack Stanley
Master Han	Bong Soo Han
Thunder Mountain	Rolling Thunder
Indian Maiden	Sandra Ego
Vision Maiden	Trinidad Hopkins
Alicia	Marianne Hall
Turning Water	Johnny West
Little Bear	Buffalo Horse
Defense Attorney	Dennis O'Flaherty
Elk's Shadow	George Aguilar
Third Trooper	Pepper Rogers
Teda	Teda Bracci
Sunshine	Susan Sosa
Karate Expert	Michael J. Shigezane

and Jason Clark, Ron Nix (Cowboys), Ken Tealor (Ken), Evans Thornton (Attorney), Jack White (Bugger), Hosea Barnett (Student), David Scott Clark (Town Boy), Jean Newburn (Militant Indian Lawyer), Debbie Hill (Debbie), Diane Webber (Belly-Dance Teacher), Oshannah Fastwolf (Oshannah), Kathy Cronkite (Kristen), DeLaura Henry (Liz), Patricia McCulloch (Girl), Alexandra Nicholson (Abby)

Left: Michael Bolland, Delores Taylor, Victor Izay, Teresa Laughlin Top: Tom Laughlin, Delores Taylor

Tom Laughlin

Tom Laughlin, Dennis O'Flaherty

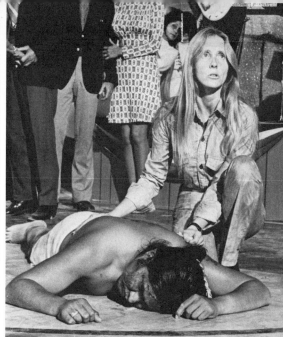

Michael Bolland, Teresa Laughlin Above: William
Wellman, Jr.(R) Top: Tom Laughlin

Delores Taylor, Tom Laughlin (also above)
Top: Gus Greymountain, Delores Taylor

EARTHQUAKE

(UNIVERSAL) Producer-Director, Mark Robson; Executive Producer, Jennings Lang; Screenplay, George Fox, Mario Puzo; Photography, Philip Lathrop; Designer, Alexander Golitzen; Art Director, E. Preston Ames; Editor, Dorothy Spencer; Music, John Williams; Costumes, Burton Miller; Assistant Directors, Fred R. Simpson, Murray Schwartz; In Panavision, Technicolor, and Sensurround; Rated PG; 129 Minutes; An MCA Presentation; November release.

CAST

Graff	Charlton Heston
Remy	Ava Gardner
Slade	George Kennedy
Royce	Lorne Greene
Denise	Genevieve Bujold
Miles	Richard Roundtree
Jody	Marjoe Gortner
Stockle	Barry Sullivan
Dr. Vance	Lloyd Nolan
Rosa	Victoria Principal
Drunk	Walter Matuschanskayasky
Barbara	Monica Lewis
Sal	Gabriel Dell
Chavez	Pedro Armendariz, Jr.
Cameron	Lloyd Gough
Mayor	John Randolph
Walter Russell	Kip Niven
Assistant Caretaker	Scott Hylands
Corry	Tiger Williams
Dr. Harvey Johnson	Donald Moffat
Buck	Jesse Vint
Ralph	Alan Vint
Hank	Lionel Johnston
Carl Leeds	John Elerick
Chief Inspector	John S. Ragin
Colonel	George Murdock
Sid	Donald Mantooth
Sandy	Michael Richardson
Pool Player	Alex A. Brown
Dr. Frank Ames	Bob Cunningham
Brawny Foreman	John Dennis
Dam Caretaker	Gene Dynarski
Farmer Mr. Griggs	Bob Gravage
Pool Player	H. B. Haggerty
Technician	Dave Morick
Laura	Inez Pedroza

1974 Academy Award for Best Sound Achievement

**Left: Richard Roundtree
Top: Ava Gardner, Charlton Heston**

Ava Gardner

Scott Hylands, Gene Dynarski Above: Gabriel
Dell, Richard Roundtree, Tiger Williams,
Genevieve Bujold (also top)

Marjoe Gortner Above: Charlton Heston,
Ava Gardner

83

A WOMAN UNDER THE INFLUENCE

(FACES INTERNATIONAL) Producer, Sam Shaw; Direction an Screenplay, John Cassavetes; Editors, David Armstrong, Elizabet Bergeron, Sheila Viseltear, Tom Cornwell; Art Director, Phedo Papamichael; Assistant Directors, Jack Corrick, Roger Slager; Mu sic, Bo Harwood; Photography, Mitch Breif; In color; Not rated; 15 minutes; November release.

CAST

Nick Longhetti	Peter Fal
Mabel Longhetti	Gena Rowland
Tony Longhetti	Matthew Cass
Angelo Longhetti	Matthew Laborteau
Maria Longhetti	Christina Grisan
Mama Longhetti	Katherine Cassavet
Martha Mortensen	Lady Rowland
George Mortensen	Fred Drap
Garson Cross	O. G. Dur
Harold Jensen	Mario Gall
Doctor Zepp	Eddie Sha
Vito Grimaldi	Angelo Grisan
Bowman	James Joy
Clancy	John Finnega
Aldo	Cliff Carne
Muriel	Joanne Moore Jord
Willie Johnson	Hugh Hu
Billy Tidrow	Leon Wagn
Joseph Morton	John Hawk
James Turner	Sil Wor
Angela	Elizabeth Deeri
Tina	Jacki Pete
Principal	Elsie Am
Adolph	Nick Cassave
Dominique Jensen	Dominique Daval
Adrienne Jensen	Xan Cassave
John Jensen	Pancho Meisenheim
Eddie the Indian	Charles Horva
Aldo	Sonny Apr
Gino	Vince Ba
Adolph	Frank Richa
Nancy	Ellen Dava

Left: Peter Falk, Gena Rowlands

Cliff Carnell, Peter Falk, Hugh
Hurd, Vince Barbi

Peter Falk, Gena Rowlands

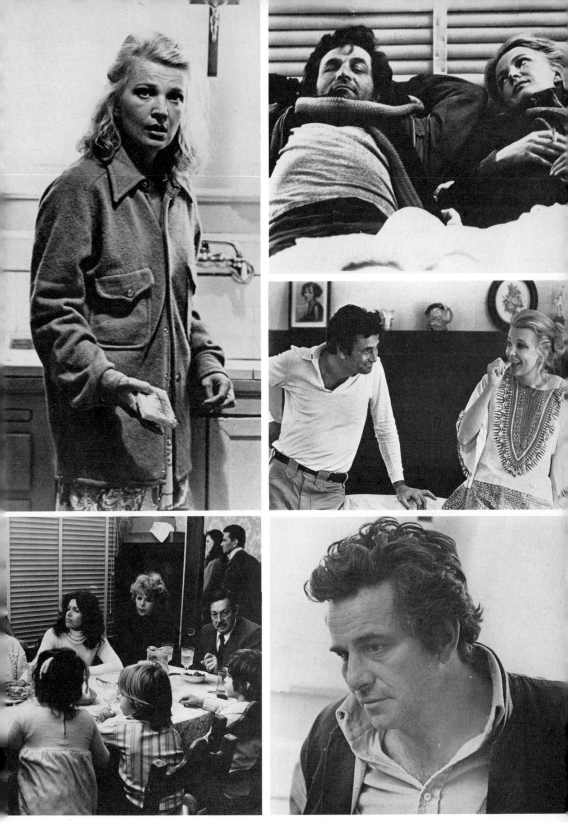

Top: Gena Rowlands

Peter Falk   Above and Top: Peter
Falk, Gena Rowlands

LENNY

(UNITED ARTISTS) Executive Producer, David V. Picker; Producer, Marvin Worth; Director, Bob Fosse; Screenplay, Julian Barry from his play of the same title; Associate Producer, Robert Greenhut; Editor, Alan Heim; Photography, Bruce Surtees; Designer, Joel Schiller; Costumes, Albert Wolsky; Assistant Directors, Ted Zachary, Douglas Green, Tommy Lofaro; In color; Rated R; 1__ minutes; November release.

CAST

Lenny Bruce	Dustin Hoffm__
Honey Bruce	Valerie Perr__
Sally Marr	Jan Mi__
Artie Silver	Stanley Be__
Sherman Hart	Gary Mort__
Aunt Mema	Rashel Novik__
Jack Goldstein	Guy Ren__
Baltimore Strip Club MC	Frankie M__
San Francisco Defense Attorney	Mark Har__
San Francisco Judge	Lee Sandm__
Kitty Bruce (at 11)	Susan Maln__
San Francisco Judge	Martin Beg__
New York Cop	Phil Phil__
New York Attorneys	Ted Sorrell, Clarence Thom__
N.Y. District Attorney	Mike Murp__
Marty	Buddy Boy__
San Francisco Cop	Mickey Gat__
Comic	George DeW__
Chorus Girl	Judy LaSc__
Hunters	Glen Wilder, Frank Ors__
Nurse's Aide	Michelle You__

Dustin Hoffman, Mickey Gatlin
Above: Dustin Hoffman, Valerie Perrine

Dustin Hoffman (also top left)

Dustin Hoffman, Valerie Perrine
Top: Dustin Hoffman

Valerie Perrine, Dustin Hoffman
Top: Ted Sorrell, Dustin Hoffman

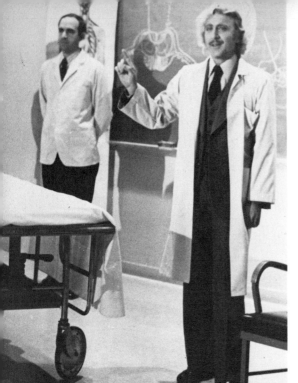

YOUNG FRANKENSTEIN

(20th CENTURY-FOX) Producer, Michael Gruskoff; Director, Mel Brooks; Screenplay, Gene Wilder, Mel Brooks; Based on characters in the novel "Frankenstein" by Mary Shelley; Photography, Gerald Hirschfeld; Music, John Morris; Violin Solo, Gerald Vinci; Editor, John Howard; Designer, Dale Hennesy; Assistant Directors, Marvin Miller, Barry Stern; Costumes, Dorothy Jeakins; In DeLuxe Color; 108 minutes; December release.

CAST

Dr. Frankenstein	Gene Wilder
Monster	Peter Boyle
Igor	Marty Feldman
Elizabeth	Madeline Kahn
Frau Blucher	Cloris Leachman
Inga	Teri Garr
Inspector Kemp	Kenneth Mars
Herr Falkstein	Richard Haydn
Mr. Hilltop	Liam Dunn
Medical Student	Danny Goldman
Herr Waldman	Leon Askin
Sadistic Jailer	Oscar Beregi
Frightened Villager	Lou Cutell
Village Elder	Arthur Malet
Inspector Kemp's Aide	Richard Roth
Gravediggers	Monte Landis, Rusty Blitz
Little Girl	Anne Beesley
First Villager	Terrence Pushman
Second Villager	Ian Abercrombie
Third Villager	Randolph Dobbs
Blindman	Gene Hackman

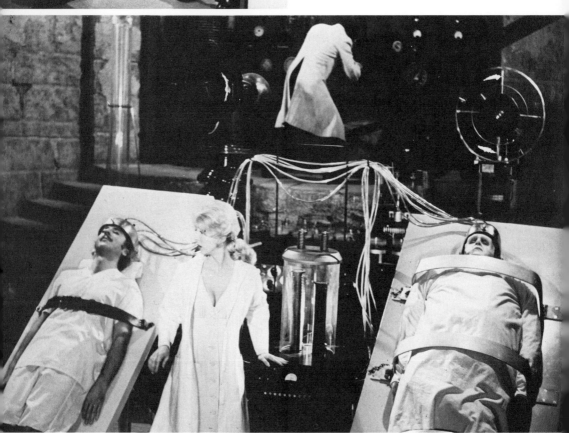

Gene Wilder, Teri Garr, Peter Boyle
Top Left: Gene Wilder

Marty Feldman
Top: Gene Wilder, Peter Boyle

Gene Wilder, Peter Boyle
Top: Madeline Kahn

THE TOWERING INFERNO

(20th CENTURY-FOX/WARNER BROS.) Producer, Irwin Allen; Director, John Guillermin; Action sequences directed by Irwin Allen; Photography, Fred Koenekamp, Joseph Biroc; Associate Producer, Sidney Marshall; Designer, William Creber; Editors, Harold F. Kress, Carl Kress; Music, John Williams; Costumes, Paul Zastupnevich; Assistant Directors, Wes McAfee, Newton Arnold, Malcolm Harding; Art Director, Ward Preston; Screenplay, Stirling Silliphant; Based on novels "The Tower" by Richard Martin Stern, and "The Glass Inferno" by Thomas N. Scortia and Frank M. Robinson. In Panavision and DeLuxe Color; Rated PG; 165 minutes; December release.

CAST

Michael O'Hallorhan	Steve McQueen
Doug Roberts	Paul Newman
James Duncan	William Holden
Susan Franklin	Faye Dunaway
Harlee Claiborne	Fred Astaire
Patty Simmons	Susan Blakely
Roger Simmons	Richard Chamberlain
Lisolette Mueller	Jennifer Jones
Jernigan	O. J. Simpson
Senator Gary Parker	Robert Vaughn
Dan Bigelow	Robert Wagner
Lorrie	Susan Flannery
Paula Ramsay	Sheila Mathews
Will Giddings	Normann Burton
Mayor Robert Ramsay	Jack Collins
Kappy	Don Gordon
Scott	Felton Perry
Carlos	Gregory Sierra
Mark	Ernie Orsatti

1974 Academy Awards for Best Cinematography, Best Editing, and Best Song ("We May Never Love Like This Again")

Steve McQueen

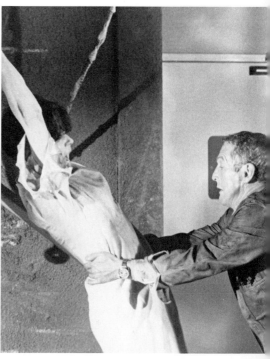

Jennifer Jones, Paul Newman

Robert Walker, Fred Astaire, Richard Chamberlain, Paul Newman, William Holden, Faye Dunaway, Steve McQueen, Jennifer Jones, O. J. Simpson, Robert Vaughn Above: (R) Steve McQueen Top: (L) Fred Astaire, Jennifer Jones (R) Susan Blakely, Richard Chamberlain

FREEBIE AND THE BEAN

(WARNER BROS.) Executive Producer, Floyd Mutrux; Producer-Director, Richard Rush; Screenplay, Robert Kaufman; Story, Floyd Mutrux; Photography, Laszlo Kovacs; Art Director, Hilyard Brown; Editors, Frederic Steinkamp, Michael McLean; Associate Producer, Tony Ray; Music, Dominic Frontiere; Assistant Directors, Chuck Bail, Chris Seitz, Lorin Salob; In Panavision and Technicolor; Rated R; 112 minutes; December release.

CAST

Bean	Alan Arkin
Freebie	James Caan
Meyer's Wife	Loretta Swit
Red Myers	Jack Kruschen
Lt. Rosen	Mike Kellin
Freebie's Girl	Linda Marsh
Whitey	Paul Koslo
Chauffeur	John Garwood
D. A.	Alex Rocco
Bean's Wife	Valerie Harper

Alan Arkin, James Caan (also top left)

Linda Marsh, James Caan Above: Alan Arkin,
James Caan Top: Kathy Witt, James Caan

Alan Arkin, James Caan Above: Paul Koslo,
James Caan Top: Monte Stickles, James Caan

THE FRONT PAGE

(UNIVERSAL) Producer, Paul Monash; Director, Billy Wilder; Executive Producer, Jennings Lang; Screenplay, Billy Wilder, I. A. L. Diamond; Based on play of same title by Ben Hecht and Charles MacArthur; Photography, Jordan S. Cronenweth; Editor, Ralph E. Winters; Art Director, Henry Bumstead; Costumes, Burton Miller; Music, Billy May; Assistant Directors, Howard G. Kazanjian, Howard G. Dismukes; In Panavision and Technicolor; Rated PG; 105 minutes; December release.

CAST

Hildy Johnson	Jack Lemmon
Walter Burns	Walter Matthau
Mollie Malloy	Carol Burnett
Peggy Grant	Susan Sarandon
Sheriff	Vincent Gardenia
Bensinger	David Wayne
Kruger	Allen Garfield
Earl Williams	Austin Pendleton
Murphy	Charles Durning
Schwartz	Herbert Edelman
Dr. Eggelhofer	Martin Gabel
The Mayor	Harold Gould
Jacobi	Cliff Osmond
McHugh	Dick O'Neill
Rudy Keppler	Jon Korkes
Endicott	Lou Frizzell
Plunkett	Paul Benedict
Jennie	Doro Merande
Wilson	Noam Pitlik
Cab Driver	Joshua Shelley
Telegrapher	Allen Jenkins
Duffy	John Furlong
Police Dispatcher	Biff Elliot
Myrtle	Barbara Davis
Butch	Leonard Breman

Left: Jack Lemmon, Cliff Osmond, Walter Matthau

Carol Burnett

Susan Sarandon, Walter Matthau

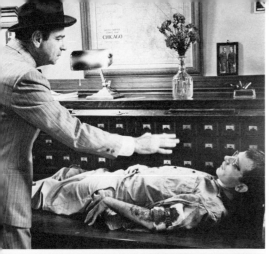

Carol Burnett (L) Above: Jack Lemmon, Walter
Matthau Top: Matthau, Austin Pendleton

Jack Lemmon Above: Walter Matthau
Top: Austin Pendleton

THE GODFATHER, PART II

(PARAMOUNT) Producer-Director, Francis Ford Coppol; Screenplay, Francis Ford Coppola, Mario Puzo; Based on nov "The Godfather" by Mario Puzo; Co-Producers, Gray Frederic son, Fred Roos; Photography, Gordon Willis; Designer, Dea Tavoularis; Editors, Peter Zinner, Barry Malkin, Richard Mark Costumes, Theadora Van Runkle; Associate Producer, Mor Skager; Music, Nino Rota; Art Director, Angelo Graham; Assista Directors, Newton Arnold, Henry J. Lange, Jr., Chuck Myers, Ala Hopkins, Burt Bluestein, Tony Brandt; Additional Music, Carmir Coppola; In Technicolor; Rated R; December release.

CAST

Michael	Al Pacir
Tom Hagen	Robert Duva
Kay	Diane Keatc
Vito Corleone	Robert De Ni
Fredo Corleone	John Caza
Connie Corleone	Talia Shi
Hyman Roth	Lee Strasbe
Frankie Pentangeli	Michael V. Gazz
Senator Pat Geary	G. D. Spradl
Al Neri	Richard Brig
Fanucci	Gaston Mosch
Rocco Lampone	Tom Rosq
Young Clemenza	B. Kirby,
Genco	Frank Sive
Young Mama Corleone	Francesca De Sap
Mama Corleone	Morgana Kir
Deanna Corleone	Mariana H
Signor Roberto	Leopoldo Tries
Johnny Ola	Dominic Chiane
Michael's Bodyguard	Amerigo T
Merle Johnson	Troy Donah
Young Tessio	John Apr
Willi Cicci	Joe Spin
Tessio	Abe Vigo
Theresa Hagen	Tere Livran
Carlo	Gianni Rus
Vito's Mother	Maria Car
Vito Andolini as a boy	Oreste Baldi
Don Francesco	Giuseppe Silla
Don Tommasino	Mario Coto
Anthony Corleone	James Gouna
Mrs. Marcia Roth	Fay Spa
F.B.I. Man #1	Harry Dean Stant
F.B.I. Man #2	David Bak
Carmine Rosato	Carmine Car
Tony Rosato	Danny Aiel
Policeman	Carmine Fores
Bartender	Nick Discen
Father Carmelo	Father Joseph Medeg

and William Bowers (Senate Committee Chairman), Joe Della Sor Carmen Argenziano, Joe Lo Grippo (Michael's Buttonmen), E; Flagello (Impressario), Livio Giorgi (Tenor), Kathy Beller (Girl "Senza Mamma"), Saveria Mazzola (Signora Colombo), Tito Al (Cuban President), Johnny Naranjo (Translator), Elda Maida (Pe tangeli's Wife), Salvatore Po (Pentangeli's Brother), Ignazio Pa palardo (Mosca), Andrea Maugeri (Strollo), Peter La Co (Abandando), Vincent Coppola (Vendor), Peter Donat (Questad Tom Dahlgren (Corngold), Paul B. Brown (Senator Ream), P Feldman, Roger Corman (Senators), Yvonne Coll (Yolanda), J. Nichols (Attendant), Edward Van Sickle (Ellis Island Docto Gabria Belloni (Nurse), Richard Watson (Custom Official), V nancia Grangerard (Cuban Nurse), Erica Yohn (Governess), Th resa Tirelli (Midwife), and special participation by James Caan

1974 Academy Awards for Best Picture,
Best Supporting Actor (Robert De Niro), Be.
Director, Best Screenplay, Best Art Directiol
Best Set Direction, Best Musical Score

Top Left: Al Pacino Below: Robert Duvall, Tere Livrano, Mariana Hill, John Cazale, Troy Donahue Talia Shire, Morgana King, Diane Keaton, Al Pacine B. J. Topol, Tony Lucatorto, Julie Gregg, Janet anc Jeanne Savarino, Scott Summers

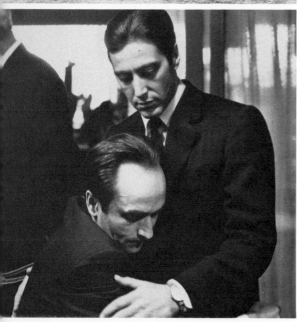

John Cazale, Al Pacino

Al Pacino, Morgana King Above: Lee Strasberg,
Pacino Top: B. Kirby, Jr., Robert De Niro

Diane Keaton, Al Pacino Above: James
Gounaris, Pacino Top: Robert De Niro

97

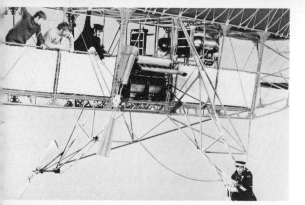

THE ISLAND AT THE TOP OF THE WORLD

(BUENA VISTA) Producer, Winston Hibler; Director, Robert Stevenson; Screenplay, John Whedon; Based on "The Lost Ones" by Ian Cameron; Photography, Frank Phillips; Music, Maurice Jarre; Designer, Peter Ellenshaw; Art Directors, John B. Mansbridge, Walter Tyler, Al Roelofs; Editor, Robert Stafford; Costumes, Bill Thomas; Assistant Directors, Ronald R. Grow, Dorothy Kieffer; A Walt Disney Production; In Technicolor; Rated G; 95 minutes; December release.

CAST

Prof. Ivarsson	David Hartman
Sir Anthony Ross	Donald Sinden
Captain Brieux	Jacques Marin
Oomiak	Mako
Donald Ross	David Gwillim
Freyja	Agneta Eckemyr
The Godi	Gunnar Ohlund
Erik	Lasse Kolstad
Torvald	Erik Silju
Lawspeaker	Rolf Soder
Sven	Torsten Wahlund
Gunnar	Sverre Ousdal
Sigurd	Niels Hinrichsen
Town Guard	Denny Miller
The Factor	Brendan Dillon
French Engineer	James Almanzar
The Butler	Ivor Barry
Chief of Boat Archers	Lee Paul

David Gwillim, Donald Sinden, David Hartman, Jacques Marin, Mako Above: Hartman, Marin, Sinden

Lasse Kolstad, Agneta Eckemyr, David Gwillim

98

Jim Kelly
in "Black Belt Jones"

Gloria Hendry
in "Black Belt Jones"

BLACK BELT JONES (Warner Bros.) Producers, Fred Weintraub, Paul Heller; Associate Producer, Oscar Williams; Director, Robert Clouse; Screenplay, Oscar Williams; Story, Alex Rose, Fred Weintraub; Photography, Kent Wakeford; Editor, Michael Kahn; Score, Luchi De Jesus; Costumes, Ann McCarthy; Decorator, Charles Pierce; Assistant Directors, Martin Hornstein, Al Sheppard; A Sequoia Pictures Production in color; Rated R; 87 minutes; January release. CAST: Jim Kelly (Black Belt Jones), Gloria Hendry (Sydney), Scatman Crothers (Pop), Alan Weeks (Toppy), Eric Laneuville (Quincy), Andre Phillipe (Don), Vincent Barbi (Big Tuna), Nate Esformes (Roberts), Malik Carter (Pinky), Mel Novak (Blue Eyes), Eddie Smith (Oscar), Alex Brown (Plummer), Clarence Barnes (Tango), Earl Brown (Jelly), Esther Sutherland (Lucy), Sid Kaiser (Ellis), Doug Sides (Militant)

THE FIGHTERS (Walter Reade) Produced, Directed, and Edited by William Greaves; Photography, Joseph Consentino, Steven Larner, Terrence Macartney-Filgate, Jimmy Mannas, Roland Mitchell; Music, David Matthews; In color; Rated G; 114 minutes; January release. A documentary on the first Muhammad Ali-Joe Frazier fight.

THE CASE OF THE SMILING STIFFS (Seaberg) Title changed from "The Case of the Full Moon Murders"; Produced and Directed by Sean S. Cunningham, Bud Talbot; Screenplay, Jerry Hayling; Photography, Gus Graham; Editor, Stephen Miner; Music, Bud Lanton, Jacques Urbont; In color; Rated X; 72 minutes; January release. CAST: Sheila Stuart (Emma), Jed Ziegler (Ice Cream Vendor), Cathy Walker (Caroline), Kenny Abston (Chuck), Geoffrey Knowles (Beau), Victoria Holloway (Daisy), Fred Lincoln (Joe), Ron Browne (Frank), Harry Reems (Silverman), Sally Ziegler (Joe's Mother), Ann Marshall (Nora)

BRUTE CORPS. (General Film Corp.) In color; Rated R; No other credits available; January release. CAST: Paul Carr, Joseph Kaufman, Jennifer Billingsley, Alex Rocco

WELCOME HOME, JOHNNY (United Films International) Producer, Hugh Corcoran; Direction and Screenplay, James Howard; Photography, Stan Slate; Executive Producer, Robert Lee; Editor, S. Lomax; Costumes, Alan Jones; A Gentlemen II Production; Rated X; January release. CAST: John Boyd, Rene Bond, Jane DeSantis, Lowell Pence, Saudi Lynn, U. Heidi Sohler, Patty Beresford, Tracy Handsuff

SNAPSHOTS (Schwartz) Producer, Kenneth E. Schwartz; Director, Irwing Horowitz; Screenplay, Mel Howard, Kenneth E. Schwartz; Photography, Paul Goldsmith; Editor-Associate Producer, L. L. Mlott; In color; Not rated; 84 minutes; January release. CAST: Kenneth E. Schwartz (Narrator), Burt Barnet, Consuela Arostegui, Mel Howard, William Czeisler, Rose Czeisler, Judy Sobol, Turid Aarsted, Billy Superball, Paul Goldsmith, Harvey Marks, Wendy Appel

A GAME OF LOVE (Virgo 3) Produced, Directed, Written, Photographed, and Edited by James Wood; Music, John Yow; In Movielab Color; Rated X; 87 minutes; January release. CAST: Fred Lincoln (Man), Sheila Stuart (Woman)

MARCO (Cinerama) Producers, Arthur Ranking, Jr., Jules Bass; Director, Seymour Robbie; Screenplay and Lyrics, Romeo Muller; Music, Maury Laws; Photography, Richard R. Nishigaki; Art Director, Shinobu Muraki; A Tomorrow Entertainment Production; In Eastmancolor; Rated G; 109 minutes; January release. CAST: Desi Arnaz, Jr. (Marco Polo), Zero Mostel (Kublai Khan), Jack Weston (Maffio), Cie Cie Win (Aigiarm), Aimee Eccles (Kuklatoi), Fred Sadoff (Niccolo), Mafumi Sakamoto (Letanpoing), Tetsu Nakamura (Captain), Van Christie (Chontosai), Osamu Ohkawa (Ling), Masumi Okada (Ti Wai), Romeo Muller (Pitai), Yuka Kamebuchi (Mme. Tung), Ikio Sawamura (Lomar)

"The Case of the Smiling Stiffs"

Muhammad Ali
in "The Fighters"

99

Angus Duncan, Jo Anne Meredith
in "How to Seduce a Woman"

Stewart Moss, Marianne McAndrew
in "The Bat People"

HOW TO SEDUCE A WOMAN (Cinerama) Direction and Screenplay, Charles Martin; Associate Producer, Stanford Gourman; Photography, William H. Cronjager; Music, Stu Phillips; Editor, William A. Sawyer; Art Director, Jack Senter; Choreography, Yuri Smaltzoff; Assistant Directors, Robert Templeton, Val Raset; Production Assistant, Dorothy Whitney; A Forward Films Presentation; In color; Rated R; 106 minutes; January release. CAST: Angus Duncan (Luther), Angel Tompkins (Pamela), Heidi Bruhl (Dr. Sisters), Alexandra Hay (Nell), Jo Anne Meredith (Melissa), Judith McConnell (Ramona), Vito Scotti (Bill), Marty Ingels (Jim), Janice Carroll (Estelle), Hope Holiday (Mary), Lillian Randolph (Matilda), Kay Peters (Jane), Dita Cobb (Fanny), James Bacon (Himself), Jack Bailey (Toklas), Fran Ryan (Mrs. Toklas), Joe E. Ross (Bartender), Joe Alfasa (Guido), Jackie Brett (Sally), Dave Barry (Ticket Seller), Eve Brent (Dr. Sisters' Sister), Herb Vigran, John Craig (Policemen), Billy Curtis (Toulouse) Billy Frick (Hitler), Jerry Mann (Rental Agent), Marvin Miller (Announcer), Ilona Wilson (Girl at party), Maurice Dallimore (Butler), Eileen McDonough (Little Girl), Angus Duncan Mackintosh (Little Boy), Schoneberg (Himself)

BIG ZAPPER (Levitt-Pickman) Producer-Director, Lindsey Shonteff; Screenplay, Hugh Brody; Music, Colin Pearson; A Syn-Frank Enterprises Presentation; In Technicolor; Rated R; January release. CAST: Linda Marlow, Gary Hope, Sean Hewett, Michael O'Malley, Jack May

SKY HIGH (Concord) Produced, Directed, and Written by Manuel Arango; In association with Robert Amram Films; Photography, Tex Zeigler; Editors, Dick Weber, Patrick Kennedy; Music, Mariano Moreno; Song, Eldad Peery; In CFI Color; Rated G; 83 minutes; January release. A documentary of airborn sports narrated by Tom McKay.

GARDEN OF THE DEAD (Entertainment Pyramid) Producer, Daniel Cady; Director, John Hayes; In color; Rated PG; No other credits available; January release. CAST: John Dennis, Duncan McCloud, Marland Proctor, Eric Stern

GRAVE OF THE VAMPIRE (Entertainment Pyramid) Director, John Hayes; In color; Rated PG; 95 minutes; No other credits available; January release. CAST: William Smith, Michael Pataki, Lynn Peters, Diane Holden, Jay Adler, Kitty Vallacher, Jay Scott, Lieux Dressler

VANISHING WILDERNESS (Pacific International Enterprises) Producers-Directors, Arthur R. Dubs, Heinz Seilman; Screenplay, Lee Chaney, Peter Scott; Narration, Rex Allen; Photography, Heinz Seilman; In color; Rated G; 90 minutes; January release. A documentary on nature and wildlife from the Arctic to the Everglades.

WONDER OF IT ALL (Pacific International Enterprises) Producer, Director, Editor, Arthur R. Dubs; Screenplay, James T. Flocker; Photography, Eugene Schumacher, Stewart Raffil; Music, William Loose; Song, Doug Dowdle; In Eastmancolor; Rated G; 95 minutes; January release. A documentary of wildlife narrated by Les Biegel.

NOT JUST ANOTHER WOMAN (Extravagant Films) Produced, Directed, and Written by Toby Ross; Associate Producer, Daniel Brooks; Photography, Bob Fletcher; Editor, Ed Rothkowitz; Music, Harold Ousley; In color; Rated X; 77 minutes; January release. CAST: Don Allen (Husband), Darby Lloyd Rains (Wife), Tina Russell (Sister), Arlana Blue, Eric Edwards, Davy Jones, Inga Kissen, Helen Madigan, Any Mattheiu, Hal Morris, Marc Stevens, Cindy West

Ilona Wilson, Vito Scotti
in "How to Seduce a Woman"

Pam Grier, Margaret Markov
in "The Arena"

Michael Pataki, Stewart Moss
in "The Bat People"

Candice Rialson
in "Pets"

THE BAT PEOPLE (American International) Original release title "It Lives by Night"; Producer, Lou Shaw; Director, Jerry Jameson; Screenplay, Lou Shaw; Executive Producers, Nicolas Jenne, Matthew Lionetti; Associate Producer, Dante Cuccinello; Photography, Matthew Leonetti; Assistant Director, Bill Lukather; Music, Artie Kane; Editor, Tom Stevens; Song, Artie Kane, Morgan Ames; Sung by Sally Stevens; In DeLuxe Color; Rated PG; 95 minutes; January release. CAST: Stewart Moss (Dr. John Beck), Marianne McAndrew (Cathy), Michael Pataki (Sgt.), Paul Carr (Dr. Kipling), Arthur Space (Tramp), Robert Berk (Motel Owner), Pat Delaney (Ms. Jax), George Paulsin (Youth in car), Bonnie Van Dyke (Girl in car), Jeni Kulik (Nurse attacked), Laurie Brooks Jefferson (Nurse).

THE ARENA (New World) Producer, Mark Damon; Director, Steve Carver; Screenplay, John and Joyce Corrington; Photography, Aristide Massacessi; Music, Francesco De Masi; Editors, Joe Dante, Jann Carver; Assistant Director, Romano Scandariato; Designer, Mimmo Scavia; In Techniscope and Technicolor; Rated R; 85 minutes; January release. CAST: Pam Grier (Mamawi), Margaret Markov (Bodicia), Lucretia Love (Deirde), Paul Muller, Daniel Vargas, Marie Louise, Mary Count, Sara Bay, Vic Karis, Sid Lawrence, Anthony Vernon, Dick Palmer, Anna Melita, Christopher Oakes, Peter Cester, Jho Jhenkins, Ivan Gasper, Piertro Torrisi, Salvatore Baccaro

LIALEH Producer, Kenneth Elliot; Direction and Screenplay, Barron Bercovichy; Photography, Paul Goldsmith; Music, Bernard Purdie; No other credits; In Technicolor; Rated X; 75 minutes; January release. CAST: Jennifer Leigh, Larry Pertillar, Darryl Speer, John D. Montgomery, Any Mathieu, Doli Abroms, Inger Kissin, Helen Highwater, Rosetta Garies, Bernard Purdie

DIABOLIC WEDDING (Ellman Enterprises) In color; Rated R; No other credits available; February release; Starring Margaret O'Brien

THE FREE LIFE Producer, Trout Fishing in America Films; Directors, Ronnie Hersh, Russ Schwartz, Richard Searls; Photography, Ronnie Hersh; Screenplay, Russ Schwartz; Editors, Russ Schwartz, Richard Searls; Not rated; 63 minutes; February release. A documentary on the unsuccessful attempt at a first trans-Atlantic crossing in a balloon.

PETS (Dahlia) Producer-Director, Raphael Nussbaum; Screenplay, Richard Reich; In color; Rated R; February release. CAST: Joan Blackman, Candy Rialson, Teri Guzman, Ed Bishop, K. T. Stevens, Berry Kroeger

FRINGE BENEFITS (Distribpic) Producers, Ed Reese, Al Gordon; Director, Al Gordon; Screenplay, Ed Reese; Photography, Ian Cordell; Music, Ed Reese, Steve Ziplow; Editor, Al Gordon; In Eastmancolor; Rated X; February release. CAST: Georgina Spelvin, Kevin Andre, Michelle Magazine, Eric Edwards, Hardy Harrison, Angel Street, Susie Mathews, Tania Tittle, Barbra Cole, Jeffrey Hurst

ROAD MOVIE (Grove Press) Producer-Director, Joseph Strick; Screenplay, Judith Rascoe; Editor, Sylvia Sarner; Photography, Don Lenzer; Music, Stanley Meyers; In color; Rated R; 88 minutes; February release. CAST: Robert Drivas (Gil), Regina Baff (Janice), Barry Bostwick (Hank), David Bauer (Harry)

TEARS OF HAPPINESS (Mutual) Producer, John Kurkjian; Direction and Screenplay, Sarky Mouradian; Photography, Gregory Sandor; Editor, Sergio Murad; Music, Jaime Mendoza; In Eastmancolor; Not rated; 105 minutes; February release. CAST: Manuel (Raffi), Sosie Kodjian (Silva), S. Sepian (Son), Levon Yergat (Father), Jon Kouzouyan (Brother), Lynne Guthrie (Lisa), Jack D. Boghaossian (Manager), Adam Aivazian (Artist)

Georgina Spelvin
in "Fringe Benefits"

Barry Bostwick
in "Road Movie"

101

Roberts Blossom
in "Deranged"

Linda Lovelace
in "Deep Throat Part II"

WHO FEARS THE DEVIL (Jack H. Harris) Title changed to "Legend of Hillbilly John"; Producer, Barney Rosenzweig; Director, John Newland; Screenplay, Melvin Levy; Based on book by Manly Wade Wellman; Photography, Flemming Olsen; Music, Roger Kellaway; Editor, Russell Schoengarth; Assistant Director, Jack Barry; In Metrocolor; A Two's Company Production; Rated PG; 89 minutes; February release. CAST: Severn Darden (Marduke), Sharon Henesy (Lily), Honor Hound (Himself), Sidney Clute (Charles), Denver Pyle (Grandpappy), White Lightnin' (Themselves), William Traylor (Rev. Millen), Harris Yulin (Zebulon), Susan Strasberg (Polly), Alfred Ryder (Onselm), R. G. Armstrong (Bristowe), Chester Jones (Uncle), Val Avery (Cobart), Percy Rodriguez (Captain), Hedges Capers (John)

THE HOUSE OF SEVEN CORPSES (International Amusements) Produced, Directed and Written by Paul Harrison; A TCA Production; In color; Rated PG; 90 minutes; February release. CAST: John Ireland, Faith Domergue, John Carradine, Carole Wells

THE DOLL SQUAD (Feature-Faire) Producer-Director, Ted V. Mikels; In color; Rated R; February release. CAST: Michael Ansara, Francine York, Anthony Eisley, John Carter, Lisa Todd

SUGAR HILL (American International) Executive Producer, Samuel Z. Arkoff; Producer, Elliot Schick; Director, Paul Maslansky; Screenplay, Tim Kelly; Photography, Bob Jessup; Editor, Karl Kress; In Movielab West Color; Rated PG; 91 minutes; February release. CAST: Marki Bey (Diana "Sugar" Hill), Robert Quarry (Morgan), Don Pedro Colley (Baron), Richard Lawson (Valentine), Betty Anne Rees (Celeste), Zara Culley (Mama Maitresse), Larry D. Johnson (Langston), Charles Robinson (Fabulous), Rick Hagood (Tank), Ed Geldhart (O'Brien), Thomas C. Carroll (Baker), Albert J. Baker (George), Raymond E. Simpson (King), Charles Krohn (Capt.), Jack Bell (Parkhurst), Peter Harrell III (Photographer), Walter Price (Preacher), Judy Hanson (Masseuse), Tony Brubaker (Head Zombie)

DEEP THROAT PART II (Bryanson) A Damiano Production i color; Rated R; February release; Starring Linda Lovelace. No othe details available.

DERANGED (American International) Producer, Tom Karr; D rectors, Jeff Gillen, Alan Ormsby; Photography, Jack McGowan Screenplay, Alan Ormsby; Music, Carl Zittrer; Assistant Directors Ken Goch, Martin Gillen; Art Director, Albert Fisher; A Kar International Picture; In Movielab Color; Rated R; 83 minute February release. CAST: Roberts Blossom (Ezra), Cosette Lee (Ma Leslie Carlson (Narrator), Robert Warner (Harlan), Marcia Dia mond (Jenny), Brian Sneagle (Brad), Arlene Gillen (Miss Johnson Robert McHeady (Sheriff), Marion Waldman (Maureen), Jac Mather (Drunk), Micki Moore (Mary), Pat Orr (Sally)

CHARIOTS OF THE GODS (Sun International) Producer, Man fred Barthel; Director, Harald Reigl; Commentary by Wilhelm Pe gersdorff; From the book by Erich von Daniken; Photography, Erns Wild; Music, Peter Thomas; Editor, Herman Haller; In color; 9 minutes; February release. A documentary that attempts to prov outer space visits on earth in the distant past.

THE WRESTLER (Entertainment Ventures) Producer, W. R Frank; Executive Producer, Verne Gagne; Director, Jim Westman Screenplay, Eugene Gump; Photography, Gil Hubbs; Editor, Nea Chastain; Music, William Loose, William Allen Castleman; Assi tant Director, Art Levinson; Song, Howard Arthur; Performed b Mona Brandt and Pat McKee; In color; Rated PG; 95 minute February release. CAST: Billy Robinson (Billy), Edward Asne (Frank), Elaine Giftos (Debbie), Verne Gagne (Mike), Sara Mille (Betty), Harold Sakata (Odd Job), Sam Menecker (Mobster), Hard boiled Haggerty (Bartender), Themselves: Dusty Rhodes, Dic Murdoch, The Crusher, The Bruiser, Lord James Blears, Supersta Billy Grahm

Zara Cully, Marki Bey, Don Pedro Colley
in "Sugar Hill"

Henry Winkler, Paula Prentiss, Peter
Boyle, Fred Williamson in "Crazy Joe"

Paula Prentiss, Peter Boyle
in "Crazy Joe"

Sian Barbara Allen, Desi Arnaz, Jr.
in "Billy Two Hats"

CRAZY JOE (Columbia) Executive Producer, Nino E. Krisman; Director, Carlo Lizzani; Screenplay, Lewis John Carlino; Based on story by Nicholas Gage; Photography, Aldo Tonti; Art Director, Robert Gundlach; Music, Gian Carlo Caramello; Editor, Peter Zinner; A Dino De Laurentiis Presentation of a B-P Associates Production; In color; Rated R; 100 minutes; February release. CAST: Peter Boyle (Crazy Joe), Paula Prentiss (Anne), Fred Williamson (Willy), Charles Cioffi (Coletti), Rip Torn (Richie), Luther Adler (Falco), Fausto Tozzi (Frank), Franco Lantieri (Nunzio), Eli Wallach (Don Vittorio), Louis Guss (Magliocco), Carmine Caridi (Jelly), Henry Winkler (Mannie), Gabriele Torrei (Cheech), Guido Leontini (Angelo), Sam Coppola (Chick), Mario Erpichini (Danny), Adam Wade (J.D.), Timothy Holley (Lou), Ralph Wilcox (Sam), Peter Savage (DeMarco), Herve Villechaize (Samson), Robert Riesel, Dan Resin (FBI Agents), Nella Dina (Mrs. Falco)

SUPERDAD (Buena Vist) Producer, Bill Anderson; Director, Vincent McEveety; Screenplay, Joseph L. McEveety; Based on story by Harlan Ware; Photography, Andrew Jackson; Music, Buddy Baker; Songs, Shane Tatum; Sung by Bobby Goldsboro; Art Directors, John B. Mansbridge, William J. Creber; Editor, Ray de Leuw; Costumes, Shelby Tatum; Associate Producer, Christopher Hibler; Assistant Directors, Bud Grace, Dorothy Kieffer; A Walt Disney Production; In Technicolor; Rated G; 96 minutes; February release. CAST: Bob Crane (Charlie), Kurt Russell (Bart), Barbara Rush (Sue), Joe Flynn (Hershberger), Kathleen Cody (Wendy), Joby Baker (Klutch), and Dick Van Patten, B. Kirby, Jr., Judith Lowry, Ivor Francis, Jonathan Daly, Naomi Stevens, Nicholas Hammond, Jack Manning, Jim Wakefield, Ed McCready, Larry Gelman, Steve Dunne, Allison McKay, Leon Belasco, Sarah Fankboner, Christina Anderson, Ed Begley, Jr., Don Carter, Joy Ellison, Ann Marshall, Mike Rupert

PANORAMA BLUE (Ellman Film Enterprises) Executive Producer, Richard Ellman; Producer-Director, Alan Roberts; Screenplay and Music, Steve Michaels; Photography, Bob Brownell; Editor, James Walters; In Eastmancolor; Rated X: 85 minutes; February release. CAST: Carona Faoro, Stephen Nave, Sue Moses, Dennis Zlamal, Rene Bond, Sandy Dempsey, John Paul Jones, Rich Loots, Linda York, Charlotte Ruse, Bob Taylor, Reg Bartram, Con Covert, Johna Lee, Cyndee Summers, Rich Cassidy, Richard S. Ellman

HORROR HIGH (Crown International) Producer, James P. Graham; Director, Larry Stouffer; In color; Rated PG; March release. CAST: Pat Cardi (Vernon), Rosie Holotik (Girlfriend), Joyce Hash (Miss Grinstaf), Austin Stoker (Lt. Bozeman)

ALWAYS A NEW BEGINNING (Goodell) Produced, Directed, Photographed by John D. Goodell; Editor, Greg Goodell; Narration, James Lawless; Music, Herb Pilhofer; In color; Not rated; 90 minutes; March release. A documentary about brain-damaged children.

THE CONFESSOR Produced, Directed, Photographed, Edited by Edward Bergman, Alan Soffin; Music, Chico Hamilton; 73 minutes; March release.

BILLY TWO HATS (United Artists) Producer, Norman Jewison, Patrick Palmer; Director, Ted Kotcheff; Photography, Brian West; Art Director, Tony Pratt; In color; Rated PG; 99 minutes; March release. CAST: Gregory Peck (Deans), Desi Arnaz, Jr. (Billy), Jack Warden (Gifford), Sian Barbara Allen (Esther), David Huddleston (Copeland), John Pearce (Spencer), Dawn Littlesky (Squaw)

Bob Crane, Barbara Rush, Kathleen Cody,
Kurt Russell in "Superdad"

Sian Barbara Allen, Gregory Peck, Desi
Arnaz, Jr. in "Billy Two Hats"

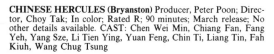
Season Hubley, Richie Havens
in "Catch My Soul"

"The Black Six"

CHINESE HERCULES (Bryanston) Producer, Peter Poon; Director, Choy Tak; In color; Rated R; 90 minutes; March release; No other details available. CAST: Chen Wei Min, Chiang Fan, Fang Yeh, Yang Sze, Li Tien Ying, Yuan Feng, Chin Ti, Liang Tin, Fah Kiuh, Wang Chug Tsung

THE KILLING KIND (Media Trend) Producer, George Edwards; Director, Curtis Harrington; Executive Producer, Leon Mirell; Screenplay, Lony Crechales, George Edwards; Photography, Maric Losi; Music, Andrew Belling; In color; Rated R; 95 minutes; March release. CAST: Ann Sothern (Thelma), John Savage (Terry), Ruth Roman (Rhea), Luana Anders (Librarian), Cindy Williams (Roomer), Sue Bernard (Raped Girl)

JANIE (Cine Flicks) In Eastmancolor; Rated X; No other credits available; March release: Starring Mary Jane Carpenter

HOUSE OF A THOUSAND DELIGHTS (Group I) Director, Ted Roter; In color; Rated X; No other credits available; March release. CAST: Byron Anderson, Mikki Damwyk, Jim Martin

CHILDREN SHOULDN'T PLAY WITH DEAD THINGS (Europix International) Producers, Benjamin Clark, Gary Goch; Direction and Screenplay, Benjamin Clark; Rated PG; March release. CAST: Alan Ormsby, Jane Daly, Anya Ormsby, Jeffrey Gillen, Valerie Mamches, Paul Cronin, Seth Sklarey

TIME TO RUN (World Wide) Rated PG; In color; No other credits available; March release. CAST: Ed Nelson, Randall Carver, Barbara Sigel, Joan Winmill, Gordon Rigsby, Billy Graham

THE TOUCH OF SATAN (Dundee) Producer, George E. Carey; Director, Don Henderson; Screenplay, James E. McLarty; In Deluxe Color; Rated PG; 87 minutes; March release. CAST: Michael Berry, Emby Mellay, Lee Amber, Yvonne Winslow, Jeanne Gerson

THE BLACK SIX (Cinemation) Producer-Director, Matt Cimber; Screenplay, George Theakos; Associate Producer, Rafer Johnson; Photography, William Swenning; Music, David Moscoe; Assistant Director, Jeff Richard; Editor, William Swenning; In color; Rated R; 90 minutes; March release. CAST: Gene Washington (Bubba), Carl Eller (Junior Bro), Lem Barney (Frenchy), Mercury Morris (Bookie), Willie Lanier (Tommy), Joe Greene (Kevin), Rosalind Miles (Ceal), John Isenbarger (Moose), Ben Davidson (Thor), Maury Wills (Coach)

CATCH MY SOUL (Cinerama) Producers, Richard Rosenbloom, Jack Good; Director, Patrick McGoohan; Screenplay, Jack Good; Adapted from Shakespeare's "Othello"; Associate Producer, Huw Davies; Executive Producer, Charles W. Fries; Music, Richie Havens, Tony Joe White, Bonnie and Delaney; Photography, Conrad Hall; Production Executive, Art Stolnitz; Presented by Metromedia Producers Corp.; In color; Rated PG; 97 minutes; March release. CAST: Richie Havens (Othello), Lance LaGault (Iago), Season Hubley (Desdemona), Susan Tyrrell (Emilia), Tony Joe White (Cassio), Bonnie Bramlett, Delaney Bramlett, Raleigh Gardenhire, Wayne Eagle Waterhouse, Family Lotus

IN THE BEGINNING. ... (Poolemar) Title changed from "Bible!"; Producer, Marvin Shulman; Directed and Photographed by Wakefield Poole; Editors, Joseph Nelson, Peter Schneckenburger; Costumes, Stanley Simmons; Presented by Joseph Green; In color; Rated X; 84 minutes; March release. CAST: Bo White (Adam), Caprice Couselle (Eve), Georgina Spelvin (Bathsheba), Nicholas Flamel (David), Robert Benes (Uriah), Nancy Wachter (Handmaiden), Brahm van Zetten (Samson), Gloria Grant (Delilah), Bonnie Mathis (Mary), Dennis Wayne (Angel), Allison Fields, Dan Johnson, Patti Perkins, Oscar Shulman, Jane Sobel, Willie Hermine, Cathy Hermine, Leopoldo Aldea de Zea, Don Farr, John Parr, Bruce Shenton, Julio Velez

Dennis Wayne, Bonnie Mathis
in "In the Beginning . . ."

Brian Narelle, Cal Kuniholm, Dan O'Bannon
in "Dark Star"

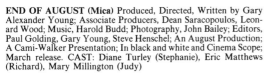

Tony Giorgio, Pam Grier, Fred Lerner
in "Foxy Brown"

Mick Jagger and The Rolling Stones

END OF AUGUST (Mica) Produced, Directed, Written by Gary Alexander Young; Associate Producers, Dean Saracopoulos, Leonard Wood; Music, Harold Budd; Photography, John Bailey; Editors, Paul Golding, Gary Young, Steve Henschel; An August Production; A Cami-Walker Presentation; In black and white and Cinema Scope; March release. CAST: Diane Turley (Stephanie), Eric Matthews (Richard), Mary Millington (Judy).

DARK STAR (Jack H. Harris Enterprises) Producer-Director, John Carpenter; Executive Producer, Jack H. Harris; Screenplay, John Carpenter, Dan O'Bannon; Photography, Douglas Knapp; Editor, Designer, Dan O'Bannon; Assistant Director, J. Stein Kaplan; In Metrocolor; Rated G; 83 minutes; March release. CAST: Brian Narelle (Doolittle), Andreijah Pahich (Talby), Carl Kuniholm (Boiler), Dan O'Bannon (Pinback)

THE GREAT AMERICAN COWBOY (Sun International) Executive Producer, Albert P. Heiner; Producer-Director-Editor, Keith Merrill; Screenplay, Douglas Kent Hall; Photography, Keith Merrill, Preston Fox, Reed Smoot, Alan Cassidy; Music, Harold Farberman; In DeLuxe Color; Not rated; 90 minutes; March release. A documentary of today's rodeo world narrated by Joel McCrea.

SEX FREAKS (Rainbow) Produced, Directed and Written by M. C. Von Hellen; Photography, Pierre Contran; Editor, Norman Fox; Music, Laslo Brundic; In Eastmancolor; Rated X; 79 minutes; March release. CAST: John Holmes, Rich Cassidy, Joan Morrissey, Robert Chatham, Tina Hakansson, Leona Raphael, Noelle Cooper, Dirk Lenz, Viola James

MEMORIES WITHIN MISS AGGIE (Inish Kae Ltd) Director, Gerard Damiano; Screenplay, Ron Wertheim, Gerard Damiano; Photography, Harry Flecks; Editor, St. Marks Place; Music, Rupert Holmes; In color; Rated X; 78 minutes; April release. CAST: Deborah Ashira (Aggie), Patrick Ferrelly (Richard), Kim Pope (Aggie 1), Mary Stuart (Aggie 2), Darby Lloyd Rains (Aggie 3), Eric Edwards (Boyfriend 1), Harry Reems (Boyfriend 2), Leo Zorba (Voyeur), Ralph Herman, Christopher Kersen, Rolf Beck

LADIES AND GENTLEMEN, THE ROLLING STONES (Dragon Aire) Executive Producer, Marshall Chess; Producers, Rollin Binzer, Marshall Chess, Bob Fries, Steve Gebhardt; Director, Rollin Binzer; Editor, Laura Lesser; Photography, Jay Cassidy, Bob Fries, Steve Gebhardt, D. P. Doug Ibold, George Manupelli, Joe Pipher; A Musifilm/Chessco-Bingo/Butterfly Production: In color; Not rated; 90 minutes; April release. A documentary filmed and recorded live during the Rolling Stones 1972 U.S. Tour, featuring Mick Jagger.

FOXY BROWN (American International) Producer, Buzz Feitshans; Direction and Screenplay, Jack Hill; Photography, Brick Marquard; Assistant Directors, Frank Beetson, Michael Messinger; Editor, Chuck McClelland; Art Director, Kirk Axtel; Songs composed and sung by Willie Hutch; In Movielab Color; Rated R: 94 minutes; April release. CAST: Pam Grier (Foxy Brown), Antonio Fargas (Link), Peter Brown (Steve), Terry Carter (Michael), Kathryn Loder (Katherine), Harry Holcombe (Judge), Sid Haig (Hays), Juanita Brown (Claudia), Sally Ann Stroud (Deb), Bob Minor (Oscar), Tony Giorgio (Eddie), Fred Lerner (Bunyan), Judy Cassmore (Vicki)

ATTICA (Attica) Produced, Directed, and Edited by Cinda Firestone; Assistant Director-Editor, Tucker Ashworth; Photography, Roland Barnes, Jay Lamarch, Mary Lampson, Jesse Goodman, Carol Stein, Kevin Keating; In color; Not rated; 80 minutes; April release. A documentary on the rebellion of the inmates at Attica Prison on Sept. 13, 1971.

SILENCE (Cinema Financial of America) Producer, James Polakof; Co-Producer, H. Kaye Dyal; Director, John Korty; Screenplay, Mary Mackey, Ellen Geer; Photography, Hiro Morikawa; Editor, Vivien Hillgrove; Music, Ed Bogus, High Country; Designer, Joe Guerena; Assistant Director, Dan McCann; In Eastmancolor; Rated G; 88 minutes; April release. CAST: Will Geer (Crazy Jack), Ellen Geer (Barbara), Richard Kelton (Al), Ian Geer Flanders (Eric), Craig Kelly (Sheriff), Sam Robustelli (Deputy), Tad Geer, Raleigh Geer (Car Thieves)

Patrick Farrelly, Deborah Ashira
in "Memories within Miss Aggie"

"Attica"

105

Felice Orlandi, Robert Duvall, Karen
Black in "The Outfit"

Richard Jaeckel, Sheree North
in "The Outfit"

THE OUTFIT (MGM) Producer, Carter De Haven; Direction and Screenplay, John Flynn; Based on novel by Richard Stark; Music, Jerry Fielding; Photography, Bruce Surtees; Art Director, Tambi Larsen; Editor, Ralph E. Winters; Assistant Directors, William McGarry, John Thomas Lenox, William F. Sheehan; Prison Music, Steve Gillette, Jeremy Kronsberg; In Metrocolor; Rated PG; 103 minutes; April release. CAST: Robert Duvall (Macklin), Karen Black (Bett), Joe Don Baker (Cody), Robert Ryan (Mailer), Timothy Carey (Menner), Richard Jaeckel (Chemey), Sheree North (Buck's wife), Felice Orlandi (Frank), Marie Windsor (Madge), Jane Greer (Alma), Henry Jones (Doctor), Joanna Cassidy (Rita), Tom Reese (1st man), Elisha Cook (Carl), Bill McKinney (Buck), Anita O'Day (Herself), Archie Moore (Packard), Tony Young (Accountant), Roland La Starza (Hit man), Edward Ness (Ed), Roy Roberts (Bob), Toby Andersen (Attendant), Emile Meyer (Amos), Roy Jenson (Al), Philip Kenneally (Bartender), Bern Hoffman (Jim), John Steadman (Attendant), Paul Genge (Pay-off Man), Francis de Sales (Jim), James Bacon (Bookie), Army Archerd (Butler), Tony Trabert (Himself)

NIGHT OF THE COBRA WOMAN (New World) Producers, Kerry Magness, Harvey Marks; Director, Andrew Meyer; Screenplay, Andrew Meyer, Kerry Magness; In Metrocolor; Rated R; 85 minutes; April release. CAST: Joy Bang (Joanna), Marlene Clark (Lena), Roger Garrett (Duff), Slash Marks (Sgt. Merkle)

OUR TIME (Warner Bros.) Producer, Richard A. Roth; Director, Peter Hyams; Screenplay, Jane C. Stanton; Photography, Jules Brenner; Art Director, Peter Wooley; Editor, James Mitchell; Music, Michel Legrand; Assistant Directors, Hal Galli, Herb Dufine; In Technicolor; Rated PG; 90 minutes; April release. CAST: Pamela Sue Martin (Abby), Betsy Slade (Muffy), Parker Stevenson (Michael), George O'Hanlon, Jr. (Malcolm), Karen Balkin (Laura), Debralee Scott (Ann), Nora Heflin (Emmy), Kathryn Holcomb (Helen), Roderick Cook (Headmaster), Edith Atwater (Mrs. Pendleton), Marijane Maricle (Miss Picard), Meg Wyllie (Nurse), Mary Jackson (Miss Moran), Carol Arthur (Gym Teacher), Hope Summers (Biology Teacher), Jerry Hardin (Keats), Robert Walden (Frank), Michael Gray (Buzzy)

THE INNERVIEW (Beymer) Produced, Directed, Written, Photographed, Edited by Richard Beymer; In black and white, and color; Not rated; 90 minutes; April release. CAST: Joanna Bochco, Richard Beymer, Antranig Mahakian

DREAMS AND NIGHTMARES (New Yorker) Produced and Written by Abe Osheroff; Directed and Edited by Larry Klingman; In color; Not rated; 60 minutes; April release. A documentary on the Spanish Civil War.

VISIT TO A CHIEF'S SON (United Artists) Producer, Robert Halmi; Director, Lamont Johnson; Screenplay, Albert Reuben; Based on novel by Robert Halmi; Music, Francis Lai; Photography, Ernest Day; Editor, Tom Rolf; Entertainment from Transamerica Corp.; In color; Rated G; 92 minutes; April release. CAST: Richard Mulligan (Robert), Johnny Sekka (Nemolok), Philip Hodgdon (Kevin), Jesse Kinaru (Kondonyo), Jock Anderson (Jock), Chief Lomoiro and his Masai Tribespeople for Kenya, East Africa.

THE SPIKES GANG (United Artists) Producer, Walter Mirisch; Director, Richard Fleischer; Screenplay, Irving Ravetch, Harriet Frank, Jr.; Music, Fred Karlin; Editors, Ralph Winters, Frank J. Urioste; Photography, Brian West; A Mirisch Corp. Presentation; United Artists Entertainment from Transamerica Corp.; In DeLuxe Color; Rated PG; 96 minutes; April release. CAST: Lee Marvin (Spikes), Gary Grimes (Will), Ron Howard (Les), Charlie Martin Smith (Tod), Arthur Hunnicutt (Kid White), Noah Beery (Jack), Marc Smith (Abel), Don Fellows (Cowboy), Elliott Sullivan (Billy), Robert Beatty (Sheriff), Ralph Brown (Posse Leader), Bill Curran (Gillis), Ricardo Palacios (Doctor), David Thomson (Sheriff), Bert Conway (Teller), Adolfo Thous (Pawnbroker), Allen E. Russell (Morton), Frances O'Flynn (Mrs. Young)

THE LAST PORNO FLICK (Bryanston) Title changed to "The Mad Mad Movie Makers"; Producer, Steve Bono; Director, Ray Marsh; Screenplay, Larry Ditillio; In color; Rated PG; April release. CAST: Frank Calcagnini, Michael Pataki, Mike Kellin, Jo Anne Meredith, Robyn Hilton, Tom Signorelli, Marianna Hill

Pamela Sue Martin, Parker Stevenson
in "Our Time"

Gary Grimes, Ron Howard, Lee Marvin, Charlie
Martin Smith in "The Spikes Gang"

Vonetta McGee, Max Julien
in "Thomasine and Bushrod"

"Caged Heat"

THOMASINE AND BUSHROD (Columbia) Producers, Harvey Bernhard, Max Julien; Director, Gordon Parks, Jr.; Screenplay, Max Julien; Photography, Lucien Ballard; Music, Coleridge-Taylor Perkinson; Editor, Frank C. Decot; Designer, Dale Beldin; Title Song, Arthur Lee; Associate Producer, Vonetta McGee; Assistant Directors, Robert Anderson, Gene Anderson, Jr.; Costumes, Andra Lilly; In color; Rated PG; 93 minutes; April release. CAST: Max Julien (Bushrod), Vonetta McGee (Thomasine), George Murdock (Bogardie), Glynn Turman (Jomo), Juanita Moore (Pecolia), Joel Fluellen (Nathaniel), Jackson D. Kane (Adolph), Bud Conlan (Tyler), Kip Allen (Jenkins), Ben Zeller (Scruggs), Herb Robins (Dodson), Harry Luck (Sheriff), Jason Bernard (Seldon), Paul Barby (Teller), Scott Britt (Frank), Geno Silva (Taffy), John Gill (Dealer), Dave Burleson (Card Player), James Sargeant (Farley), Leigh Potter, Tedi Altice (Washerwomen), Charles Gaines (Bank Customer), Katy Martin (Mrs. Tyler), Patricia Milner (Mrs. Carter), Brad Woolley (Ricky), Lilybell Crawford (Lady in bank), Max Cisneros (Kane), Neil Davis (Barber), Raleigh Gardenhire (Renegade)

SING SING THANKSGIVING (Varied Directions) Producer, Harry Wiland; Director, David Hoffman, Harry Wiland; Photography, David Hoffman, Joe Constantino, Bob Fiori, Jerry Cotts; Editors, David Hoffman, Ruth Schell; In color; Not rated; 78 minutes; April release. A documentary of a pop concert inside Sing Sing prison with Joan Baez, Mimi Farina, B. B. King, The Voices of East Harlem, Jimmy Walker, Joe Williams

THE HOT BOX (New World) Director, Joseph Viola; In Metrocolor; Rated R: April release. No other details available. CAST: Carmen Argenziano, Andrea Cagan, Margaret Markov, Rickey Richardson, Laurie Rose, Charles Dierkop

I DISREMEMBER MAMA (Europix International) Director, Paul Leder; Music, Herschel Burke Gilbert; Screenplay, William Norton; In color; Rated R; April release. CAST: Zooey Hall, Geri Reischl, Joanne Moore Jordan, Marlene Tracy

SILENT NIGHT, BLOODY NIGHT (Cannon) Director, Ted Gershuny; In color; Rated R; 88 minutes; April release. CAST: Patrick O'Neal, James Patterson, Astrid Heeren, John Carradine, Walter Abel, Mary Woronov, Candy Darling, Ondine

THE SINGLE GIRLS (Dimension) Produced and Directed by Ferd and Beverly Sebastion; Story and Screenplay, Ann Cawthorne; In color; Rated R; April release. CAST: Claudia Jennings (Allison), Jean Marie Ingels (Phyllis), Cheri Howell (Shannon), Joan Prather (Lola), Gregg Mullavey (George), Ed Blessington (Bud), Victor Izay (Andrew), Jason Ledger (Blue), Robyn Hilton (Denise), Wayne Dvorak (Stevens), Albert Popwell (Morris), Mercy Rooney (Kathy)

CAGED HEAT (New World) Producer, Evelyn Purcell; Direction and Screenplay, Jonathan Demme; Executive Producer, Samuel Gelfman; Photography, Tak Fujimoto; Editors, Johanna Demetrakis, Carolyn Hicks; Music, John Cale; Art Director, Eric Thiermann; Assistant Director, David Osterhout; In DeLuxe Color; Rated R; 83 minutes; May release. CAST: Juanita Brown, Roberta Collins, Erica Gavin, Ella Reid, Rainbeaux Smith, Barbara Steele, Warren Miller, Lynda Gold, Mickey Fox, Tobi Carr Rafelson, Ann Stockdale, Irene Stokes, Cynthia Songey, Carmen Argenziano, John Aprea, Leslie Otis, Mike Shack, George Armitage, Patrick Wright, Joe Viola, Gary Littlejohn, Hal Marshall, Carol Miller, Cindy Cale, Essie Hayes, Layla Gallaway, Dorothy Love, Bob Reese, Valley Hoffman, Amy Randall, Keisha

BLACK EYE (Warner Bros.) Producer, Pat Rooney; Director, Jack Arnold; Screenplay, Mark Haggard, Jim Martin; From novel "Murder on the Wild Side" by Jeff Jacks; Photography, Ralph Woolsey; Editor, Gene Rurriero; Executive Producer, Jack Reeves; Associate Producer, Larry Noble; Assistant Producer, Anne Reeves; Music, Mort Garson; Assistant Directors, Clark Paylow, David Hamburger; A Jerry Buss Presentation; In Technicolor; Rated PG; 98 minutes; May release. CAST: Fred Williamson (Stone), Rosemary Forsyth (Francis), Teresa Graves (Cynthia), Floy Dean (Diane), Richard Anderson (Dole), Cyril Delevanti (Talbot), Richard X. Slattery (Bowen), Larry Mann (Avery), Bret Morrison (Majors), Susan Arnold (Amy)

Jesse Kinaru, Johnny Sekka, Richard Mulligan,
Philip Hodgdon in "Visit to a Chief's Son"

Sue Ann Arnold, Fred Williamson
in "Black Eye"

107

Candice Rialson, Kimberly Hyde, Maria Rojo
in "Candy Stripe Nurses"

Tom Drake, Robert Walker, Jr., Cesar Romero
in "Spectre of Edgar Allan Poe"

CANDY STRIPE NURSES (New World) Producer, Julie Corman; Direction and Screenplay, Allan Holleb; Photography, Colin Campbell; Art Director, Jane Ruhm; Editor, Allan Holzman; Assistant Director, Teri Schwartz; Music, Eron Tabor, Ron Thompson; In Metrocolor; Rated R; 80 minutes; May release. CAST: Candice Rialson, Robin Mattson, Maria Rojo, Kimberly Hyde, Roger Cruz, Rick Gates, Rod Haase, Don Keefer, Dick Miller, Stanley Ralph Ross, Monte Landis, Tom Baker, John David Garfield, Alma Beltran, Kendrew Lascelles, Michael Ross Verona, Elana Casey, John Hudson, Ruth Warshawsky, June Christopher, Al Alu, Ray Galvin, Frank Lugo, Rick Garcia, Bill Erwin, Tara Strohmeier

THE SPECTRE OF EDGAR ALLAN POE (Cinerama) Produced, Directed, Written by Mohy Quandour; Photography, Robert Birchal; Music, Allen D. Allen; A Cintel Production; In color; Rated PG; 89 minutes; May release. CAST: Robert Walker, Jr. (Poe), Cesar Romero (Grimaldi), Tom Drake (Forrest), Carol Ohmart (Lisa), Mary Grover (Lenore), Mario Milano (Joseph), Karen Hartford (Nurse), Dennis Fimple (Farron), Paul Bryar (White), Frank Packard (Jonah), Marsha Mae Jones (Sarah)

THE DYNAMITE BROTHERS (Cinemation) Director, Al Adamson; In DeLuxe Color; Rated R; May release. CAST: Alan Tang, Timothy Brown, James Hong, Aldo Ray, Carolyn Ann Speed, Don Oliver.

DIRTY O'NEIL (American International) Producer, John C. Broderick; Directors, Howard Freen, Lewis Teague; Executive Producer, Leonidas Capetanos; Screenplay, Howard Freen; Music, Raoul Kraushaar; A United Producers Production; In Movielab Color; Rated R; 89 minutes; May release. CAST: Morgan Paull (O'Neil), Art Metrano (Lassiter), Pat Anderson (Lisa), Jean Manson (Ruby), Katie Saylor (Vera), Raymond O'Keefe (Lou), Tom Huff (Bennie), Bob Potter (Al), Sam Laws (Clyde), Liv Lindeland (Mrs. Crawford)

THE STOOLIE (Continental) Producer, Chase Mellen 3d; Executive Producer, Jackie Mason; Director, John G. Avidsen; Screenplay, Eugene Price, Larry Alexander, Marc B. Ray; Photography, Ralf Bode; Editor, Gerald Greenberg, Stanley Bochner; Music, William Goldstein; Rated PG; 90 minutes; May release. CAST: Jackie Mason (Roger), Josip Elic (1st Hijacker), Reid Cruikshank (2nd Hijacker), Dan Frazer (Alex), Leonard York (Maxie), Marcia Jean Kurtz (Sheila), Richard Casballo (Marco), Babette New (Sylvia)

WHERE THE RED FERN GROWS (Doty-Dayton) Executive Producer, George Ellis Doty; Producer, Lyman Dayton; Director, Norman Tokar; Screenplay, Douglas Stewart, Eleanor Lamb; From novel by Wilson Rawls; Photography, Dean Cundey; Editors, Marsh Hendry, Bob Bring; Music, Lex De Azevedo; Songs, The Osmonds; Assistant Director, William H. White; In DeLuxe Color; Rated G; 97 minutes; May release. CAST: James Whitmore (Grandpa), Beverly Garland (Mother), Jack Ging (Father), Lonny Chapman (Sheriff), Stewart Petersen (Billy), Jill Clark (Alice), Jeanna Wilson (Sara)

WELCOME TO ARROW BEACH (Warner Bros.) Producers, Jack Cushingham, Steven North; Director, Laurence Harvey; Screenplay, Wallace C. Bennett; Adapted by Jack Gross, Jr.; Photography, Gerald Perry Finnerman; Editor, James Potter; Music, Tony Camillo; Song, Bert Keyes and George Barrie, Sammy Cahn; Assistant Director, George Templeton; A Brut Production; In Eastmancolor; Rated R; 99 minutes; May release. CAST: Laurence Harvey (Jason), Joanna Pettet (Grace), Stuart Whitman (Deputy), John Ireland (Sheriff), Gloria LeRoy (Ginger), David Macklin (Alex), Dody Heath (Felice), Meg Foster (Robbin), Altovise Gore (Deputy Molly), Elizabeth St. Clair (Head Nurse), Jesse Vint (Hot Rod Driver)

PARDON MY BLOOPER (K-Tel International) Producer, Kermit Schafer; Song, Sam Coslow; Sung by Danny Street; Rated R; 82 minutes; No other details available; May release. Radio and TV's most hilarious boners.

Morgan Paull, Pat Anderson
in "Dirty O'Neil"

John Ireland, Joanna Pettet, Laurence Harvey
in "Welcome to Arrow Beach"

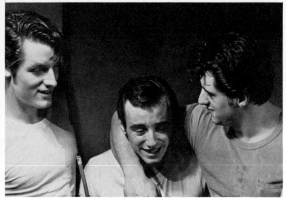

Perry King, Paul Mace, Sylvester Stallone
in "The Lords of Flatbush"

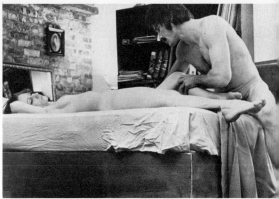

"Happy Days"

THE LORDS OF FLATBUSH (Columbia) Producer, Stephen F. Verona; Directors, Stephen F Verona, Martin Davidson; Screenplay, Stephen F. Verona, Gayle Gleckler, Martin Davidson; Music, Joe Brooks; Photography, Joseph Mangine, Edward Lachman; Editors, Stan Siegel, Muffie Meyer; Associate Producer, Richard Millman; Art Director, Glenda Miller; Additional Dialogue, Sylvester Stallone; Additional Music, Paul Jabara, Paul Nicholas; In color; Rated PG; 86 minutes, May release. CAST: Perry King (Chico), Sylvester Stallone (Stanley), Henry Winkler (Butchey), Paul Mace (Wimpy), Susie Blakely (Jane), Maria Smith (Frannie), Renee Paris (Annie), Paul Jabara (Crazy Cohen), Bruce Reed (Mike), Frank Stiefel (Arnie), Martin Davidson (Birnbaum), Joe Stern (Eddie), Ruth Klinger (Mrs. Tyrell), Joan Neuman (Miss Molina), Dolph Sweet (Rosiello), Lou Byrne (Mrs. Bradshaw), Bill Van Sleet (Bradshaw), Margaret Bauer (Nancy), Lillian Davidson, Ann Lefkowitz, Florence Schissler, Mildred Deutsch (Mah Jong Players), Ralph Rogers Trio (Wedding Band), Students: Ray Sharkey, Geraldine Smith, Darryl Peck, Bernardo Hiller, Karen Kaye, Phyllis Gibbs, Helen Calahan, Dana Foley, Barbara Foley, Thomas Clarke, Bonnie Sylvano, Linda Troiano, Mark Flanagan, Wedding Guests: Armand Assanti, Antonia Rey, Rose Rothman, George Goomishian, Arlene Gelb, Jamie Gelb, Stacy Gelb, Peter Mints, Tom Bauer, David Stein

THE TAKE (Columbia) Executive Producer, Stanley Rubin; Producer, Howard Brandy; Director, Robert Hartford-Davis; Screenplay, Del Reisman, Franklin Coen; From novel "Sir, You Bastard" by G. F. Newman; Photography, Duke Callaghan; Editor, Aaron Stell; Music, Fred Karlin; Art Director, Kirk Axtel; Assistant Director, Robin Clark; A World Film Services Production; In Metrocolor; Rated PG; 91 minutes; May release. CAST: Billy Dee Williams (Sneed), Eddie Albert (Chief Berrigan), Frankie Avalon (Danny), Sorrell Booke (Oscar), Tracy Reed (Nancy), Albert Salmi (Dolek), Vic Morrow (Manso), A. Martinez (Tallbear), James Luisi (Benedetto)

SWEET AGONY (Unique Films) Produced, Directed, and Written by Alex de Renzy; In color; Rated X; 73 minutes; May release. No other credits available.

HAPPY DAYS (Anonymous Releasing Triumvirate) Executive Producer, Beula Brown; Director, Beau Buchanan; Screenplay, Trixie Morris, Beau Buchanan; Photography, Gary Alexander; Editor, Jim Holiday; Music and Lyrics performed by Marcus Anthony; A Skinny Pictures Production; In color: Rated X; 95 minutes; May release. CAST: Georgina Spelvin, Cindy West, Arlana Blue, Joe O'Brien, Joyce Alan, Sonny Landham, Barbara Schwartz, Jenny Carlton, Caroline Denner, Douglas Drew, Pat Edwards, Raoul Foster, Curt Gerad, Harding Harrison, Nina Lasko, Rick Livermore, Jean Palmer, Celina Schneider, Peter Rabit

INTERNATIONAL STEWARDESSES (Rumson) Formerly "Supersonic Supergirls." In Stereovision 3-D and Eastmancolor; Rated X; 92 minutes; May release. No other credits available. CAST: Mary Pat Bonney (Candice), Phyllis Denike (Pixie), Adrienne Stroud, Goncha Ondemir (Mira), Peggy Church (Deeanne), Corona Faoro (Pam), Delana Bissonette, Sallie Stevens, Maurie Reese, Vicky Christy, Kathy Francis, Kitty Holcomb

MRS. BARRINGTON (Monarch) Producer, Allan Shackleton; Director, Chuck Vincent; Screenplay, Chuck Vincent, James Vidos; Photography, Stephen Colwell; Editor, Marc Ubell; Music, Richard Billay; Costumes, Robert Pusilo; In Cinefrects Color; Rated X; 86 minutes; May release. CAST: Kim Pope (Mrs. Barrington), Ida Klein (Eloise), David Hausman (Roberto), Marlow Ferguson (Ralph/James), David Kirk, Jack Sylva, Jennifer Welles, Jeffrey Hurst, Rebecca Brooke, Guy Thomas, Chris Jordan, Eric Edwards, Steve Tucker, Joseph Corral, Paul Giacobbe

A KNIFE FOR THE LADIES (Bryanston) Director, Larry G. Spangler; Screenplay, George Arthur Bloom; In Movielab Color; Rated R; May release. CAST: Jack Elam, Ruth Roman, Jeff Cooper, John Kellogg, Gene Evans, Diana Ewing, Joe Santos, Jon Spangler

MOON CHILD (Filmakers Ltd.) Direction and Screenplay, Alan Gadney; In color; Rated R; May release. CAST: John Carradine, Mark Travis, Janet Landgard, Victor Buono, Pat Renella, Marie Dunn, William Challee, Frank Corsentino

Billy Dee Williams, Albert Salmi, Vernon Weddle,
Eddie Albert in "The Take"

"International Stewardesses"

**Burt Lancaster, Catherine Bach
in "The Midnight Man"**

**Jeff East, Paul Winfield
in "Huckleberry Finn"**

THE MIDNIGHT MAN (Universal) Produced, Directed, and Written by Roland Kibbee, Burt Lancaster; Based on novel "The Midnight Lady and the Mourning Man" by David Anthony; Photography, Jack Priestley; Designer, James D. Vance; Editor, Frank Morriss; Music, Dave Grusin; Song, Morgan Ames, Dave Grusin; Sung by Yvonne Elliman. In Panavision and Technicolor; A Norlan Production; Rated R; 117 minutes; May release. CAST: Burt Lancaster (Jim), Susan Clark (Linda), Cameron Mitchell (Quartz), Morgan Woodward (Clayborn), Harris Yulin (Casey), Robert Quarry (Dr. Pritchet), Joan Lorring (Judy), Lawrence Dobkin (Mason), Ed Lauter (Leroy), Mills Watson (Cash), Charles Tyner (Ewing), Catherine Bach (Natalie), William Lancaster (King), Quinn Redeker (Swanson), Eleanor Ross (Nell), Richard Winterstein (Virgil), William T. Hicks (Charlie), Peter Dane (Metterman), Linda Kelsey (Betty), William Splawn (Lamar), Susan MacDonald (Elaine), Joel Gordon Kravitz (Pearlman), Nick Cravat (Gardener), Rodney Stevens (Jimmy), Weems Oliver Baskin III (Bartender), Jean Perkins (Nurse), Harold N. Cooledge, Jr. (Collins), Gene Lehfeldt (Casey's Driver), William Clark (Deputy), Elizabeth Black (Bus Dispatcher), Rachel Ray (Parolee), David Garrison (Photographer), Hugh Parsons (Grocery Clerk), Lonnie Kay (Hostess), G. Warren Smith (Director), Lucille Meredith (Radio Evangelist), Mal Alberts (Basketball Announcer), Alan Gibbs, Jim Burke, Frank Orsatti, Julie Johnson (Stunts)

MEMORY OF US (Cinema Financial of America) Producer, James P. Polakof; Executive Producer, Ronald Peck; Director, H. Kaye Dyal; Screenplay, Ellen Geer; Photography, Hiro Morikawa; Editors, Robert Estrin, Verna Fields, Harry Keramidas; Music, Ed Bogas; Song, Ed Bogas, Ellen Geer; Art Director, Joe Guerena; Assistant Director, David Holden; In DeLuxe Color; Rated PG; 93 minutes; May release. CAST: Ellen Geer (Betty), Will Geer (Motel Manager), Jon Cypher (Brad), Barbara Colby (Iris), Robert Hogan (John), Charlene Polite (Stella), Joyce Easton (Lisa), Rose Marie (Housekeeper), Robbie Rist, Ann Elizabeth Beesley (Betty's children), Peter Brown (Winston)

HUCKLEBERRY FINN (United Artists) Producer, Arthur P. Jacobs; Director, J. Lee Thompson; Screenplay, Music and Lyrics, Richard M. Sherman, Robert B. Sherman; Associate Producer, Robert Greenhut; Designer, Philip Jefferies; Costumes, Donfeld; Choreographer, Marc Breaux; Editor, Michael F. Anderson; Photography, Laszlo Kovacs; Assistant Directors, Newton Arnold, Ron Wright; In Panavision and DeLuxe Color; An APJAC International Picture; Rated G; 118 minutes; May release. CAST: Jeff East (Huckleberry Finn), Paul Winfield (Jim), Harvey Korman (King), David Wayne (Duke), Arthur O'Connell (Col. Grangerford), Gary Merrill (Pap), Natalie Trundy (Mrs. Loftus), Lucille Benson (Widder Douglas), Kim O'Brien (Maryjane), Jean Fay (Susan), Ruby Leftwich (Miss Watson), Odessa Cleveland (Jim's Wife), Joe Boris (Jason), Danny Lantrip (Kyle), Van Bennett (Wayne), Linda Watkins (Mrs. Grangerford), Jean Combs (Miss Emmeline), Frances Fawcett (Miss Charlotte), Suzanne Prystup (Miss Maryanne), H. L. Rowley (Horatio), Doris Owens (Marybelle), Frank Mills (Buck), Sherree Sinquefield (Miss Sophia), Morris Denton (Boat Capt.), Hoskins Deterly (Lot), Elliott Trimble (Uncle Harvey), Forrest Colebank (Abner), Charles C. Burns (Sheriff), Orville Meyer (Tomkins), and R. Norwood Smith, Jack Millstein, Larry Ferney, Albert Schilling, Clayton Starling, Rex Commack, George Prescott, Mrs. James Torrey, Rose Pansano, John Schwartzman, Gray Montgomery, Pat O'Connor, Sam Blackmon, Ron Wright, Louis Wentworth III, Andrew Knight, Ken Wannberg

JOURNEY THROUGH THE PAST (New Line) A Neil Young Film in color; Rated R; No other credits available; May release. CAST: Neil Young, Crosby, Stills & Nash, Buffalo Springfield

THE TEACHER (Crown International) Produced, Directed and Written by Hikmet Avedis; Executive Producer, Lenke Romanszky; Music, Sammy Fain; Lyrics, Paul Francis Webster; In color; Rated R; May release. CAST: Angel Tompkins, Jay North, Anthony James, Marlene Schmidt

THE DIVINE MR. J. Produced and Directed by Peter Alexander; May release; No other details available. CAST: Bette Midler, John Bassberger, among others.

**Joan Lorring, Susan Clark, Cameron Mitchell,
Burt Lancaster in "The Midnight Man"**

**Harvey Korman, David Wayne
in "Huckleberry Finn"**

110

Moms Mabley, Slappy White
in "Amazing Grace"

James Garner, Vera Miles
in "The Castaway Cowboy"

FORGOTTEN ISLAND OF SANTOSHA (Santosha) Produced, Directed and Written by Larry Yates; Photography, Spider Wills, Tom Cousins, Greg Weaver, Tom Jewel, Ralph Meyers, Scott Preiss; Editor, Lewis Teague; Music, Carlos Pardeiro; In DeLuxe Color; not rated; 84 minutes; July release. A surfing documentary narrated by Rick Ely

SUMMER RUN (Lighthouse) Producer, Steven Graham; Executive Producer, Patrick Ferrell; Directed and Written by Leon Capetanos; Photography, Klaus Konig; Editors, Antranig Mahakian, Lewis Teague; Music, Patrick Ferrell; Assistant Director, Charles Himes; A Movie and Music Corp. of Texas Presentation; In Metrocolor; Rated PG; 96 minutes; August release. CAST: Andy Parks (Harry), Ina Lund (Kristina), Dennis Redfield (Felix), Gail Joy (Sam), Judith Nugent (Debbie), Juliet Berto (Juliet), Leon Capetanos, Roda Rassmussen, John Broderick, Phyllis Altenhaus

AMAZING GRACE (United Artists) Produced and Written by Matt Robinson; Director, Stan Lathan; Photography, Sol Negrin; Art Director, Robert Wrightman; Costumes, Ceil Bryant; In color; Rated G; 99 minutes; August release. CAST: Moms Mabley (Grace), Slappy White (Forthwith), Moses Gunn (Welton), Rosalind Cash (Creola), James Karen (Annenberg), George Miles (Laney), Gary Bolling (William), Dolph Sweet (Mayor Scott), Stepin Fetchit (Cousin Lincoln), Butterfly McQueen (Clarine)

BRING ME THE HEAD OF ALFREDO GARCIA (United Artists) Producer, Martin Baum; Executive Producer, Helmut Dantine; Director, Sam Peckinpah; Screenplay, Gordon Dawson, Sam Peckinpah; Story, Frank Kowalski, Sam Peckinpah; Music, Jerry Fielding; Photography, Alex Phillips, Jr.; Associate Producer, Gordon Dawson; Editors, Robbe Roberts, Sergio Ortega, Dennis E. Dolan; An Optimus Productions/Estudios Churubusco Co-Production; In color; Rated R; 112 minutes; August release. CAST: Warren Oates (Bennie), Isela Vega (Elita), Gig Young (Quill), Robert Webber (Sappensly), Helmut Dantine (Max), Emilio Fernandez (El Jefe), Kris Kristofferson (Paco), Chano Urueta (One-armed Bartender), Jorge Russek (Cueto)

THE CASTAWAY COWBOY (Buena Vista) Producers, Ron Miller, Winston Hibler; Director, Vincent McEveety; Screenplay, Don Tait; Story, Don Tait, Richard Bluel, Hugh Benson; Photography, Andrew Jackson; Music, Robert F. Brunner; Associate Producer-2nd Unit Director, Christopher Hibler; Art Director, John B. Mansbridge; Designer, Robert Clatworthy; Editor, Cotton Warburton; Assistant Directors, Dick Caffey, Gary Daigler; Costumes, Chuck Keehne, Emily Sundby; A Walt Disney Production; In Technicolor; Rated G; 91 minutes; August release. CAST: James Garner (Costain), Vera Miles (Henrietta), Robert Culp (Bryson), Eric Shea (Booton), Elizabeth Smith (Liliha), Manu Tupou (Kimo), Gregory Sierra (Marrujo), Shug Fisher (Capt. Cary), Nephi Hannemann (Malakoma), Lito Capina (Leleo), Ralph Hanalei (Hopu), Kahana (Oka), Lee Wood (Palani), Luis Delgado (Hatman), Buddy Joe Hooker (Boatman), Patrick Sullivan Burke (Sea Captain)

OPEN SEASON (Columbia) Producer, Jose S. Vicuna; Executive Producer, George H. Brown; Director, Peter Collinson; Screenplay, David Osborn, Liz Charles-Williams; Music, Ruggero Cini; Assistant Director, Adolfo Aristarain; Photography, Fernando Arribas; Art Director, Gil Parrondo; Editor, Alan Pattillo; An Impala-Arpa Production; In color; Rated R; 103 minutes; August release. CAST: Peter Fonda (Ken), William Holden (Wolkowski), Cornelia Sharpe (Nancy), John Phillip Law (Greg), Richard Lynch (Art), Albert Mendoza (Martin), Helga Line (Sue), Didi Sherman (Helen), Conchita Cuetos (Joyce), Norma Castel (Annie), May Heatherly (Pat), Blanca Estrada (Alicia), Gudrun McLeary (Mrs. Rennick), Simon Andreu (Barman), William Layton (D.A.), Beatriz Savon (Sandy), Loretta Tovar (Moonmaid), Mabel Escano (Waitress), Scott Miller (Purcell), Jaime Doria (Carter), Lorraine Clewes (Hostess), Judith Stephen (Manageress), Amory Fitzpatric (Connie), Jerry Boudreaux (Tommy), Mike Sambeck (Petey)

TERROR CIRCUS (CNC) Director, Gerald Comier; In color; Rated R; August release. CAST: Andrew Prine, Gyl Roland, Maneela Thiess, Jennifer Ashley

Donny Fritts, Isela Verga, Kris Kristofferson
in "Bring Me the Head of Alfredo Garcia"

Richard Lynch, John Phillip Law, Lorraine Clewes,
Peter Fonda in "Open Season"

Peter Brown, Ginger Mason
in "Act of Vengeance"

Gerald Grant, Calvin Culver,
Claire Wilbur in "Score"

TOGETHER BROTHERS (20th Century-Fox) Executive Producer, Sanford Howard; Producer, Robert L. Rosen; Director, William A. Graham; Screenplay, Jack DeWitt, Joe Greene; Story, Jack DeWitt; Photography, Philip Lanthrop, Charles Rosher; Music, Barry White; Sung by Love Unlimited; Associate Producer, Alan Levine; Editor, Stanley E. Johnson; Assistant Directors, James H. Brown, Jay Daniel; Costumes, Raymond H. Summers; In DeLuxe Color; Rated PG; 94 minutes; August release. CAST: Ahmad Nurradin (H.J.), Anthony Wilson (Tommy), Nelson Sims (A.P.), Kenneth Bell (Mau), Owen Pace (Monk), Kim Dorsey (Gri), Ed Bernard (Kool), Lincoln Kilpatrick (Billy), Glynn Turman (Dr. Johnson), Richard Yniguez (Vega), Angela Gibbs (Francine), Mwako Cumbuka (Strokes), Frances Williams (Mama Wes), Craig Campfield (Maria), Bessie Griffin (Rev. Brown), Lynne Holmes (Sugar), Danny Big Black (Armstrong), Gloria Calomee (Alice), Howard Picard (Detective), Charles Lemons (Matthew), Joe Zapata (Chicano), Leah Ward (Clutie), William Dagg (Desk Officer), Ernest Boyd (Harry), Roberta Ester (Nurse), John Jennings (Policeman), Lane Mitchell (Dude).

COCKFIGHTER (New World) Producer, Roger Corman; Co-Producer, Samuel Gelfman; Director, Monte Hellman; Screenplay, Charles Willeford from his novel; Photography, Nestor Almendros; Editor, Lewis Teague; Music, Michael Franks; Assistant Director, Don Walters; An Artists Entertainment Complex Picture; In Metrocolor; Rated R; 85 minutes; August release. CAST: Warren Oates (Frank), Richard B. Shull (Omar), Harry Dean Stanton (Jack), Ed Begley, Jr. (Tom), Laurie Bird (Dody), Troy Donahue (Randall), Warren Finnerty (Sanders), Robert Earl Jones (Buford), Patricia Pearcy (Mary Elizabeth), Millie Perkins (Frances), Steve Railsback (Junior), Tom Sprately (Milam), Charles Willeford (Ed), Pete Munro (Packard), Kermit Echols (Fred), Ed Smith (Whipple), Jimmy Williams (Buddy), John Trotter (Hansen), Lois Zeitlin (Lucille), Joe Bently (Peach), A. B. Greeson (Pete), Bob Earl Hannah (Deputy), Sara Rickman (Martha), Meg Brush (Mary's Mother), Oliver Coleman (Senator), Donnie Fritts (Gangleader), Bobby Dunn, Kim Bernard (Gamblers), Ank Carleton (Capt. Mack), Billy Abbott (Referee)

CAPTAIN CELLULOID VS THE FILM PIRATES (Mica) Produced, Directed, Photographed, and Edited by Louis A. McMahon; Screenplay, Robert Miller, Louis McMahon, Alan G. Barbour; Idea, William K. Everson; Associate Producer-Assistant Director, Robert Miller; An Adventur Pictures Production; A Cami-Walker Presentation; In black and white; 65 minutes; August release. CAST: Robert Clayton (Larry), Doris Burnell (Dale), Alan G. Barbour (Duncan), Barney Noto (Paul), John Cullen (Martin), Jean Barbour (Satanya), Al Kilgore (Vance), Grant Willis (Tom), William K. Everson (D. W.), George Labes, John Kirk (Bit Men), Ken Kipperman, Brian Salisbury, Sam Crowther, Jr., Art Maddaloni (Stunt Artists)

ACT OF VENGEANCE (American International) Producer, Buzz Feitshans; Director, Robert Kelljchian; Screenplay, Betty Conklin, H. R. Christian; Music, Bill Marx; Photography, Brick Marquard; Editor, Carl Kress; In Movielab Color; Rated R; 90 minutes; August release. CAST: Jo Ann Harris (Linda), Peter Brown (Jack), Jennifer Lee (Nancy), Lisa Moore (Karen), Connie Strickland (Teresa), Patricia Estrin (Angie), Lada Edmund, Jr. (Tiny), Tony Young (Bud), Steve Kanaly (Tom), Ross Elliot (Sgt. Long), John Pickard (Dr. Schetman), Ninette Bravo (Joyce), Stanley Adams (Bernie/Foulmouth), Joan McCall (Gloria)

SCORE (Audubon) Director, Radley Metzger; Screenplay, Jerry Douglas; Based on his play; Associate Producer, Ava Leighton; Photography, Franjo Vodopivec; Editor, Doris Tourmarine; In Eastmancolor; Rated X; 90 minutes; August release. CAST: Claire Wilbur, Calvin Culver, Lynn Lowry, Gerald Grant, Carl Parker

BLACK SAMSON (Warner Bros.) Producer, Daniel B. Cady; Director, Charles Bail; Screenplay, Warren Hamilton, Jr.; Story, Daniel B. Cady; Photography, Henning Schellerup; Art Director, E. Cosby; Editor, Duane Hartzell; Music, Allen Toussaint; Assistant Director, Eddie Donno; An Omni Picture; In Technicolor; Rated R; 87 minutes; August release. CAST: Rockne Tarkington (Samson), William Smith (Johnny), Connie Strickland (Tina), Carol Speed (Leslie), Michael Payne (Arthur), Joe Tornatore (Harry), Titos Vandis (Joseph), Napoleon Whiting (Old Henry), John Alderman (Michael)

Warren Oates
in "Cockfighter"

Rockne Tarkington
in "Black Samson"

"The Naughty Nymphs"

"The Sinful Bed"

UPER SPOOK (Levitt-Pickman) Producer, Ed Dessisso; Execu-
ve Producer-Director, Anthony Major; Music, Rheet Taylor;
reenplay, Ed Dessisso, Leonard Jackson, Bill Jay, Tony King;
nthony Major; A Syn-Frank Enterprises Presentation; In color;
ated R; August release. CAST: Leonard Jackson, Bill Jay, Tony
ing

NCE Producers, Marianne Heilig, Morton Heilig; Direction, Pho-
graphy, Morton Heilig; Music, Aminadav Aloni; In
lor; 100 minutes; August release. CAST: Christopher Mitchum,
arta Kristen, Jim Malinda

HE HARRAD SUMMER (Cinerama) Executive Producer, Duke
oldstone; Producer, Dennis F. Stevens; Director, Steven H. Stern;
reenplay, Morth Thaw, Steven Zacharias; Photography, Richard
line; Editor, Bill Brame; Music, Pat Williams; Assistant Directors,
sse Corallo, George Marshall, Jr.; In color; Rated R; 105 minutes;
ugust release. CAST: Robert Reiser (Stanley), Laurie Walters
heila), Richard Doran (Harry), Victoria Thompson (Beth), Em-
aline Henry (Margaret), Bill Dana (Jack), Jode an Russo (Paula),
ngela Clarke (Mrs. Kolasukas), Tito Vandis (Kolasukas), Walter
ooke (Sam), Mimi Saffian (Diane), Lisa Moore (Arnae), James
ach (Brad), Pearl Shear (Fritzi), Jane Lambert (Florence), Marty
len (Bert), Lili Valenty (Great Grandma), Sherry Miles (Dee),
trice Rohmer (Marcia), Sylvia Walden, Chuckie Bradley (Wom-
s Consciousness Group)

NDER LOVING CARE (New World) Produced, Directed, and
ritten by Don Edmonds; Co-Producer, Chako Van Leeuwen; Pho-
graphy, William B. Kaplan; Editor, Robert Freeman; Music, Steve
chaels; Associate Producer, Bethel G. Buckalew; Art Director,
en Prince; In color; Rated R; 77 minutes; August release. CAST:
nna Desmond (Karen), Michael Asher (Ben), Leah Simon
racy), Tony Victor (David), Anita King (Lynn), John Daniels
ckie), Laurence Cohen (Gino), C. D. Lafleur (Simpson), Tim
ylor (Reno), Roger Pancake (Dr. Beal), Tim Paola (Lt.), Carona
oro, Kathy Hilton (Nude Girls), Ellen Prince (Nurse Brandon),
f Burton (Braddock), Brad Peterson (McLean)

FUNNY CAR SUMMER (Ambassador) Procedures, Ron Phillips,
John Brooks; Director, Ron Phillips; Executive Producer, Jack
Yopp; In DeLuxe Color; Rated G; August release. CAST: Jim Dunn

MAMA'S DIRTY GIRLS (Premiere) Producers, Gil Lasky, Ed
Carlin; Rated R; In color; August release. CAST: Gloria Grahame,
Paul Lambert, Sandra Currie, Candice Rialson

NAUGHTY NYMPHS (Centaur) Producer, TV 13; Director,
Frank Antel; Screenplay, Hans Billian; In color; Rated R; September
release. CAST: Eve Garden, Christine Mayback, Clark Tinney

THE SINFUL BED (United Film) Producer, City-Film; Director,
Ilja von Anutroff; Music, Ralf Bauer; Story, Michael Wildberger;
Photography, Michael Alexander; In color; Rated X; 90 minutes;
September release. CAST: Heidi Kramer, Ken Rich, Edie Mann,
Frank Summers, Karen Kaiser

BLACK GODFATHER (Cinemation) Produced, Directed, and
Written by John Evans; Music, Martin Yarbrough; A Jerry Gross
Presentation; A Cougar Production; In color; Rated R; 97 minutes;
September release. CAST: Rod Perry, Damu King, Don Chastain,
Diane Sommerfield, Jimmy Witherspoon

U.F.O.: TARGET EARTH (Centrum International) Producer-
Director, Michael A. de Gaetano; In color; Rated G; 80 minutes;
September release. CAST: Nick Plakias, Cynthia Cline; Phil Erick-
son

SOLOMON KING (Sal/Wa) Producer, Sal Watts in association
with Stage Struck Inc.; Directors, Sal Watts, Jack Bomay; Screen-
play, Sal Watts; Story, Jim Alston; Photography, Chuck Colwell,
Phil Caplan; Editors, Chuck Colwell, Sal Watts; Music, Jimmy
Lewis; Art Director, Al Brown; In color; Rated R; 110 minutes;
September release. CAST: Sal Watts (Solomon), Little Jamie Watts
(Maney), Claudia Russo (Princess), Felice Kinchelow (Albert),
Samaki Bennett (Samaki), Louis Zito (O'Malley), Bernard B. Burton
(Abdulla), Richard Scarso (Hassan), Tito Fuentes (Himself), C. B.
Lyars (Preacher)

"Tender Loving Care"

"The Black Godfather"

"The Girls Who Do"

Linda Marsh, William Hansen
in "Homebodies"

THE GIRLS WHO DO (Centaur) Producer, Robert Leichtmann; Director, Hans Billian; A Regina Film; In Eastmancolor; Rated X; 80 minutes; September release. CAST: Alena Penz, Gunther Ziegler, Margot Mahler, Joseph Mosholzer

HOMEBODIES (Avco Embassy) Producer, Marshal Backlar; Director, Larry Yust; Executive Producer, James R. Levitt; Screenplay, Larry Yust, Howard Kaminsky, Bennett Sims; Music, Bernardo Segall; Song, Bernardo Segall, Jeremy Kronsberg; Photography, Isidore Mankofsky; Editor, Peter Parasheles; Art Director, John Retsek; Costumes, Lynn Bernay; In color; Rated PG; 96 minutes; September release. CAST: Peter Brocco (Blakely), Frances Fuller (Emily), William Hansen (Sandy), Ruth McDevitt (Mrs. Loomis), Paula Trueman (Mattie), Ian Wolfe (Loomis), Linda Marsh (Miss Pollack), Douglas Fowley (Crawford), Kenneth Tobey (Construction Boss), Wesley Lau (Foreman), Norman Gottschalk (Superintendent), Ireene Webster (Woman in floppy hat), Nicholas Lewis, John Craig, Joe De Meo (Construction Workers), Michael Johnson (Policeman), Alma Du Bus (Super's Wife), Eldon Quick (Insurance Inspector), William Benedict (Watchman)

THE LIFE AND TIMES OF XAVIERA HOLLANDER (Mature Pictures) Producer-Director, Larry G. Spangler; Screenplay, Lawrence Pickwick, David Loin; Photography, Philip Kaplan; Editors, Bob McDaniels, Arthur Jay, Harvey Martin; Music, Ken Sutherland, Adrian Beamer; Art Director, Leroy Basset; Associate Producer, Robert Manning; Rated X; In color; 76 minutes; September release. CAST: Samantha McClearn (Xaviera), Rick Cassidy, John Wadd, Rick Lutz, Paula Stone, Sylvia Reasoner, Betty Hunt, Russel Stover, Bert Finneberg, Larry Laurence, Al Husson, James Walch, John Roach, Marvin Finch, Tad Dood

WATCHED (Penthouse) Executive Producer, David Goldman; Directed and Written by John Parsons; Photography, Hart Perry, Ed Lynch, Keavin Keating, Jack Wright; Editor, Ed Deitch; Music, Weather Report, Bob Carpenter; In color; Rated R; 93 minutes; September release. CAST: Stacy Keach (Mike/Sonny), Harris Yulin (Gordon), Bridget Pole (Informer), Turid Aarstd (Blonde), Valeri Parker (Hitchhiker), Denver John Collins (Hippie)

I'M A STRANGER HERE MYSELF (October Films) Produce James C. Gutman; Director, David Helpern, Jr.; Screenplay, Dav Helpern, Jr., James C. Gutman, Myrin Meisel; Photography, Aus Debesche; Editors, Frank Galvin, Richard Bock; In color; N rated; 60 minutes; September release. A documentary on Nichol Ray narrated by Howard Da Silva.

GETTIN' BACK (Crabtree Films/McCulloch Enterprises) P ducer, Ronald L. McCulloch; Director, Gary L. Crabtree; Photogr phy, Gary L. Crabtree, Bryan Rankin, Ronald L. McCulloch, D McClendon; Editor, Hank Lam; In Eastmancolor; Rated GP; minutes; September release. CAST: Earl Scruggs Revue, Oza Mountain Daredevils, Clifton Chenier and The Red Hot Caj Band, Big Mama Thornton, John Lee Hooker, The Lewis Fami Michael Murphey, Talbot Brothers, Mason Proffit, Leo Kottke

TWO (Colmar Ltd) Produced, Directed, and Written by Char Trieschmann; Photography, Vilis Lapenieks; Music, Akiva Taln Editor, David McKenna; In Movielab Color; Not rated; 93 minut September release. CAST: Evelyn Venable (Ellen), Douglas Tra (Steven), Clifford Villeneuve (Irate Driver), Ray Houle (Docto Florence Hadley (Hardware Customer), William Green (Husban Thelma Green (Wife), Sylvia Harman (Bank Teller), Elwyn Mil (Guard), Jack Dykeman (Man in bank), Stanley McIntire (Chief Police), Fred Gilbert (Policeman), Winston Merrill (Postal Cler

THE HENRY MILLER ODYSSEY (Grove Press) Produc Director, Robert Snyder; Photography, Baylis Glascock; Edit Ray Laurent; Not rated; In color; 110 minutes; September relea A documentary on the life of writer Henry Miller.

PHASE IV (Paramount) Producer, Paul Radin; Director, Saul Ba Screenplay, Mayo Simon; Photography, Dick Bush; Art Direct John Barry; Music, Brian Gascoigne; Assistant Director, Bill Ca lidge; Costumes, Verena Coleman; Editor, Wally Kemplen; Alced Production; In color; Rated PG; 91 minutes; September lease. CAST: Nigel Davenport (Hubbs), Lynne Frederick (Kendr Michael Murphy (Lesko), Alan Gifford (Eldridge), Helen Hort (Mrs. Eldridge), Robert Henderson (Clete)

Ruth McDevitt, William Hansen, Peter Brocco,
Ian Wolfe, Paula Trueman, Frances Fuller
in "Homebodies"

Nigel Davenport, Michael Murphy,
Lynne Frederick in "Phase IV"

Britt Ekland, Barry Brown
in "The Ultimate Thrill"

"Rivers of Sand"

THE DEVIL'S TRIANGLE (Maron) Director, Richard Winer; Music, King Crimson; Narrator, Vincent Price; In color; Rated G; 2 minutes; September release. No other credits available.

A PLACE WITHOUT PARENTS (Dimension) Title changed from Pigeon"; Director, Ken Handler; Screenplay, Michael Thomas; In Metrocolor; Rated PG; September release. CAST: Albert Salmi, Nicholas Wahler, Craig Horrall

NIGHT CALL NURSES (New World) Producer, Julie Corman; Director, Jonathan Kaplan; Screenplay, George Armitage; In Metrocolor; September release. CAST: Patti T. Byrne, Alana Collins, Mitti Lawrence, Clint Kimbrough, Felton Perry, Richard Young, Dennis Dugan, Christopher Law, Stack Pierce, Dick Miller

THE CENTERFOLD GIRLS (General Film) Executive Producer, William Silberkleit; Producer, Charles Stroud; Director, John Peyser; Screenplay, Robert Peete; Arthur Marks Presentation; In color; Rated R; September release. CAST: Andrew Prine, Tiffany Bolling, Ray Danton, Aldo Ray, Francine York, Jaime Lyn Bauer, Mike Mazurki

THE BLACK ALLEYCATS (Entertainment Pyramid) Producer, John Munchkin; Director, Henning Schellerup; In color; Rated X; September release. CAST: Sunshine Woods, Sandy Dempsey, Charlene Miles, Johnny Rhodes, Marsha Jordan

HONEYBABY, HONEYBABY (Kelly-Jordan) Producer, Jack Jordan; Director, Michael Schultz; Executive Producers, Quentin Kelly, Jack Jordan; Associate Producer, Saladin Jammal; Screenplay, Brian Phelan; Story, Leonard Kantor; Music, Michael Tschudin; Photography, Andreas Bellis; Assistant Director, Kurt Baker; Editor, Hortense Beveridge; In color; Rated PG; 88 minutes; October release. CAST: Diana Sands (Laura), Calvin Lockhart (Liv), Seth Allen (Sam), J. Eric Bell (Skiggy), Brian Phelan (Harry), Bricktop (Harry's mother), Thomas Baptiste (Gen. Awani), Gay Suilin (Mme. Chan), Nabih Aboul Hoson (Herb), Mr. Sunshine (Real Takuba)

RIVERS OF SAND (Phoenix) Produced, Directed, Photographed, Edited, and Written by Robert Gardner; Translation, I. K. Eikeberians, Ivo Strecker, Jean Strecker; Music, Michel Chalufour; In color; 83 minutes; October release. A documentary on the daily life of the Hamar people of Ethiopia.

HELEN HAYES: PORTRAIT OF AN AMERICAN ACTRESS (Phoenix) Producer-Director, Nathan Kroll; Written by Claire Birsh Merrill; In color; 90 minutes; October release. A documentary with Helen Hayes narrating the story of her life.

THE ULTIMATE THRILL (General Cinema) Producers, Peter S. Traynor, William D. Sklar; Director, Robert Butler; Screenplay, John W. Zodrow; Story, Jim McGinn; Photography, Isidore Mankofsky; Associate Producer, Mel Frohman; Music, Ed Townsend; Editor, Peter Parasheles; Assistant Director, Ron Schwary; Costumes, Ray Summers A Centaur Film; In Eastmancolor; Rated PG; October release. CAST: Barry Brown (Joe), Britt Ekland (Michele), Eric Braeden (Roland), Michael Blodgett (Tom), John Davis Chandler (Evans), Ed Baierlein (Webster), Paul Felix (Fielder), Gary Tessler (Night Clerk), Ron Schwary (Danny), Mary Hampton (Woman at deli), Carol Adams (Secretary), June Goodman (Pretzel), David Kahn (Denver Clerk), Hallie McCollum (Day Clerk), Sam Darling (Bartender)

THE HOUSE ON SKULL MOUNTAIN (20th Century-Fox) Executive Producer, Joe R. Hartsfield; Producer, Ray Storey; Co-Producer, Tom Boutross; Director, Ron Honthaner; Screenplay, Mildred Pares; Art Director, James Newport; Photography, Monroe Askins; Music, Jerrold Immel; Editor, Gerard Wilson; Assistant Director, Stephen P. Dunn; Associate Producers, Monroe Askins, Albert Shepard; In color; Rated PG; 89 minutes; October release.

Calvin Lockhart
in "Honeybaby, Honeybaby"

Janee Michelle, Jean Durand
in "The House on Skull Mountain"

Gunnar Hansen, Marilyn Burns
in "The Texas Chainsaw Massacre"

"Pinocchio's Birthday Party"

THE TEXAS CHAINSAW MASSACRE (Bryanston) Executive Producer, Jay Parsley; Producer-Director, Tobe Hooper; Associate Producers, Kim Henkel, Richard Saenz; Assistant Director, Sallye Richardson; Story and Screenplay, Kim Henkel, Tobe Hooper; Photography, Daniel Pearl; Art Director, Robert A. Burns; Editors, Sallye Richardson, Larry Carroll; Music, Tobe Hooper, Wayne Bell; In color; Rated R; 83 minutes; October release. CAST: Marilyn Burns (Sally), Allen Danziger (Jerry), Paul A. Partain (Franklin), William Vail (Kirk), Teri McMinn (Pam), Edwin Neal (Hitchhiker), Jim Siedow (Old Man), Gunnar Hansen (Leatherface), John Dugan (Grandfather), Jerry Lorenz (Pickup Driver)

THE CRAZY WORLD OF JULIUS VROODER (20th Century-Fox) Executive Producer, Hugh M. Hefner; Producers, Edward Rissien, Arthur Hiller; Director, Arthur Hiller; Associate Producer-Screenplay, Daryl Henry; Associate Producer, Peter V. Herald; Music, Bob Alcivar; Assistant Directors, Peter Bogart, David S. Hamburger; Photography, David M. Walsh; Art Director, Hilyard Brown; Editor, Robert C. Jones; In DeLuxe Color; Rated PG; 98 minutes; October release. CAST: Timothy Bottoms (Julius Vrooder), Barbara Seagull (Zanni), Lawrence Pressman (Dr. Passki), Albert Salmi (Splint), Richard A. Dysart (Father), Dena Dietrich (Mother), Debralee Scott (Sister), Lou Frizzell (Fowler), Jack Murdock (Millard), Michael Ivan Cristofer (Allessini), Dewayne Jessie (Rodali), Ron Glass (Quintus), Barbara Douglas (Roberta), Andrew Duncan (Chaplain), Jack Colvin (Sergeant), Jarion Monroe (Mosby), George Marshall (Corky)

MIXED COMPANY (United Artists) Producer-Director, Melville Shavelson; Screenplay, Melville Shavelson, Mort Lachman; Photography, Stan Lazan; Music, Fred Karlin; Associate Producer, Mike Moder; Designer, Stan Jolley; Editors, Walter Thompson, Ralph James Hall; A Llenroc Production; In color; Rated PG; 109 minutes; October release. CAST: Barbara Harris (Kathy), Joseph Bologna (Peter), Tom Bosley (Al), Lisa Gerritsen (Liz), Dorothy Shay (Marge), Ruth McDevitt (Miss Bergquist), Arianne Heller (Mary), Stephen Honanie (Joe), Haywood Nelson (Freddie), Eric Olson (Rob), Jina Tan (Quan), Bob G. Anthony (Krause), Roger Price (Doctor), Keith Hamilton (Milton)

PINOCCHIO'S GREATEST ADVENTURE (K-Tel International) A Family Entertainment Corp. Production in association with Intercom Films; Music and Lyrics, Karen Cohl, Susie Unga In color; Rated G; No other details available; October release CAST: Nancy Belle Fuller, Sean Sullivan, Danny McIlravey

KATO AND THE GREEN HORNET (20th Century-Fox) Rated PG; 83 minutes; October release. Three installments of the TV serie put together and prefaced with footage from the late Bruce Lee screen test.

GIRLS FOR RENT (Independent International) Producer, Samuel M. Sherman; Director, Al Adamson; Rated R; In Metrocolor; October release. CAST: Georgina Spelvin, Susan McIver, Rosalind Mile Preston Pierce, Kent Taylor, Robert Livingston

CHALLENGE (Cinemation) Producer, Earl Owensby; Director Martin Beck; A Jerry Gross Presentation; In Technicolor; Rated PG; October release. CAST: Earl Owensby, William T. Hicks, K theryn Thompson, Johnny Popwell

THE WORKING GIRLS (Dimension) Producer, Charles Swartz; Direction and Screenplay, Stephanie Rothman; Executive Producer, Laurence H. Woolner; In Metrocolor; Rated R; Octob release. CAST: Sarah Kennedy (Honey), Mary Beth Hughes (M Borden), Laurie Rose (Denise), Mark Thomas (Nick), Lynne Gut rie (Jill), Ken Del Conte (Mike), Solomon Sturges (Vernon), Ge Elman (Sidney), Cassandra Peterson (Stripper), Lou Tiano, B Schott

DEAD OF NIGHT (Europix International) Producer-Directo Bob Clark; Executive Producers, John Trent, Peter James; A Qua rant Film; In color; Rated PG; 88 minutes; October release. CAS John Marley, Lynn Carlin, Richard Backus, Henderson Forsyt William Shatner, Ruth Roman, Harold Sakata, Kim Nicholas, Je nifer Bishop, James Dobbs

IMPULSE (Conqueror) Director, William Grefe; In Technicolo Rated PG; October release. No other details available.

Barbara Harris, Joseph Bologna
in "Mixed Company"

Timothy Bottoms, George Marshall
in "The Crazy World of Julius Vrooder"

John Ryan, Sharon Farrell
in "It's Alive"

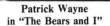

Patrick Wayne
in "The Bears and I"

IT'S ALIVE (Warner Bros.) Produced, Directed, and Written by Larry Cohen; Photography, Fenton Hamilton; Editor, Peter Honess; Executive Producer, Peter Sabiston; Co-Producer, Janelle Cohen; Music, Bernard Herrmann; A Larco Production; In Panavision and Technicolor; Rated R; 90 minutes; October release. CAST: John Ryan (Frank), Sharon Farrell (Lenore), Andrew Duggan (Professor), Guy Stockwell (Clayton), James Dixon (Perkins), Michael Ansara (Captain), Robert Emhardt (Executive), William Wellman, Jr. (Charlie), Shamus Locke (Doctor), Mary Nancy Burnett (Nurse), Diana Hale (Secretary), Daniel Holzman (Boy), Patrick Macallister, Gerald York, Jerry Taft, Gwil Richards, W. Allen York (Expectant Fathers)

THE BEARS AND I (Buena Vista) Producer, Winston Hibler; Director, Bernard McEveety; Screenplay, John Whedon; Based on book by Robert Franklin Leslie; Narration written by Jack Speirs; Music, Buddy Baker; Song "Sweet Surrender" composed and performed by John Denver; Art Directors, John B. Mansbridge, LeRoy G. Deane; Editor, Gregg McLaughlin; Assistant Director, Don Torpin; Costumes, Chuck Keehne; A Walt Disney Production; In Technicolor; Rated G; 89 minutes; October release. CAST: Patrick Wayne (Bob/Narrator), Chief Dan George (Chief Peter), Andrew Duggan (Commissioner), Michael Ansara (Oliver), Robert Pine (John), Val DeVargas (Sam), Hal Baylor (Foreman)

WET RAINBOW (Variety Films) Executive Producer, Robert Trenton; Producer, Roger Wald; Director, Duddy Kane; Photography, Pierre Schwartz II; Editor, Natasha Gottlieb; In Eastmancolor; Rated X; 74 minutes; October release. CAST: Georgina Spelvin, Harry Reems, Valerie Marron, Mary Stuart, Alan Marlo

LICKITY SPLIT (MSW) Producer-Director, Carter Stevens; Assistant Director, Chuck Mills; Editor, Malcolm S. Worob; In color; Rated X; 71 minutes; October release. CAST: Linda Lovemore, Mark Andrews, Niomi Jason, Max Packs, Sandi Fox, Don Allen, Mary Stuart, Mark Anthony, Leokavidia Olszewski, Cedar Houston, Francis X. Bush, Peches Flambe, Leo Lovelace, Laurie Suesan, Vic Dare

THE SECOND COMING OF SUZANNE (Barry) Executive Producer, Gene Barry; Producer, Ralph Burris; Directed and Written by Michael Barry; Photography, Isidore Mankofsky; Editor, Frank Mazzola; Music, Don Caverhill; Art Director, Elayne Ceder; Assistant Director, David McGiffert; In color; Not rated; 90 minutes; October release. CAST: Sondra Locke (Suzanne), Paul Sand (Artist), Jared Martin (Filmmaker), Richard Dreyfuss (Clavius), Gene Barry (TV Commentator)

BENJI (Mulberry Square) Produced, Directed, and Written by Joe Camp; Photography, Don Reddy; Music, Euel Box; Editor, Leon Smith; Designer, Harland Wright; In CFI Color; Rated G; 85 minutes; October release. CAST: Higgins (Benji), Patsy Garrett (Mary), Allen Fiuzat (Paul), Cynthia Smith (Cindy), Peter Breck (Dr. Chapman), Frances Bavier (Lady with cat), Terry Carter (Tuttle), Edgar Buchanan (Bill), Tom Lester (Riley), Christopher Connelly (Henry), Deborah Walley (Linda), Mark Slade (Mitch), Herb Bigran (Samuels), Larry Swartz (Floyd), J. D. Young (2nd Policeman), Edwin Hearne (Harvey), Katie Hearne (Mrs. Harvey), Don Puckett (Plainclothesman), Ed DeLatte (Bob), Victor Raider-Wexler (Payton), Charles Starkey (Custodian), Ben Vaughn (Man)

HANGUP (Warner Bros.) Director, Henry Hathaway; Screenplay, John B. Sherry, Lee Lazich; Based on novel "The Face of Night" by Bernard Brunner; Photography, Robert Houser; Art Director, Jim Halsey; Editor, Chris Kaeselau; Music, Tony Camillo; Title Song, George Barrie; Associate Producer, T. W. Sewell; Assistant Directors, Anthony Brand, Pepi Lenzi; In Technicolor; A Brut Production; Rated R; 94 minutes; October release. CAST: William Elliott (Ken), Marki Bey (Julie), Cliff Potts (Lou), Michael Lerner (Richards), Wally Taylor (Sgt. Becker), Timothy Blake (Gwen), Fredd Wayne (Felder), Midori (Sally), David A. Renard (Bud), Pepe Serna (Enrique), Rafael Campos (Longnose), Lynn Hamilton (Mrs. Ramsey), William Bramley (Simpson), Bob Delegall (Jennings), Barbara Baldavin (Beverly), Morris Buchanan (Dave), Danny "Big" Black (Jim Jim), Herbert Jefferson, Jr. (Ben), Jerry Ayres (Jerry), Joe Renteria (Paul), Sy Prescott (Morton), George Murdock (Capt. Gorney)

Chief Dan George, Michael Ansara, Patrick Wayne
in "The Bears and I"

William Elliott, Cliff Potts
in "Hangup"

121

William Finley, Paul Williams
in "Phantom of the Paradise"

Jason Miller, Bo Hopkins
in "The Nickel Ride"

PHANTOM OF THE PARADISE (20th Century-Fox) Producer, Edward R. Pressman; Direction-Screenplay, Brian DePalma; Executive Producer, Gustave Berne; Photography, Larry Pizer; Music, Paul Williams; Sung by Ray Kennedy; Associate Producers, Paul Lewis, Bill Scott, Jeffrey Hayes, Michael Arciaga; Assistant Producer, Lynn Raymond; Assistant Directors, Michael Dmytryk, Robert Enrietto; Costumes, Peter Jamison; Choreography, William Shephard; In movielab Color; Rated PG; 91 minutes; October release. CAST: Paul Williams (Swan), William Finley (Phantom), Jessica Harper (Phoenix), George Memmoli (Philbin), Gerrit Graham (Beef), Jeffrey Comanor, Archie Hahn, Harold Oblong (The Juicy Fruits, The Beach Bums, The Undeads), Gene Gross (Warden), Henry Calvert (Nightwatchman), Ken Carpenter, Sam Forney (Stagehands), Leslie Brewer, Celia Derr, Linda Larimer, Roseanne Romine (Surfgirls), Nydia Amagas, Sara Ballantine, Kristi Bird, Cathy Buttner, Linda Cox, Jane Deford, Bibi Hansen, Robin Jeep, Deen Summers, Judy Washington, Susan Weiser (Dancers), Janet and Jean Savarino (Singing Twins), Keith Allison (Country and Western Singer), Bobby Birkenfeld (Guy), Sandy Catton (Black Singer), William Donovan, Scott Lane, Dennis Olivieri, Adam Wade (Reporters), Nancy Moses, Diana Walden (Backup Singers), Sherri Adeline (Girl in ticket line), Carol O'Leary (Betty), Mary Bongfeld, Coleen Crudden, Bridgett Dunn (Mini-boppers), William Shephard (Rock Freak), Andrew Epper, Jim Lovelett (Winslow's Doubles), Steven Richmond, James Gambino (Swan's Doubles)

BLOOD COUPLE (Kelly-Jordan) Executive Producers, Quentin Kelly, Jack Jordan; Director, F. H. Novikov; Screenplay, Hamm Parker, Al Condrey; Photography, James E. Hinton; Designer, Tom John; Editor, Pima Novek; Associate Producer, Joan Shigekawa; Assistant Director, Anthony Major; March Blues sung by Mabel King; Costumes, Scott Barrie; Rated R; 86 minutes; October release. CAST: Duane Jones (Dr. Green), Marlene Clark (Ganja), Leonard Jackson (Archie), Mabel King (Queen of Myrthia), Candece Tarpley (Girl in bar), Richard Harrow (Dinner guest), John Hoffmeister (Man in mask), Betty Barney (Singer in church), Tommy Lane (Pimp), Tara Fields (Woman with baby), Congregation of the Evangel Revivaltime Church

THE NICKEL RIDE (20th Century-Fox) Producer-Director, Robert Mulligan; Executive Producers, David Foster, Lawrence Turman; Screenplay, Eric Roth; Photography, Jordan Cronenweth; Editor, O. Nicholas Brown; Art Director, Larry Paull; Assistant Directors, Danny McCauley, Jerry Grandey; Music, Dave Grusin; In DeLuxe Color; Rated PG; 106 minutes; October release. CAST: Jason Miller (Cooper), Linda Haynes (Sarah), Victor French (Paddie), John Hillerman (Carl), Bo Hopkins (Turner), Richard Evans (Bobby), Bart Burns (Elias), Lou Frizzell (Paulie), Brendan Burns (Larry), Mark Gordon (Tonozzi), Harvey Gold (Chester), Lee Debroux (Harry), Jeanne Lange (Jeannie)

LET THE CHURCH SAY AMEN! Producer-Director, St. Clair Bourne; 78 minutes; No other details available. November release. A documentary on the discoveries and dilemmas of a young seminarian.

LENNY BRUCE PERFORMANCE FILM (Grove Press Evergreen) Producer-Director, John Magnuson; 65 minutes; No other details available; November release. A documentary on the controversial comic's next-to-last nightclub performance in 1965 at the Basin Street West in San Francisco.

PINK FLAMINGOS (Saliva) Produced, Directed, Written, Photographed, and Edited by John Waters; A Dreamland Production; In color; Rated X; 95 minutes; November release. CAST: Divine (Divine/Babs), David Lochary (Raymond), Mink Stole (Connie), Mary Vivian Pearce (Cotton), Edith Massey (Mama Edie), Danny Mills (Crackers), Channing Wilroy (Channing), Cookie Mueller (Cookie), Paul Swift (Eggman), Susan Walsh, Linda Olgeirson (Kidnapped Girls)

JOURNEY BACK TO OZ (Filmation) Producers, Norm Prescott, Lou Scheimer; Director, Hal Sutherland; Lyrics and Music, James Van Heusen, Sammy Cahn; Screenplay, Fred Ladd, Norm Prescott; In Technicolor; Rated G; November release. CAST: Milton Berle, Herschel Bernardi, Paul Ford, Margaret Hamilton, Jackie Leonard, Paul Lynde, Ethel Merman, Liza Minnelli, Mickey Rooney, Rise Stevens, Danny Thomas, Mel Blanc, Dallas McKennon, Larry Storch

Marlene Clark
in "Blood Couple"

William Finley, Jessica Harper
in "Phantom of the Paradise"

Jason Miller, Linda Haynes
in "The Nickel Ride"

Divine
in "Pink Flamingos"

TRUCK STOP WOMEN (LT Films) Producer-Director, Mark L. Lester; Executive Producer, Peter S. Traynor; Screenplay, Mark L. Lester, Paul Deason; Story, Paul Deason; Photography, John A. Morrill; Editor, Marvin Wallowitz; Music, Big Mack and The Truckstoppers; Songs, Red Simpson, Jerry Chestnut, Bob Stanton, Bobby Hart, Jimmy Haskell, Danny Janssen, Guy Hemric; Performed by Bobby Hart; Art Director, Tom Hassen; Assistant Director, Mark Levinson; In Technicolor; Rated R; 82 minutes; November release. CAST: Claudia Jennings (Rose), Lieux Dressler (Anna), John Martino (Smith), Dennis Fimple (Curly), Dolores Dorn (Trish), Gene Drew (Mac), Paul Carr (Seago), Jennifer Burton (Tina)

ANGEL NUMBER 9 (Monarch) Produced, Directed, Written, Photographed by Roberta Findlay; Editor, Anna Riva; Art Director, Tyrone Green; In Cinneffects Color; Rated X; 75 minutes; November release. CAST: Darby Lloyd Rains (Stephanie), Jamie Gillis (Photographer), Jennifer Jordan (Angel #9), Mark Stevens (Driver), Alan Marlo, Eric Edwards, Elmen Steel, Judy Craven, Regina Lee, Sandy Fox

SEIZURE (Cinerama) Producers, Garrad Glenn, Jeffrey Kapelman; Director, Oliver Stone; Screenplay, Edward Mann, Oliver Stone; Photography, Roger Racine; Editors, Nobuko Oganesoff, Oliver Stone; Music, Lee Gagnon; Art Director, Najwa Stone; Assistant Director, Timothy Rowse; Presented by Euro-American-Intercontinental Leisure Industries; In DeLuxe Color; Rated PG; 93 minutes; November release. CAST: Jonathan Frid (Edmund), Martine Beswick (Queen of Evil), Joe Sirola (Charlie), Christina Pickles (Nicole), Herve Villechaize (Spider), Anne Meacham (Eunice), Roger DeKoven (Serge), Troy Donahue (Mark), Mary Woronov (Mikki), Henry Baker (Jackal)

HORIZONS Produced, Directed, Photographed, Edited by Larry Gottheim; In color; 80 minutes; November release. A documentary on upstate New York during a two year period.

BLACK HOOKER (Wheeler) Director, Arthur Roberson; In color; Rated R; November release. CAST: Sandra Alexandra, Kathryn Jackson, Jeff Burton, Teddy Quinn, Durey Mason

CURSE OF THE HEADLESS HORSEMAN (Kirt) Producer, Leonard Kirtman; Director, John Kirkland; In color; Rated PG; November release. CAST: Ultra Violet, Marland Proctor, Claudia Dean

THE SWITCH (Scotia American) Producers, Sidney Ginsberg, Peter Kares; Direction and Screenplay, Joe Sarno; Rated X; In color; November release. CAST: Veronica Parrish, Sonny Landham, Eric Edwards, Cris Jordan

BABY NEEDS A NEW PAIR OF SHOES (Alert Films) Producer, Howard Ransom; In Technicolor; Rated R; November release. CAST: Paul Harris, Reginald Farmer, Frances Williams, Frank de Kova

DEADLY WEAPONS (Hallmark) Producer, Doris Wishman; In color; Rated R; November release; Starring Chesty Morgan

THE THREE STOOGES FOLLIES (Columbia) A collection of The Three Stooges shorts including "Violent Is the Word for Curly," "Yes, We Have No Bananza," "You Natzy Spy," "Crystal Gazebo," "Strife of the Party," "Nothing but Pleasure," "Batman," "America Sings with Kate Smith"

MOVING (Poolemar) Producer, Marvin Shulman; Directed, Photographed, and Edited by Wakefield Poole; In color; Rated X; 70 minutes; December release. CAST: "House for Sale" with Casey Donovan (Calvin Culver), Val Martin, "Room for Rent" with Burt Edouards, Kurt Gerard, "Apartment for Rent" with Peter Fisk, Tom Wright

HOT TIMES (William Mishkin) Producer, Lew Mishkin; Directed and Written by Jim McBride; Associate Producer-Editor, Jack Baran; Executive Producer, William Mishkin; Photography, Affonso Beato; In color; Rated R; 82 minutes; December release. CAST: Henry Cory (Archie), Gail Lorber (Ronnie), Amy Farber (Bette), Bob Lesser (Coach/Guru), Steve Curry (Mughead), Clarissa Ainley (Kate), Bonnie Gondel (Gloria), Jack Baran (Alex), Betty Mur (La Chochita), Irving Horowitz (Potemkin)

Calvin Culver
in "Moving"

Henry Cory
in "Hot Times"

Michael Moriarty
in "Shoot It: Black, Shoot It: Blue!"

Arthur Hunnicutt, James Mitchum
in "Moonrunners"

SHOOT IT: BLACK, SHOOT IT: BLUE (Levitt-Pickman) Direction and Screenplay, Dennis McGuire; From the novel "Shoot It" by Paul Tyner, Photography, Bob Bailin; Editor, Bob Brady; Music, Terry Stockdale; Produced by The Shoot It Company; A Harbour Properties Associates Presentation; In color; Rated R; 93 minutes; December release. CAST: Michael Moriarty (Herbert Rucker), Eric Laneuville (Lamont), Paul Sorvino (Ring), Earl Hindman (Garrity), Linda Scruggs (Stacy), Bruce Kornbluth (Buddy), Anthony Charnota (Sal), Fred Burrell (Teacher), Lynda Wescott (Hattie), Val Pringle (Wardell), Buck Buchanan (Mark), George DiCenzo (George), Molly McGreevy (Salesgirl), Michael Shannon (Purcell), Joella Deffenbaugh (Brenda), John Quastler (Karl), Art Ellison (Heon), Gilbert Milton (Pops), Bob Phillips (Dougie), Cecil Burton (Old Woman), Linda McGuire (Victim in park), Irene Ballinger (Bernice), LeRoy Vaughn (Coach), Don Peterson (Sniper), Tom Turner (Hot camera dealer), Ronnie Sellers (Black Cop)

THEY SHALL OVERCOME (Mister and Johnson) Producer-Director, Peter Savage; Music, Bruce Roberts; In color; Rated X; 70 minutes; December release. CAST: Linda Lovemore, Jennifer Jordan, Ophelia Rass, Susann Teretitoff, Studs Longer, Aaron Wadd, Ima Kooze, Sarah Digsit

BLACK STARLET (Omni) Producer, Daniel Cady; Director, Chris Munger; Screenplay, Howard Ostroff; Music, Dee Ervin, Joe Hinton; In color; Rated R; December release. CAST: Juanita Brown, Rockne Tarkington, Eric Mason, Damu King, Diane Holden, Noah Keen, Al Lewis, James Broadhead, Peter Dana, Gary Battaglia

THE LIFE AND TIMES OF GRIZZLY ADAMS (Sun International) Producer, Charles E. Sellier, Jr.; Director, Richard Friedenberg; Screenplay, Larry Dobkin; Music, Thom Pace; In DeLuxe Color; Rated G: December release. CAST: Dan Haggerty (Adams)

GOSH (Tom Scheuer) Produced, Directed, Written by Tom Scheuer; Photography, Ken Gibb; Editors, Tom Scheuer, Gary R. Maxwell; Music, Vic Caesar; Art Director, Charles French; Assistant Director, Michael Heit; In Pacific Color; Rated R; 80 minutes; December release. CAST: Sharon Kelly (Alice), Daniel Kauffman (Myron), Keith McConnell (Rex), Arem Fisher (Manny), Norma Field (J. C.), Lorna Thayer (Yvonne), Maurice Millard, William Wanrooy, Vic Caesar, Irving Wasserman, Angela Carnon

SOMETIME SWEET SUSAN (Variety) Producer, Craig Baumgarten, Joel Scott; Directed and Edited by Fred Donaldson; Photography, Saul Casella; Music, Scott Mansfield; A Lothar Production; In color; Rated X; 76 minutes; December release. CAST: Shawn Harris (Susan), Harry Reems (Mark), Neil Flanagan (Bill), Sarah Nicholson (Leslie), Craig Baumgarten (Johnny), Kirsten Steen (Nurse Carrie), Rod Loomis (Father), Carole Holland (Mother), Tom Skowron (Orderly), Jamie Gillis, Alex Mann (Rapists)

MOONRUNNERS (United Artists) Executive Producer, Robert B. Clark; Direction and Screenplay, Gy Waldron; Photography, Brian Roy; Editor, Avrum Fine; Art Director, Pat Mann; Costumes, Patty Shaw; In color; Rated PG; 102 minutes; December release. CAST: James Mitchum, Kiel Martin, Arthur Hunnicutt, Chris Forbes, George Ellis, Pete Munro, Joan Blackman, Waylon Jennings, Spanky McFarlan, Joey Giondello, Rick Hunter, Dick Steinborn, Happy Humphery

ABBY (American International) Producers, William Girdler, Mike Henry, Gordon C. Layne; Director, William Girdler; Screenplay, G. Cornell Layne; Story, William Girdler, G. Cornell Layne; Photography, William Asman; Editors, Corky Ehlers, Henry Asman; Assistant Director, Hugh Smith; Designer, J. Patrick Kelly III; Song written and sung by Carol Speed; A Mid-America Picture; Presented by Samuel Z. Arkoff; In Movielab Color; Rated R; 91 minutes; December release. CAST: William Marshall (Garnet Williams), Carol Speed (Abby), Terry Carter (Emmett), Austin Stoker (Cass), Juanita Moore (Momma), Charles Kissinger (Dr. Hennings), Elliott Moffitt (Russell), Nathan Cook (Tafa), Nancy Lee Owen (Mrs. Wiggins), Bob Holt (Voice of the Demon)

Kiel Martin, Chris Forbes
in "Moonrunners"

Austin Stoker, Carol Speed, William Marshall,
Terry Carter in "Abby"

PROMISING NEW ACTORS OF 1974

MAUD ADAMS

WILLIAM ATHERTON

RICHARD DREYFUSS

LINDA BLAIR

JOANNA CASSIDY

CLEAVON LITTLE

DAVID SELBY

LOLA FALANA

VALERIE PERRINE

MARTIN SHEEN

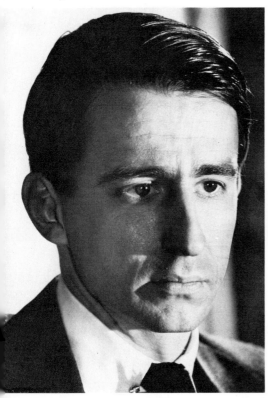

SAM WATERSTON

BERNADETTE PETERS

127

THE STING

(UNIVERSAL) Producers, Tony Bill, Michael and Julia Phillips: Director, George Roy Hill; Screenplay, David S. Ward; Photography, Robert Surtees; Editor, William Reynolds; Music, Marvin Hamlisch; Art Director, Henry Bumstead; Assistant Director, Ray Gosnell; A Richard D. Zanuck-David Brown presentation; In Technicolor; Rated PG; 129 minutes; December 1973 release.

CAST

Henry Gondorff	Paul Newman
Johnny Hooker	Robert Redford
Doyle Lonnegan	Robert Shaw
Lt. Snyder	Charles Durning
Singleton	Ray Walston
Billie	Eileen Brennan
Kid Twist	Harold Gould
Niles	John Heffernan
FBI Agent	Dana Elcar
Erie Kid	Jack Kohoe
Loretta	Dimitra Arliss

Robert Redford, Paul Newman, (also top)
Above: Ray Walston, Eileen Brennan, Paul
Newman

Robert Redford, Eileen Brennan Above: Redford,
Robert Shaw, Robert Dierkop

*1973 Academy Award winner for Best Film, Best Director, Best Story and Screenplay, Best
Editing, Best Scoring, Best Art and Set Direction, Best Costume Design*

JACK LEMMON
in "Save the Tiger"
BEST PERFORMANCE BY AN ACTOR IN 1973

GLENDA JACKSON
in "A Touch of Class"
BEST PERFORMANCE BY AN ACTRESS IN 1973

JOHN HOUSEMAN
in "The Paper Chase"
BEST PERFORMANCE BY A SUPPORTING ACTOR IN 1973

131

TATUM O'NEAL
in "Paper Moon"
BEST PERFORMANCE BY A SUPPORTING ACTRESS IN 1973

DAY FOR NIGHT

(WARNER BROTHERS) Director, Francois Truffaut; Screenplay, Mr. Truffaut, Jean-Louis Richard, Suzanne Schiffman; Executive Producer, Marcel Berbert; Photography, Pierre-William Glenn; Editors, Yann Dedet, Martine Barraque; Music, Georges Delerue; In color; 116 minutes; Rated PG; September 1973 release.

CAST

Ferrand	Francois Truffaut
Julie	Jacqueline Bisset
Alphonse	Jean-Pierre Leaud
Severine	Valentina Cortese
Alexandre	Jean-Pierre Aumont
Lilianna	Dani
Stacey	Alexandra Stewart
Bertrand	Jean Champion

Right: Jean Champion, Francois Truffaut
Below: Jean-Pierre Leaud, Jean-Pierre Aumont, Jacqueline Bisset, Valentina Cortese

Jacqueline Bisset, Jean-Pierre Aumont

Dani, Jean-Pierre Leaud

1973 ACADEMY AWARD FOR BEST FOREIGN LANGUAGE FILM

| Marlon Brando | Anne Baxter | Bob Fosse | Jane Fonda | Charles Chaplin |

PREVIOUS ACADEMY AWARD WINNERS

(1) Best Picture, (2) Actor, (3) Actress, (4) Supporting Actor, (5) Supporting Actress, (6) Director, (7) Special Award, (8) Best Foreign Language Film

1927–28: (1) "Wings" (2) Emil Jannings in "The Way of All Flesh", (3) Janet Gaynor in "Seventh Heaven", (6) Frank Borzage for "Seventh Heaven", (7) Charles Chaplin.

1928–29: (1) "Broadway Melody", (2) Warner Baxter in "Old Arizona", (3) Mary Pickford in "Coquette", (6) Frank Lloyd for "The Divine Lady".

1929–30: (1) "All Quiet on the Western Front", (2) George Arliss in "Disraeli", (3) Norma Shearer in "The Divorcee", (6) Lewis Milestone for "All Quiet on the Western Front".

1930–31: (1) "Cimarron", (2) Lionel Barrymore in "A Free Soul", (3) Marie Dressler in "Min and Bill", (6) Norman Taurog for "Skippy".

1931–32: (1) "Grand Hotel", (2) Fredric March in "Dr. Jekyll and Mr. Hyde", tied with Wallace Beery in "The Champ", (3) Helen Hayes in "The Sin of Madelon Claudet", (6) Frank Borzage for "Bad Girl".

1932–33: (1) "Cavalcade", (2) Charles Laughton in "The Private Life of Henry VIII", (3) Katharine Hepburn in "Morning Glory", (6) Frank Lloyd for "Cavalcade".

1934: (1) "It Happened One Night", (2) Clark Gable in "It Happened One Night", (3) Claudette Colbert in "It Happened One Night", (6) Frank Capra for "It Happened One Night", (7) Shirley Temple.

1935: (1) "Mutiny on the Bounty", (2) Victor McLaglen in "The Informer" (3) Bette Davis in "Dangerous", (6) John Ford for "The Informer", (7) D. W. Griffith.

1936: (1) "The Great Ziegfeld", (2) Paul Muni in "The Story of Louis Pasteur", (3) Luise Rainer in "The Great Ziegfeld", (4) Walter Brennan in "Come and Get It", (5) Gale Sondergaard in "Anthony Adverse", (6) Frank Capra for "Mr. Deeds Goes to Town".

1937: (1) "The Life of Emile Zola", (2) Spencer Tracy in "Captains Courageous", (3) Luise Rainer in "The Good Earth", (4) Joseph Schildkraut in "The Life of Emile Zola", (5) Alice Brady in "In Old Chicago", (6) Leo McCarey for "The Awful Truth", (7) Mack Sennett, Edgar Bergen.

1938: (1) "You Can't Take It with You", (2) Spencer Tracy in "Boys' Town", (3) Bette Davis in "Jezebel", (4) Walter Brennan in "Kentucky", (5) Fay Bainter in "Jezebel", (6) Frank Capra for "You Can't Take It with You", (7) Deanna Durbin, Mickey Rooney, Harry M. Warner, Walt Disney.

1939: (1) "Gone with the Wind", (2) Robert Donat in "Goodbye, Mr. Chips", (3) Vivien Leigh in "Gone with the Wind", (4) Thomas Mitchell in "Stagecoach", (5) Hattie McDaniel in "Gone with the Wind", (6) Victor Fleming for "Gone with the Wind", (7) Douglas Fairbanks, Judy Garland.

1940: (1) "Rebecca", (2) James Stewart in "The Philadelphia Story", (3) Ginger Rogers in "Kitty Foyle", (4) Walter Brennan in "The Westerner", (5) Jane Darwell in "The Grapes of Wrath", (6) John Ford for "The Grapes of Wrath", (7) Bob Hope.

1941: (1) "How Green Was My Valley", (2) Gary Cooper in "Sergeant York", (3) Joan Fontaine in "Suspicion", (4) Donald Crisp in "How Green Was My Valley", (5) Mary Astor in "The Great Lie", (6) John Ford for "How Green Was My Valley", (7) Leopold Stokowski, Walt Disney.

1942: (1) "Mrs. Miniver", (2) James Cagney in "Yankee Doodle Dandy", (3) Greer Garson in "Mrs. Miniver", (4) Van Heflin in "Johnny Eager", (5) Teresa Wright in "Mrs. Miniver", (6) William Wyler for "Mrs. Miniver", (7) Charles Boyer, Noel Coward.

1943: (1) "Casablanca", (2) Paul Lukas in "Watch on the Rhine", (3) Jennifer Jones in "The Song of Bernadette", (4) Charles Coburn in "The More the Merrier", (5) Katina Paxinou in "For Whom the Bell Tolls", (6) Michael Curtiz for "Casablanca".

1944: (1) "Going My Way", (2) Bing Crosby in "Going My Way", (3) Ingrid Bergman in "Gaslight", (4) Barry Fitzgerald in "Going My Way", (5) Ethel Barrymore in "None but the Lonely Heart", (6) Leo McCarey for "Going My Way", (7) Margaret O'Brien, Bob Hope.

1945: (1) "The Lost Weekend", (2) Ray Milland in "The Lost Weekend", (3) Joan Crawford in "Mildred Pierce", (4) James Dunn in "A Tree Grows in Brooklyn", (5) Anne Revere in "National Velvet", (6) Billy Wilder for "The Lost Weekend", (7) Walter Wanger, Peggy Ann Garner.

1946: (1) "The Best Years of Our Lives", (2) Fredric March in "The Best Years of Our Lives", (3) Olivia de Havilland in "To Each His Own", (4) Harold Russell in "The Best Years of Our Lives", (5) Anne Baxter in "The Razor's Edge", (7) Laurence Olivier, Harold Russell, Ernst Lubitsch, Claude Jarman, Jr.

1947: (1) "Gentleman's Agreement", (2) Ronald Colman in "A Double Life", (3) Loretta Young in "The Farmer's Daughter", (4) Edmund Gwenn in "Miracle On 34th Street", (5) Celeste Holm in "Gentleman's Agreement", (6) Elia Kazan for "Gentleman's Agreement", (7) James Baskette, (8) "Shoe Shine".

1948: (1) "Hamlet", (2) Laurence Olivier in "Hamlet", (3) Jane Wyman in "Johnny Belinda", (4) Walter Huston in "The Treasure of the Sierra Madre", (5) Claire Trevor in "Key Largo", (6) John Huston for "The Treasure of the Sierra Madre", (7) Ivan Jandl, Sid Grauman, Adolph Zukor, Walter Wanger, (8) "Monsieur Vincent".

1949: (1) "All the King's Men", (2) Broderick Crawford in "All the King's Men", (3) Olivia de Havilland in "The Heiress", (4) Dean Jagger in "Twelve O'Clock High", (5) Mercedes McCambridge in "All the King's Men", (6) Joseph L. Mankiewicz for "A Letter to Three Wives", (7) Bobby Driscoll, Fred Astaire, Cecil B. DeMille, Jean Hersholt, (8) "The Bicycle Thief".

1950: "All about Eve", (2) Jose Ferrer in "Cyrano de Bergerac", (3) Judy Holliday in "Born Yesterday", (4) George Sanders in "All about Eve", (5) Josephine Hull in "Harvey", (6) Joseph L. Mankiewicz for "All about Eve", (7) George Murphy, Louis B. Mayer, (8) "The Walls of Malapaga".

1951: (1) "An American in Paris", (2) Humphrey Bogart in "The African Queen", (3) Vivien Leigh in "A Streetcar Named Desire", (4) Karl Malden in "A Streetcar Named Desire", (5) Kim Hunter in "A Streetcar Named Desire", (6) George Stevens for "A Place in the Sun", (7) Gene Kelly, (8) "Rashomon."

1952: (1) "The Greatest Show on Earth", (2) Gary Cooper in "High Noon", (3) Shirley Booth in "Come Back, Little Sheba", (4) Anthony Quinn in "Viva Zapata", (5) Gloria Grahame in "The Bad and the Beautiful", (6) John Ford for "The Quiet Man", (7) Joseph M. Schenck, Merian C. Cooper, Harold Lloyd, Bob Hope, George Alfred Mitchell, (8) "Forbidden Games."

1953: (1) "From Here to Eternity", (2) William Holden in "Stalag 17", (3) Audrey Hepburn in "Roman Holiday", (4) Frank Sinatra in "From Here to Eternity", (5) Donna Reed in "From Here to Eternity", (6) Fred Zinnemann for "From Here to Eternity", (7) Pete Smith, Joseph Breen.

Lillian Gish **Gene Hackman** **Goldie Hawn** **Bob Hope** **Eileen Heckart**

1954: (1) "On the Waterfront", (2) Marlon Brando in "On the Waterfront", (3) Grace Kelly in "The Country Girl", (4) Edmond O'Brien in "The Barefoot Contessa", (5) Eva Marie Saint in "On the Waterfront", (6) Elia Kazan for "On the Waterfront", (7) Greta Garbo, Danny Kaye, Jon Whitely, Vincent Winter, (8) "Gate of Hell."

1955: (1) "Marty", (2) Ernest Borgnine in "Marty", (3) Anna Magnani in "The Rose Tattoo", (4) Jack Lemmon in "Mister Roberts", (5) Jo Van Fleet in "East of Eden", (6) Delbert Mann for "Marty", (8) "Samurai."

1956: (1) "Around the World in 80 Days", (2) Yul Brynner in "The King and I", (3) Ingrid Bergman in "Anastasia", (4) Anthony Quinn in "Lust for Life", (5) Dorothy Malone in "Written on the Wind", (6) George Stevens for "Giant", (7) Eddie Cantor, (8) "La Strada."

1957: (1) "The Bridge on the River Kwai", (2) Alec Guinness in "The Bridge on the River Kwai", (3) Joanne Woodward in "The Three Faces of Eve", (4) Red Buttons in "Sayonara", (5) Miyoshi Umeki in "Sayonara", (6) David Lean for "The Bridge on the River Kwai", (7) Charles Brackett, B. B. Kahane, Gilbert M. (Bronco Billy) Anderson, (8) "The Nights of Cabiria."

1958: (1) "Gigi", (2) David Niven in "Separate Tables", (3) Susan Hayward in "I Want to Live", (4) Burl Ives in "The Big Country", (5) Wendy Hiller in "Separate Tables", (6) Vincente Minnelli for "Gigi", (7) Maurice Chevalier, (8) "My Uncle."

1959: (1) "Ben-Hur", (2) Charlton Heston in "Ben-Hur", (3) Simone Signoret in "Room at the Top", (4) Hugh Griffith in "Ben-Hur", (5) Shelley Winters in "The Diary of Anne Frank", (6) William Wyler for "Ben-Hur", (7) Lee de Forest, Buster Keaton, (8) "Black Orpheus."

1960: (1) "The Apartment", (2) Burt Lancaster in "Elmer Gantry", (3) Elizabeth Taylor in "Butterfield 8", (4) Peter Ustinov in "Spartacus", (5) Shirley Jones in "Elmer Gantry", (6) Billy Wilder for "The Apartment", (7) Gary Cooper, Stan Laurel, Hayley Mills, (8) "The Virgin Spring."

1961: (1) "West Side Story", (2) Maximilian Schell in "Judgment at Nuremberg", (3) Sophia Loren in "Two Women", (4) George Chakiris in "West Side Story", (5) Rita Moreno in "West Side Story", (6) Robert Wise for "West Side Story", (7) Jerome Robbins, Fred L. Metzler, (8) "Through a Glass Darkly."

1962: (1) "Lawrence of Arabia", (2) Gregory Peck in "To Kill a Mockingbird", (3) Anne Bancroft in "The Miracle Worker", (4) Ed Begley in "Sweet Bird of Youth", (5) Patty Duke in "The Miracle Worker", (6) David Lean for "Lawrence of Arabia", (8) "Sundays and Cybele."

1963: (1) "Tom Jones", (2) Sidney Poitier in "Lilies of the Field", (3) Patricia Neal in "Hud", (4) Melvyn Douglas in "Hud", (5) Margaret Rutherford in "The V.I.P's", (6) Tony Richardson for "Tom Jones", (8) "8½".

1964: (1) "My Fair Lady", (2) Rex Harrison in "My Fair Lady", (3) Julie Andrews in "Mary Poppins", (4) Peter Ustinov in "Topkapi", (5) Lila Kedrova in "Zorba the Greek", (6) George Cukor for "My Fair Lady", (7) William Tuttle, (8) "Yesterday, Today and Tomorrow."

1965: (1) "The Sound of Music", (2) Lee Marvin in "Cat Ballou", (3) Julie Christie in "Darling", (4) Martin Balsam in "A Thousand Clowns", (5) Shelley Winters in "A Patch of Blue", (6) Robert Wise for "The Sound of Music", (7) Bob Hope, (8) "The Shop on Main Street".

1966: (1) "A Man for All Seasons", (2) Paul Scofield in "A Man for All Seasons", (3) Elizabeth Taylor in "Who's Afraid of Virginia Woolf?", (4) Walter Matthau in "The Fortune Cookie", (5) Sandy Dennis in "Who's Afraid of Virginia Woolf?", (6) Fred Zinnemann for "A Man for All Seasons", (8) "A Man and A Woman."

1967: (1) "In the Heat of the Night", (2) Rod Steiger in "In the Heat of the Night", (3) Katharine Hepburn in "Guess Who's Coming to Dinner", (4) George Kennedy in "Cool Hand Luke", (5) Estelle Parsons in "Bonnie and Clyde", (6) Mike Nichols for "The Graduate", (8) "Closely Watched Trains."

1968: (1) "Oliver!", (2) Cliff Robertson in "Charly", (3) Katharine Hepburn in "The Lion in Winter" tied with Barbra Streisand in "Funny Girl", (4) Jack Albertson in "The Subject Was Roses", (5) Ruth Gordon in "Rosemary's Baby", (6) Carol Reed for "Oliver!", (7) Onna White for "Oliver!" choreography, John Chambers for "Planet of the Apes" make-up, (8) "War and Peace."

1969: (1) "Midnight Cowboy", (2) John Wayne in "True Grit", (3) Maggie Smith in "The Prime of Miss Jean Brodie", (4) Gig Young in "They Shoot Horses, Don't They?", (5) Goldie Hawn in "Cactus Flower", (6) John Schlesinger for "Midnight Cowboy", (7) Gary Grant, (8) "Z."

1970: (1) "Patton", (2) George C. Scott in "Patton", (3) Glenda Jackson in "Women in Love", (4) John Mills in "Ryan's Daughter", (5) Helen Hayes in "Airport", (6) Franklin J. Schaffner for "Patton," (7) Lillian Gish, Orson Welles, (8) "Investigation of a Citizen above Suspicion."

1971: (1) "The French Connection," (2) Gene Hackman in "The French Connection," (3) Jane Fonda in "Klute," (4) Ben Johnson in "The Last Picture Show," (5) Cloris Leachman in "The Last Picture Show," (6) William Friedkin for "The French Connection," (7) Charles Chaplin, (8) "The Garden of the Finzi-Continis."

1972: (1) "The Godfather," (2) Marlon Brando in "The Godfather," (3) Liza Minnelli in "Cabaret," (4) Joel Grey in "Cabaret," (5) Eileen Heckart in "Butterflies Are Free," (6) Bob Fosse for "Cabaret," (7) Edward G. Robinson, (8) "The Discreet Charm of the Bourgeoisie."

1973: (1) "The Sting," (2) Jack Lemmon in "Save the Tiger," (3) Glenda Jackson in "A Touch of Class," (4) John Houseman in "The Paper Chase," (5) Tatum O'Neal in "Paper Moon," (6) George Roy Hill for "The Sting," (8) "Day for Night"

Ben Johnson **Celeste Holm** **Burt Lancaster** **Hayley Mills** **Rod Steiger**   135

1974 FOREIGN FILMS

PARTNER

(**NEW YORKER**) Director, Bernardo Bertolucci; Screenplay, Bernardo Bertolucci, Gianni Amico; Adapted from Dostoyevsky's "The Double"; Photography, Ugo Piccone; Art Director, Jean Robert Marquis; Editor, Robert Perpiagnani; Music, Ennio Morricone; In Technicolor and Techniscope; Not classified; 105 minutes; January release.

CAST

Jacob I/Jacob II ....Pierre Clementi
Clara .... Stefania Sandrelli
Salesgirl .... Tina Aumont
Petrushka .... Sergio Tofano
Professors...Giulio Cesare Castello,
Romano Costa, Antonio Maestri

Right: Pierre Clementi, Tina Aumont

Pierre Clementi

Pierre Clementi

THREE SISTERS

(AMERICAN FILM THEATRE) Producer, Alan Clore; Director, Laurence Olivier; Co-Director, John Sichel; Author, Anton Chekov; Translation, Moura Budbuerg; Associate Producers, Timothy Burrill, James C. Katz; Assistant Director, Simon Relph; Photograhy, Geoffrey Unsworth; Editor, Jack Harris; Designer, Josef Voboda; Composer, William Walton; Art Director, Bill Hutchinn; Costumes, Beatrice Dawson; In color; 165 minutes plus intermission; January release.

CAST

Olga	Jeanne Watts
Masha	Joan Plowright
Irina	Louise Purnell
Andrei	Derek Jacobi
Natasha	Sheila Reid
Kulighin	Kenneth Mackintosh
Anfissa	Daphne Heard
Ferrapont	Harry Lomax
Serving Maid	Judy Wilson
Housemaid	Mary Griffiths
Tusenbach	Ronald Pickup
Tchebutikin	Laurence Olivier
Vassili Vassilich Solloni	Frank Wylie
Vershinin	Alan Bates
Fedotik	Richard Kay
Rode	David Belcher
Orderly	George Selway
Officers	David Munro, Alan Adams, Robert Walker

Right: Joan Plowright, Louise Purnell, Jeanne Watts

Alan Bates, Joan Plowright
Above: Louise Purnell, Laurence Olivier

Laurence Olivier, also above with Derek Jacobi, Joan Plowright

137

MAN IS NOT A BIRD

(GROVE PRESS) Direction and Screenplay, Dusan Makavejev; Photography, Aleksander Petkovic; Music, Petar Bergamo; An Avala Film; In black and white; 80 minutes; February release.

CAST

Hairdresser	Milena Dravic
Truck Driver	Boris Dvornik
Rudinski	Janez Urhovec
Barbulovitch	Stojan Arandjelovic
His Wife	Efa Ras
Hypnotist	Roko

Milena Dravic

LUTHER

(AMERICAN FILM THEATRE) Producer, Ely A. Landau; Direc-
tor, Guy Green; Screenplay, Edward Anhalt; Based on play by John
Osborne; Executive Producer, Mort Abrahams; Assistant Director,
Philip Gowans; Photography, Freddie Young; Editor, Malcolm
Cooke; Designer, Peter Mullins; Music, John Addison; Costumes,
Elizabeth Haffenden, Joan Bridge; In color; Rated G; 112 minutes;
February release.

CAST

Martin Luther	Stacy Keach
Hans	Patrick Magee
Tetzel	Hugh Griffith
Von Eck	Robert Stephens
Cajetan	Alan Badel
Catherine	Judi Dench
Feinand	Leonard Rossiter
Staupitz	Maurice Denham
The Knight	Julian Glover
Prior	Peter Cellier
Lucas	Thomas Heathcote
King Charles	Malcolm Stoddard

Right: Stacy Keach

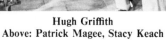

Hugh Griffith
Above: Patrick Magee, Stacy Keach

Stacy Keach
Above: Hugh Griffith, Alan Badel

THE THREE MUSKETEERS

(20th CENTURY-FOX) Producer, Alexander Salkind; Director, Richard Lester; Screenplay, George MacDonald Fraser; Based on novel by Alexander Dumas; Music, Michel Legrand; Photography, David Watkins; Editor, John Victor Smith; In Technicolor; Rated PG; 107 minutes; March release.

CAST

Athos ....Oliver Reed
Constance.. Raquel Welch
Aramis .... Richard Chamberlain
D'Artagnan .... Michael York
Porthos...Frank Finlay
Rochefort.. Christopher Lee
Louis XIII ....Jean-Pierre Cassel
Anne of Austria ....Geraldine Chaplin
Buckingham.. Simon Ward
Milady .... Faye Dunaway
Cardinal Richelieu...Charlton Heston
M. Bonancieux ....Spike Milligan
and Roy Kinnear, Nicole Calfan, Sybil Danning

Left: Raquel Welch, Michael York

Frank Finlay, Oliver Reed, Michael York, Richard Chamberlain

Faye Dunaway, Charlton Heston
Top: Jean Pierre Cassel, Geraldine Chaplin

THE PEDESTRIAN

(CINERAMA) Produced, Directed, and Written by Maximilian Schell; Photography, Wolfgang Treu, Klaus Koenig; Editor, Dagmar Hirtz; Music, Manos Hadjidakis; Assistant Directors, Ina Fritsche, Leonard Gmuer; English adaptation, David Ambrose; Co-Producer, Zev Braun; In Eastmancolor; Rated PG; 97 minutes; March release.

CAST

Heinz Alfred Giese	Gustav Rudolf Sellner
Inge Maria Giese	Ruth Hausmeister
Andreas Giese	Maximilian Schell
Hubert Giese	Manuel Sellner
Elsa Giese	Elsa Wagner
Elke Giese	Dagmar Hirtz
Michael Giese	Michael Weinert
Rudolf Hartmann	Peter Hall
Alexander Markowitz	Alexander May
Erwin Gotz	Christian Kohlund
Dr. Karl Peters	Franz Seitz
First Reporter	Herbert Mensching
Second Reporter	Peter Moland
Henriette Markowitz	Gertrud Bald
Dr. Rolf Meineke	Walter Kohut
Frau Buchmann	Margarethe Schell von Noe
Auditor	Sigfrit
Karin	Gila von Weitershausen
Greek woman	Fani Fotinou
Greek man	Gaddi Ben-Artzi
Policeman	Walter Schmidinger
Dr. Kratzer	Walter von Varndal
Housekeeper Hilde	Silvia Hurlimann
Norbert Schiller	Norbert Schiller
Angela Salloker	Angela Salloker
Lady Gray	Peggy Ashcroft
Frau Lilienthal	Elisabeth Bergner
Frau Eschenlohr	Lil Dagover
Frau von Rautenfeld	Kate Haack
Frau Bergedorf	Johanna Hofer
Frau Dechamps	Francoise Rosay

Left: Gustav Rudolf Sellner

Johanna Hofer, Kathe Haack, Peggy Ashcroft, Lil Dagover, Elsa Wagner, Francoise Rosay, Elisabeth Bergner

Gustav Rudolf Sellner, Gila Von Weitershausen
Above: Christian Kohlund, Peter Hall, Alexander May

Dagmar Hirtz, Gustav Rudolf Sellner Above: Sellner, Gila von Weitershausen Top: Sellner

LOVE AND ANARCHY

(PEPPERCORN-WORMSER) Directed and Written by Lina Wertmuller; Photography, Giuseppe Rotunno; Sets and Costumes, Enrico Job; Editor, Franco Fraticelli; Music, Nino Rota; A. Herbert R. Steinmann—Billy Baxter Presentation; In Technicolor; 108 minutes; Rated R; April release.

CAST

Tunin	Giancarlo Giannini
Salome	Mariangela Melato
Tripolina	Lina Polito
Spatoletti	Eros Pagni
Madame Aida	Pina Cei
Donna Carmela	Elena Fiore

Left: Giancarlo Giannini

Lina Polito, Giancarlo Giannini
(also above)

Giancarlo Giannini, Mariangela Melato, also
above with Lina Polito

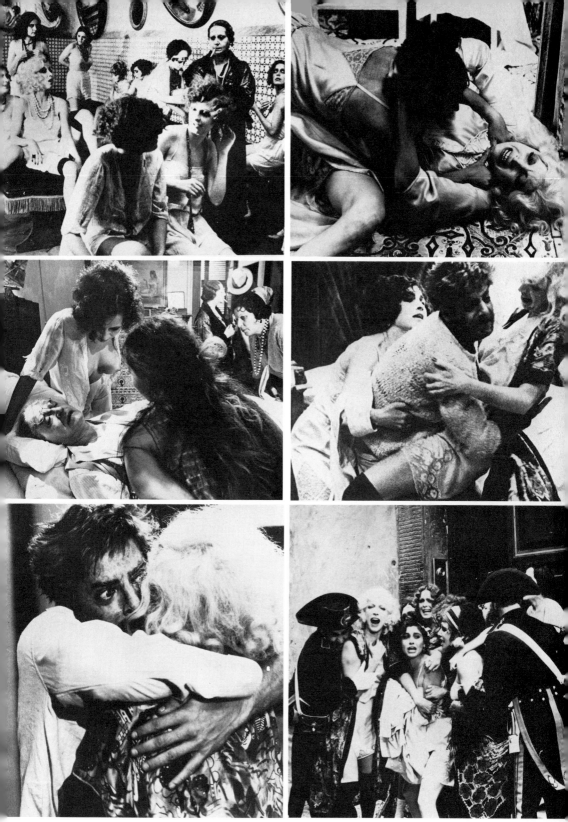

Giancarlo Giannini

BUTLEY

(AMERICAN FILM THEATRE) Producer, Ely A. Landau; Director, Harold Pinter; Screen Adaptation by Simon Gray from his play; Executive Producer, Otto Plaschkes; Assistant Director, Ted Sturgis; Photography, Gerry Fisher; Editor, Malcolm Cooke; Art Director, Carmen Dillon; In color; Rated R; 129 minutes; April release.

CAST

Ben Butley	Alan Bates
Edna Shaft	Jessica Tandy
Joey Keyston	Richard O'Callaghan
Anne Butley	Susan Engel
Reg Nuttall	Michael Byrne
Miss Heasman	Georgina Hale
Mr. Gardner	Simon Rouse
James	John Savident
Train Passenger	Oliver Maguire
Male Students	Colin Haigh, Darien Angadi
Girl Students	Susan Woodridge, Lindsay Ingram, Patti Love, Belinda Low

Top Right: Alan Bates, Simon Rouse

Alan Bates, Richard O'Callaghan, Michael Byrne
Above: Alan Bates, Jessica Tandy

Susan Engel, Alan Bates
Above: Georgina Hale, Alan Bates

WEDDING IN BLOOD

(NEW LINE CINEMA) Direction, Screenplay and Dialogue, Claude Chabrol; Photography, Jean Rabier; Music, Pierre Jansen; Executive Producer, Andre Genoves; A Franco-Italian Co-Production; In color; Not rated; 98 minutes; May release.

CAST

Lucienne	Stephane Audran
Pierre	Michel Piccoli
Paul	Claude Pieplu
Clothilde	Clothilde Joano
Helene	Eliana de Santis
Auriol	Francois Robert
Prefect	Daniel Lecourtois
Berthier	Pipo Merisi
Councillor	Ermano Casanova

Right: Stephane Audrane, Michel Piccoli

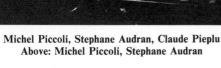

Michel Piccoli, Stephane Audran, Claude Pieplu
Above: Michel Piccoli, Stephane Audran

Michel Piccoli, Stephane Audran
(also above)

HEARTS AND MINDS

(WARNER BROS.) Producer, Marina Cicogna; Director, Michele Lupo; Screenplay, Mino Roli, Franco Bucceri, Roberto Leoni, Michele Lupo; Story, Franco Bucceri, Roberto Leoni; Art Director, Francesco Bronzi; Costumes, Enrico Sabbatini; Editor, Antonietta Zitta; Music, Ennio Morricone; Photography, Tonino Delli Colli; Executive Producer, Manolo Bolognini; In color; Rated PG; May release. Title changed from "The Master Touch."

CAST

Wallace	Kirk Douglas
Anna	Florinda Bolkan
Marco	Giuliano Gemma
Police Inspector	Rene Koldehoff
Muller	Wolfgang Preiss

Left: Kirk Douglas

Kirk Douglas, Florinda Bolkan

Giuliano Gemma, Florinda Bolkan, Kirk Douglas
Top: Kirk Douglas, Florinda Bolkan

LE PETIT THEATRE DE JEAN RENOIR

(PHOENIX FILMS) Produced, Directed, Written, and Narrated by Jean Renoir; Designer, Gilbert Margerie; Editor, Genevieve Winding; Photography, Georges Leclerc; Music, Joseph Kosma, Jean Wiener, Octave Cremieux; Subtitles, Herman Weinberg; In color; 100 minutes; May release.

CAST

"The Last Christmas Dinner"
Le Clochard .... Nino Formicola
La Clochard .... Milly
Gontran .... Roland Bertin
Le Gerant .... Andre Dumas
"The Electric Floor Waxer"
Emilie .... Marguerite Cassan
Gustave .... Pierre Olaf
Jules .... Jacques Dynam
"The King of Yvetot"
Duvallier .... Fernand Sardou
Isabelle .... Francoise Arnoul
Ferand .... Jean Carmet
Blanc .... Andrex
Paulette .... Dominique Labourier
Cesar .... Edmond Ardisson
"When Love Dies"
Interpreted by Jeanne Moreau

Left: Jean Renoir

Francoise Arnoul, Jean Carmet

Jean Carmet, Francoise Arnoul, Fernand Sardou
Top: Marguerite Cassan

THE BLACK WINDMILL

(UNIVERSAL) Producer-Director, Don Siegel; Executive Producers, Richard D. Zanuck, David Brown; Associate Producer, Scott Hale; Screenplay, Leigh Vance; From "Seven Days to a Killing" by Clive Egleton; Photography, Outsama Rawi; Art Director, Peter Murton; Editor, Antony Gibbs; Costumes, Anthony Mendleson; Music, Roy Budd; Assistant Director, Kip Gowans; In Panavision and Technicolor; Rated PG; 106 minutes; May release.

CAST

Maj. John Tarrant	Michael Caine
Sir Edward Julyan	Joseph O'Conor
Cedric Harper	Donald Pleasence
McKee	John Vernon
Alex Tarrant	Janet Suzman
Ceil Burrows	Delphine Seyrig
Chief Superintendent Wray	Joss Ackland
Alf Chestermann	Clive Revill
Mike McCarthy	Edward Hardwicke
Thickset M. I. 5 Man	David Daker
Bateson	Denis Quilley
David Tarrant	Paul Moss
James Stroud	Mark Praid
Pincus	George Cooper
Monitoring Policeman	Derek Newark
Special Policeman	John Rhys-Davies
Pleasant Secretary	Brenda Cowling
Ilkeston	Preston Lockwood
Manageress	Nancy Gabrielle
Doctor	Murray Brown
Ilkeston's Secretary	Hilary Sesta
S. P. Driver	Frank Henson
Lady Julyan	Catherine Schell
Sollars	Derek Lord
Postman	Michael Segal
Jane Harper	Maureen Pryor
Tomkins	Paul Humpoletz
Hetty	Hermione Baddeley
General St. John	Patrick Barr
Heppenstal	John Harvey
Admiral Ballentyne	Russell Napier

Anthony Verner (Magnus), Joyce Carey (Secretary), Robert Dorning (Jeweller), Mollie Urquhart (Margaret), Jon Croft (Officer), Christopher Hawkings (Auctioneer), Billy Milton (Pianist), Golda Casimir (Barmaid), Peter Halliday (Customs Official), Jessie Robins (Fat Lady), Del Baker (M.I.5 Driver), Yves Afonso (Jacques), Jacques Ciron (Prison Official), Roger Lumont (Prison Guard), Jean Michaud (Doctor), Michel Norman (Paddy Wagon Driver), Jean-Pierre Allais (Passenger in truck), Roland Neunreuther (Motorcycle Cop), Mme. Vagenende (Hurdy Gurdy Woman)

Top Right: Donald Pleasence, Michael Caine

Delphine Seyrig, John Vernon

Michael Caine, Janet Suzman
Above: Michael Caine, Delphine Seyrig

152

S*P*Y*S

(20th CENTURY-FOX) Producers, Irwin Winkler, Robert Chartoff; Director, Irvin Kershner; Associate Producer, Bob Lawrence; Screenplay, Mal Marmorstein, Laurence J. Cohen, Fred Freeman; Music, Jerry Goldsmith; Photography, Gerry Fisher; Designer, Michael Seymour; Editor, Keith Palmer; Art Director, Richard Rambeau; Costumes, Sue Yelland; Assistant Directors, Tony Way, Gerry Gavigan; In DeLuxe color; Rated PG; 87 minutes; June release.

CAST

Griff	Elliott Gould
Brulard	Donald Sutherland
Sybil	Zouzou
Martinson	Joss Ackland
Lippet	Kenneth Griffith
Borisenko	Vladek Sheybal
Grubov	Kenneth J. Warren
Yuri	Yuri Borienko
Sevitsky	Michael Petrovitch
Gaspar	Pierre Oudry
Lafayette	Jacques Marin
Hessler	Shane Rimmer
Paul	Xavier Gelin
Russian Coach	George Pravda
Stunt Man/KGB Agent	Alf Joint
Toy Ling	Andy Ho
Ellie	Melanie Ackland
Alan	James Woolley
Priest	Michael Anthony
Vet	Robert Cawdron
King of Swobodia	Raf De La Torre
Clerk	Andre Charisse
Evans	John Bardon
Head Waiter	Norman Atkyns
Seely	Jeffry Wickham
Croft	Nigel Hawthorne
Lippet's Bodyguard	Larry Taylor
Russian-speaking Lady	Marian Desmond
KGB Agent	Phillip Ross
Prostitute	Hella Petri

Right: Zouzou, Donald Sutherland
Top: Elliott Gould, Donald Sutherland

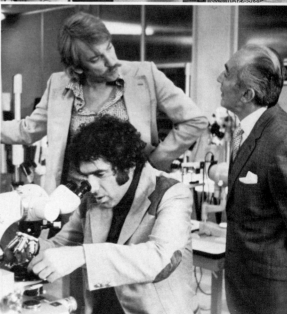

Donald Sutherland, Elliott Gould

Donald Sutherland, Elliott Gould

153

A FREE WOMAN

(NEW YORKER) Director, Volker Schlondorff; Screenplay, Volker Schlondorff, Margarethe von Trotta; Production Director, Eberhard Junkersdorf; Photography, Sven Nykvist; Editor, Suzanne Baron; Sets and Costumes, Nicos Parakis; Choreography, William Milie; Music, Stanley Myers; A Hallelujah Film Production; In Eastmancolor; Not rated: 100 minutes; June release.

CAST

Elisabeth	Margarethe von Trotta
Hans-Helmut	Friedhelm Ptok
Oskar	Martin Luttge
Personnel Director	Walter Sedlmayer
Schmollinger	Georg Marischka
Art Historian	Dr. Konrad Farner
Singing Teacher	Else Domberger
Dancing Teacher	Maria Brunner

Left: Margarethe von Trotta, Friedhelm Ptok

Margarethe von Trotta, Martin Luttge

Margarethe von Trotta, Martin Luttge Top Left: Friedhelm Ptok, Margarethe von Trotta
Top Right: Margarethe von Trotta, Konrad Farner

THE SEDUCTION OF MIMI

(NEW LINE CINEMA) Producers, Daniele Senatore, Romano Cardarelli; Direction, Story, and Screenplay, Lina Wertmuller; Music, Piero Piccioni; Photography, Blasco Giurato; Editor, Franco Fraticelli; Art Director, Amedeo Fago; Costumes, Maria Bono; A Euro International Films Production; In color; Not rated; 89 minutes; June release.

CAST

Mimi	Giancarlo Giannini
Fiore	Mariangela Melato
Rosalia	Agostina Belli
Signora Finocchiaro	Elena Fiore

Left: Giancarlo Giannini

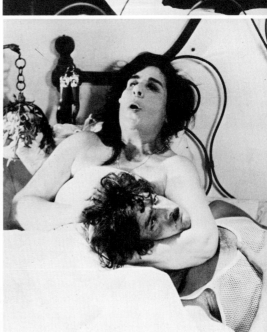

Giancarlo Giannini, Mariangela Melato
Above: Giancarlo Giannini

Giancarlo Giannini, and above

Giancarlo Giannini (L)
Top Left and Right: Giancarlo Giannini, Mariangela Melato

THE MAD ADVENTURES OF RABBI JACOB

(20th CENTURY-FOX) Producer, Bertrand Javal; Director, Gerard Oury; Screenplay, Gerard Oury, Danielle Thompson, Josy Eisenberg; Music, Vladimir Cosma; In color; Rated G; 96 minutes; July release.

CAST

Victor Pivert	Louis De Funes
Germaine Pivert	Suzy Delair
Rabbi Jacob	Marcel Dalio
Slimane	Claude Giraud
Andreani	Claude Pieplu
Fares	Renzo Montagnani
Salomon	Henry Gutbert
Tzipe	Janet Brandt
Moishe	Jean Herbert

Left: Louis De Funes

Louis De Funes

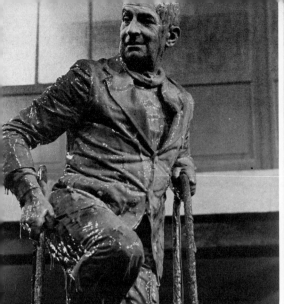

Louis De Funes (also top)

THE DESTRUCTORS

(AMERICAN INTERNATIONAL) Produced and Written by Judd Bernard; Director, Robert Parrish; Associate Producer, Patricia Casey; Music, Roy Budd; Photography, Douglas Slocombe; Art Director, Willy Holt; Assistant Director, Georges Pellegrin; Editor, Willy Kemplen; A Kettledrum-PECF Production; A Samuel Z. Arkoff Presentation; In Movielab Color; Rated PG; 89 minutes; July release

CAST

Deray	Michael Caine
Steve Ventura	Anthony Quinn
Brizard	James Mason
Lucianne	Maureen Kerwin
Calmet	Marcel Bozzuffi
Brizard's Mistress	Catherine Rouvel
Briac	Maurice Ronet
Marsac	Andre Oumansky
Rita	Alexandra Stewart
Kovakian	Patrick Floersheim
Williams	Pierre Salinger
Countess	Hella Petri
Lazar	Vernon Dobtcheff
Kurt	Jerry Brouer
Henri	Georges Lycan
Rouget	Jean Bouchaud
Minieri	Georges Beller
Matthews	Robert Rondo
Fournier	Gib Grossac
Fortuit	J. L. Fortuit
Wilson	Pierre Koulak
Kevin	Jonathan Brooks Poole
Sally	Barbara Sommers
Janet	Martine Kelly
The Girl	Dianik Zurakowska
Detective Fargas	Ed Marcus
Poker Players	Alan Rosset, Bill Kearns, James Jones, Gene Moskowitz

Top Right: Michael Caine, James Mason, Maureen Kerwin Below: Pierre Salinger, Anthony Quinn

James Mason, Maureen Kerwin

Michael Caine, Maureen Kerwin
Above: Anthony Quinn, Michael Caine

THE TAMARIND SEED

(AVCO EMBASSY) Producer, Ken Wales; Direction and Screenplay, Blake Edwards; Based on novel by Evelyn Anthony; Music, John Barry; Photography, Freddie Young; Associate Producer, Johnny Goodman; Art Director, Harry Pottle; Editor, Ernest Walter; Assistant Director, Derek Cracknell; Song, John Barry, Don Black; Sung by Wilma Reading; In Panavision and Eastmancolor; Rated PG; 123 minutes; July release.

CAST

Judith Farrow	Julie Andrews
Feodor Sverdlov	Omar Sharif
Jack Loder	Anthony Quayle
Fergus Stephenson	Daniel O'Herlihy
Margaret Stephenson	Sylvia Sims
General Golitsyn	Oscar Homolka
George MacLeod	Bryan Marshall
Richard Paterson	David Baron
Rachel Paterson	Celia Bannerman
Colonel Moreau	Roger Dann
Sandy Mitchell	Sharon Duce
Major Sukalov	George Mikell
Anna Skriabina	Kate O'Mara
Dimitri Memenov	Constantin De Goguel
First KGB Agent	John Sullivan
Second KGB Agent	Terence Plummer
Third KGB Agent	Leslie Crawford
Igor Kalinin	Alexei Jawdokimov
Embassy Section Head	Janet Henfrey

Right: Julie Andrews, Omar Sharif

Julie Andrews, Anthony Quayle
Above: Julie Andrews, Omar Sharif

Julie Andrews, Omar Sharif

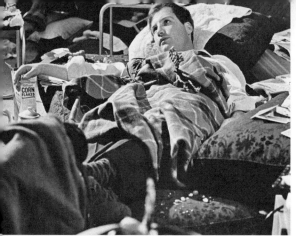

THE APPRENTICESHIP OF DUDDY KRAVITZ

(PARAMOUNT) Producer, John Kemeny; Director, Ted Kotcheff; Screenplay (based on his novel), Mordecai Richler; Adaptation, Lionel Chetwynd; Executive Producer, Gerald Schneider; Photography, Brian West; Designer, Anne Pritchard; Editor, Thom Noble; Associate Producer, Don Duprey; Assistant Directors, Timothy Rowse, Charles Braive, Robert Malenfant; In Panavision and Bellevue-Pathe Color; An International Cinemedia Center Ltd. Co-Production with the Canadian Film Development Corp.; Rated PG; 121 minutes; July release.

CAST

Duddy	Richard Dreyfuss
Yvette	Micheline Lanctot
Max	Jack Warden
Virgil	Randy Quaid
Uncle Benjy	Joseph Wiseman
Friar	Denholm Elliott
Dingleman	Henry Ramer
Farber	Joe Silver
Grandfather	Zvee Scooler
Calder	Robert Goodier
Lennie	Allan Rosenthal
Paddy	Barry Baldaro
Irwin	Allan Migicovsky
Bernie Farber	Barry Pascal
Linda	Susan Friedman
Bodyguard	Jacques Durette
Rabbi	Jonathan Robinson
Bernie Altman	Edward Resmini
Moe	Vincent Cole
Lawyer	Henry Gamer
Rubin	Lou Levitt
Cohen	Sonny Oppenheim
Arnie	Lionel Schwartz
Cuckoo	Mickey Eichen
Laplante	Robert Desroches
Tarty Woman	Judith Gault
Grandfather Farber	Norman Taviss

and Capt. L. Lussier and the cadets of the St. Basile-le-Grand Cadet Corps 2831

Left: Richard Dreyfuss, Jack Warden
Top: Richard Dreyfuss

Micheline Lanctot, Richard Dreyfuss

Richard Dreyfuss, Joe Silver

Jack Warden, Richard Dreyfuss Above: Richard
Dreyfuss, Randy Quaid Top: Denholm Elliott,
Micheline Lanctot, Richard Dreyfuss

Micheline Lanctot, Richard Dreyfuss Above: Richard
Dreyfuss, Joe Silver Top: Zvee Cooler, Richard
Dreyfuss

THE RA EXPEDITIONS

(UNIVERSAL) Executive Producer, Lennart Ehrenborg; Photog
phy, Carlo Mauri, Kei Ohara; Editor, Bengt Gunnar Eriksson; M
sic, Ed Norton; Narration, Roscoe Lee Brown, Thor Heyerdahl;
MCA Presentation; In Color; Rated G; 93 minutes; August relea

EXPEDITION MEMBERS
Thor Heyerdahl, Norway
Norman Baker, U.S.A.
Santiago Genoves, Mexico
Carlo Mauri, Italy
Yuri Senkevitch, U.S.S.R.
Georges Sourial, Egypt
Kei Ohara, Japan
Madani Ait Ouhanni, Morocco
Abdullah Djibrine, Chad, Africa
Safi
Sinbad

**Thor Heyerdahl, also above with Santiago
Genoves**

THE INTERNECINE PROJECT

(ALLIED ARTISTS) Producer, Barry Levinson; Co-Producer, Andrew Donally; Director, Ken Hughes; Screenplay, Barry Levinson, Jonathan Lynn; Based on novel by Mort W. Elkind; Photography, Geoffrey Unsworth; Assistant Director, David Bracknell; Designer, Geoffrey Drake; Art Director, David Minty; Editor, John Shirley; Music, Roy Budd; Presented by Emanuel L. Wolf; In color; Rated PG; 89 minutes; September release.

CAST

Robert Elliot	James Coburn
Jean Robertson	Lee Grant
Albert Parsons	Harry Andrews
Alex Hellman	Ian Hendry
David Baker	Michael Jayston
E. J. Farnsworth	Keenan Wynn
Christina	Christiane Kruger
Tycoon	Terence Alexander
Elliot's Secretary	Philip Anthony
Chester Drake	David Swift
Arnold Pryce Jones	Julian Glover
Producer	Ray Callaghan
Floor Manager	Geoffrey Burridge
Mixer	Robert Tayman
Production Assistant	Judy Robinson
Maxwell	Kevin Scott
German	John Savident
First Officer	Richard Cornish
Air Stewardess	Carrie Kirstein
German Delegate	Richard Marner
Executive Type	Ralph Ball
Executives	Brian Tully, Michael Knightingale
Senior Lab Technician	Ewan Roberts
Laboratory Assistant	Susan Magolier
Jean's Secretary	Mary Larkin

Right: Harry Andrews, Christiane Kruger
Top: James Coburn, Lee Grant

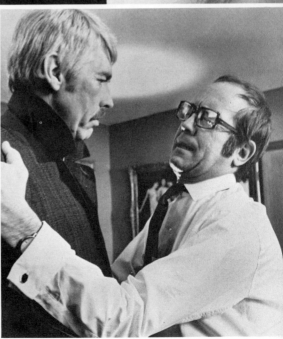

Michael Jayston

James Coburn, Ian Hendry

EARLY SPRING

(NEW YORKER) Director, Yasujiro Ozu; Screenplay, Yasujiro Ozu, Kogo Noda; Photography, Yushun Atsuta; Art Director, Tatsuo Hamada; Music, Takanobu Saito; Not rated; In black and white; 144 minutes; September release.

CAST

Shoji Sugiyama .... Ryo Ikebe
Masako, his wife .... Chikage Awashima
Chiyo Kaneko .... Keiko Kishi
Taizo Aoki .... Teiji Takahashi
Kiichi Onodera .... Chishu Ryu

Left: Chikage Awashima (L)

Keiko Kishi, Ryo Ikebe

Tiji Takahashi Top: Ryo Ikebe, Keiko Kishi

AMARCORD

(ROGER CORMAN/NEW WORLD) Producer, Franco Cristaldi; Director, Federico Fellini; Story and Screenplay, Federico Fellini, Tonino Guerra; Photography, Giuseppe Rotunno; Editor, Ruggero Mastroianni; Music, Nino Rota; Art Director-Costumes, Danilo Donati; Assistant Director, Maurizio Mein; An Italian-French Co-Production; In Panavision and Technicolor; Rated R; 127 minutes; September release.

CAST

Gradisca	Magali Noel
Titta	Bruno Zanin
Titta's Mother	Pupella Maggio
Titta's Father	Armando Brancia
Titta's Grandfather	Giuseppe Lanigro
Pataca	Nando Orfei
Uncle Teo	Ciccio Ingrassia
Lawyer	Luigi Rossi
Bisein	Gennaro Ombra
Volpina	Josiane Tanzilli
Tobacconist	Antonietta Beluzzi
Don Baravelli	Gianfilippo Carcano
Fascist Leader	Ferruccio Brembilla
Math Teacher	Dina Adorni

and Antonino Faa'DiBruno, Ferdinando Villella, Aristide Caporale, Domenico Pertica, Mauro Misul, Antonino Spaccatini, Genaro Ombra, Stefano Proietti, Bruno Scagnetti, Marcello Di Falco, Bruno Lenzi

1974 Academy Award for
Best Foreign Language Film

Left: Bruno Zanin, Magali Noel

Nando Orfei, Puppella Maggio, Armando Brancia, Giuseppe Lanigro, Bruno Zanin, Stefano Proietti

Top: Bruno Zanin
Below: Magali Noel (C)

Bruno Zanin (C) also Top (L)

169

SCENES FROM A MARRIAGE

(CINEMA 5) Producer, Cinematograph AB; Directed and Written by Ingmar Bergman; Executive Producer, Lars-Owe Carlberg; Photography, Sven Nykvist; Designer, Bjorn Thulin; Costumes, Inger Pehrsson; Editor, Siv Lundgren; In Eastmancolor; Rated PG; 168 minutes plus intermission; September release.

CAST

Marianne	Liv Ullman
Johan	Erland Josephson
Katarina	Bibi Andersson
Peter	Jan Malmsjo
Mrs. Palm	Anita Wall
Eva	Gunnel Lindblon
Mrs. Jacobi	Barbro Hiort AF Ornas

Left: Liv Ullmann, Erland Josephson

Liv Ullmann, Erland Josephson

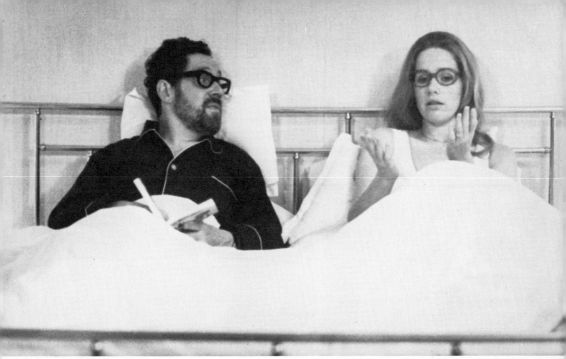

Liv Ullmann, Erland Josephson (also top)

JUGGERNAUT

(**UNITED ARTIST**) Executive Producer, David V. Picker; Associate Producer, Denis O'Dell; Produced and Written by Richard DeKoker; Director, Richard Lester; Music, Ken Thorne; Additional Dialogue, Alan Plater; Photography, Gerry Fisher; Designer, Terence Marsh; Editor, Tony Gibbs; Art Director, Alan Tomkins; In color; Rated PG; 109 minutes; September release.

CAST

Fallon	Richard Harris
Capt. Brunel	Omar Sharif
Charlie Braddock	David Hemmings
Supt. John McCleod	Anthony Hopkins
Barbara Banister	Shirley Knight
Nicholas Porter	Ian Holm
Mr. Corrigan	Clifton James
Social Director Curain	Roy Kinnear
Susan McCleod	Caroline Mortimer
First Officer Hollingsworth	Mark Burns
Hughes	John Stride
Mr. Buckland	Freddie Jones
Commander Marder	Julian Glover
Chief Engineer Mallicent	Jack Watson
Azad	Roshan Seth
Detective Brown	Kenneth Colley
Third Officer Hardy	Andrew Bradford

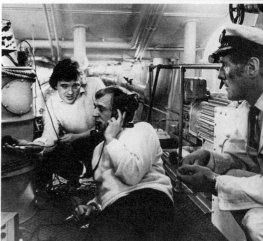

Right: David Hemmings, Richard Harris, Jack Watson Top: Shirley Knight, Omar Sharif

Rebecca Bridge, Caroline Mortimer, Adam Bridge

Doris Nolan, Clifton James

GIUSEPPE VERDI

(OPERA PRESENTATIONS) Producer, Maleno Malenotti; Director, Vittorio Glori; Photography, Tino Santoni; Designer, A. Boccianti; Costumes, D. DiBari; In Ferraniacolor; 120 minutes; October release.

CAST

Giuseppe Verdi	Pierre Cressoy
Margherita Barezzi	Anna Maria Ferrero
Giuseppina Strepponi	Gaby Andre

and Mario Del Monaco, Tito Gobbi, Irene Genna, Enzo Biliotti, Aldo Bufilandi, Guido Celano, Emilio Cigoli, Loris Gizzi, Laura Gore, Camillo Pilotto, Sandro Ruffini, Mario Ferrari, Giampaolo Rosmino, Enrico Glori, Hady DeSantis, Rosetta Pasquini, Gloria Villa, Lola Braccini, Turi Pandolfini, Teresa Franchini.

Right: Pierre Cressoy

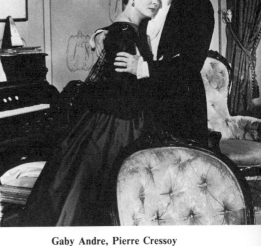

Pierre Cressoy, Anna Maria Ferrero
Above: Tito Gobbi in "Rigoletto"

Gaby Andre, Pierre Cressoy
Above: Mario Del Monaco in "Otello"

173

LACOMBE LUCIEN

(20th CENTURY-FOX) Producer-Director, Louis Malle; Associate Producer, Claude Nedjar; Screenplay, Louis Malle, Patrick Modiano; Photography, Tonino Delli Colli; Art Director, Ghislain Uhry; Editor, Suzanne Baron; Music, Django Reinhardt, Andre Claveau, Irene de Trebert; In Eastmancolor; Rated R; 141 minutes; October release.

CAST

Lucien	Pierre Blaise
France	Aurore Clement
Albert Horn	Holger Lowenadler
Bella Horn	Therese Gieshe
Jean Bernard	Stephane Bouy
Betty Beaulieu	Loumi Iacobesco
Faure	Rene Bouloc
Aubert	Pierre Decazes
Tonin	Jean Rougerie
Mme. Lacombe	Gilberte Rivet
M. Laborit	Jacques Rispal

Left: Pierre Blaise

Pierre Blaise, Aurore Clement

Holger Lowenadler, Pierre Blaise, Aurore Clement
Top: Pierre Blaise (L)

THE ODESSA FILE

(COLUMBIA) Producer, John Woolf; Director, Ronald Neame; Co-Producer, John R. Sloan; Screenplay, Kenneth Ross, George Markstein; Based on novel by Frederick Forsyth; Music, Andrew Lloyd Webber; Song, Andrew Lloyd Webber, Tim Rice and Andre Heller; Sung by Perry Como; Photography, Oswald Morris; Designer, Rolf Zehetbauer; Editor, Ralph Kemplen; Assistant Director, Colin Brewer, Wieland Liebske; Costumes, Monika Bauert; Domino/Oceanic Co-Production; In Panavision and color; Rated PG; 128 minutes; October release.

CAST

Peter Miller	Jon Voight
Eduard Roschmann	Maximilian Schell
Frau Miller	Maria Schell
Sigi	Mary Tamm
Klaus Wenzer	Derek Jacobi
David Porath	Peter Jeffrey
Gustav MacKensen	Klaus Lowitsch
Alfred Oster	Kurt Meisel
General Glucks	Hans Messemer
Israeli General	Garfield Morgan
Simon Wiesenthal	Shmuel Rodensky
Werner Deilman	Ernst Schroder
Kunik	Gunter Strack
Franz Bayer	Noel Willman
Marx	Martin Brandt
Dr. Ferdinand Schultz	Hans Caninenberg
Shapira	Heinz Ehrenfreund
Colonel	Alexander Golling
Solomon Tauber	Towje Kleiner
General Greifer	Gunter Meisner
Karl Braun	Gunnar Miller
Frau Wenzer	Elizabeth Neumann-Viertel
Gisela	Christine Wodetzky
Hoffmann	Werner Bruhns
Medal Shop Proprietor	Til Kiwe
Lawyer	Georg Marischka
Wehrmacht Captain	Joachim Dietmar Mues
Landlord	Hans Wyprachtiger
Tauber's Voice	Cyril Shaps
Esther Tauber	Miriam Mahler

Left: Jon Voight, Mary Tamm
Top: Jon Voight

Maximilian Scheli

Jon Voight

THE ABDICATION

(WARNER BROS.) Producers, Robert Fryer, James Cresson; Director, Anthony Harvey; Screenplay, Ruth Wolff; Based on her play; Photography, Geoffrey Unsworth; Designer, Terry Marsh; Art Director, Alan Tomkins; Editor, John Bloom; Associate Producer, William Hill; Music, Nino Rota; Costumes, Peter J. Hall; Costumes, Farani; Assistant Director, David Munro; In Technicolor; Rated PG; 103 minutes; October release.

CAST

Azzolino	Peter Finch
Queen Christina	Liv Ullman
Oxenstierna	Cyril Cusack
Altieri	Paul Rogers
Barberini	Graham Crowden
The Dwarf	Michael Dunn
Queen Mother	Kathleen Byron
Dominic	Lewis Flander
Pinamonti	Harold Goldblatt
Carranza	Tony Steedman
Ginetti	Noel Trevarthen
Charles	Richard Cornish
Magnus	James Faulkner
Ebba	Ania Marson
Birgito	Franz Drago
Young Christina	Suzanne Huddart
Young Ebba	Debbie Nicholson
Christina's Father	Edward Underdown

Top: Liv Ullmann, Peter Finch
Below: Michael Dunn, Liv Ullmann

Liv Ullmann, Peter Finch
Top: Liv Ullmann

GOLD

(ALLIED ARTISTS) Producer, Michael Klinger; Director, Peter Hunt; Screenplay, Wilbur Smith, Stanley Price; From novel "Goldmine" by Wilbur Smith; Designers, Alex Vetchinsky, Syd Cain; Art Director, Robert Laing; Photography, Ousama Rawi; Editor-2nd Unit Director, John Glen; Music, Elmer Bernstein; Assistant Director, Peter Price; Costumes, Marjorie Cornelius; Assistant Producer, Tony Klinger; Lyrics, Don Black; Songs sung by Jimmy Helms, Maureen McGovern, Trevor Chance; In Panavision and Technicolor; Rated PG; 118 minutes; October release.

CAST

Rod Slater	Roger Moore
Terry Steyner	Susannah York
Hurry Hirschfeld	Ray Milland
Manfred Steyner	Bradford Dillman
Farrell	John Gielgud
Big King	Simon Sabela
Stephen Marais	Tony Beckley
Kowalski	Bernard Horsfall
Tex Kiernan	Marc Smith
Plummer	John Hussey
Frank Lemmer	Norman Coombes
Doctor	George Jackson
Jackson	Michael McGovern
French Man	Andre Maranne
American	John Bay
Swiss	Paul Hansard

Right: Roger Moore, Susannah York

Roger Moore, Susannah York,
Ray Milland

Bradford Dillman, Roger Moore
Above: Ray Milland, Susannah York

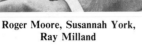

178

THE NIGHT PORTER

(AVCO EMBASSY) Producer, Robert Gordon Edwards; Director, Liliana Cavani; Screenplay, Liliana Cavani, Italo Moscati; Story, Liliana Cavani, Barbara Alberti, Amedeo Pagani; Editor, Franco Arcalli; Photography, Alfio Contini; Music, Daniele Paris; Art Directors, Nedo Azzini, Jean Marie Simon; Costumes, Piero Tosi; Assistant Directors, Franco Cirino, Paolo Tallarigo, Johann Freisinger; Joseph E. Levine Presentation; In Technicolor; Rated R; 117 minutes; October release.

CAST

Max	Dirk Bogarde
Lucia	Charlotte Rampling
Klaus	Philippe Leroy
Hans	Gabriele Ferzetti
Stumm	Giuseppe Addobbati
Countess Stein	Isa Miranda
Adolph	Nino Bignamini
Atherton	Marino Mase
Bert	Amedeo Amodio
Day Porter	Piero Vida
Kurt	Geoffrey Copleston
Dobson	Manfred Freiberger
Mario	Ugo Cardea
Greta	Hilda Gunther
The Neighbor	Nora Ricci
Concierge	Piero Mazzinghi
Jacob	Kai S. Seefield

Right: Dirk Bogarde, Isa Miranda

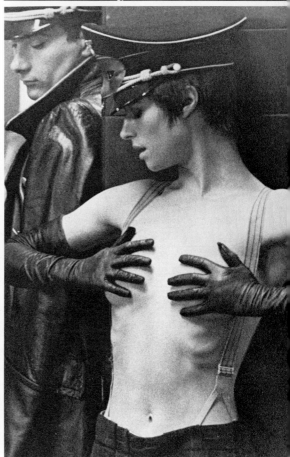

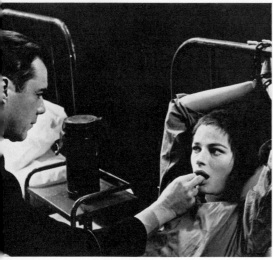

Dirk Bogarde, Charlotte Rampling
(also above)

Charlotte Rampling

MURDER ON THE ORIENT EXPRESS

(PARAMOUNT) Producers, John Brabourne, Richard Goodwin; Director, Sidney Lumet; Screenplay, Paul Dehn; From novel by Agatha Christie; Editor, Anne V. Coates; Photography, Geoffrey Unsworth; Design and Costumes, Tony Walton; Music, Richard Rodney Bennett; Art Director, Jack Stephens; Assistant Director, Ted Sturgis; In Panavision and Technicolor; Rated PG; 128 minutes; November release.

CAST

Hercule Poirot	Albert Finney
Mrs. Hubbard	Lauren Bacall
Bianchi	Martin Balsam
Greta Ohlsson	Ingrid Bergman
Countess Andrenyi	Jacqueline Bisset
Pierre Paul Michel	Jean-Pierre Cassel
Colonel Arbuthnot	Sean Connery
Beddoes	John Gielgud
Princess Dragomiroff	Wendy Hiller
Hector McQueen	Anthony Perkins
Mary Debenham	Vanessa Redgrave
Hildegarde Schmidt	Rachel Roberts
Ratchett	Richard Widmark
Count Andrenyi	Michael York
Hardman	Colin Blakely
Dr. Constantine	George Coulouris
Foscarelli	Denis Quilley
Concierge	Vernon Dobtcheff
A. D. C.	Jeremy Lloyd
Chief Attendant	John Moffatt

Ingrid Bergman received a 1974 Academy Award for Best Supporting Actress

Jean-Pierre Cassel, Anthony Perkins, Vanessa Redgrave, Sean Connery, Ingrid Bergman, George Coulouris, Rachel Roberts, Wendy Hiller, Denis Quilley, Michael York, Jacqueline Bisset, Lauren Bacall, Martin Balsam
Top Left: Albert Finney, George Coulouris, John Gielgud, Colin Blakely, Rachel Roberts, Wendy Hiller

John Gielgud, Richard Widmark Above: Wendy Hiller, Rachel Roberts, Lauren Bacall, Sean Connery, Anthony Perkins, Martin Balsam Top: Albert Finney (L)

Sean Connery, Vanessa Redgrave Above: Lauren Bacall, Ingrid Bergman Top: Michael York, Jacqueline Bisset

LE FANTOME DE LA LIBERTE

(20th CENTURY-FOX) Producer, Serge Silberman; Direction and Screenplay, Luis Bunuel; With the collaboration of Jean-Claude Carriere; Assistant Director, Pierre Lary; Photography, Edmond Richard; A Greenwich Film Production; In color; Not rated; 104 minutes; November release.

CAST

Sister of Prefect of Police	Adrianna Asti
First Prefect	Julien Bertheau
Mr. Foucauld	Jean-Claude Brialy
Dr. Legendre	Adolfo Celi
Innkeeper	Paul Frankeur
Hatter	Michel Lonsdale
Policeman Gerard	Pierre Maguelon
Professor	Francois Maistre
Aunt	Helene Perdriere
Second Prefect	Michel Piccoli
Commissioner	Claude Pieplu
Mr. Legendre	Jean Rochefort
Captain	Bernard Verley
Nurse	Milena Vukotic
Mrs. Foucauld	Monica Vitti

Left: Michel Piccoli

Jean-Claude Brialy, Monica Vitti

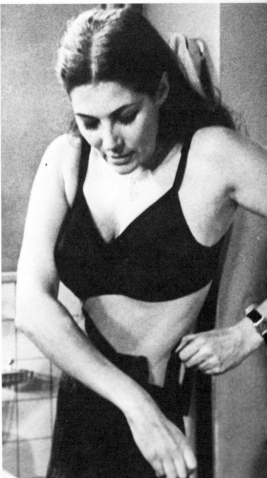

Ann-Marie Deschott

183

THE LITTLE PRINCE

(PARAMOUNT) Producer-Director, Stanley Donen; Screenplay and Lyrics, Alan Jay Lerner; Music, Frederick Loewe; Associate Producer, A. Joseph Tandet; Based on story by Antoine de Saint Exupery; Photography, Christopher Challis; Designer, John Barry; Choreography, Ronn Forella, Bob Fosse; Art Director, Norman Reynolds; Costumes, Shirley Russell, Tim Goodchild; Editors, Peter Boita, John Guthridge; Assistant Directors, Allan James, Al Burgess; In Technicolor; Rated G; 88 minutes; November release.

CAST

The Pilot	Richard Kiley
The Little Prince	Steven Warner
The Snake	Bob Fosse
The Fox	Gene Wilder
The King	Joss Ackland
The Businessman	Clive Revill
The Historian	Victor Spinetti
The General	Graham Crowden
The Rose	Donna McKechnie

Right: Steven Warner, Richard Kiley

Steven Warner, Gene Wilder
Above: Steven Warner, Richard Kiley

Bob Fosse, Steven Warner
Above: Steven Warner, Clive Revill

BLACK THURSDAY

(LEVITT-PICKMAN) Producers, Carole Weisweiller, Roger Fley-tous; Director, Michel Mitrani; Based on the book "Les Guichets du Louvre: by Roger Boussinot; Screenplay, Albert Cossery, Michel Mitrani; Music, Mort Shuman; A Louvre Associates Limited Presentation; In color; Not rated; 92 minutes; December release.

CAST

Jeanne	Christine Pascal
Paul	Christian Rist
Old Lady	Alice Sapritch
Mr. Edmond	Michel Auclair
Mrs. Ash	Judith Magre
The Cousin	Michel Robin
The Officer	Henri Garcin
Gestapo Man	Andre Thorent
The Priest	Jacques De Bary

Right: Christian Rist, Christine Pascal

Christian Rist, Christine Pascal

LES VIOLONS DU BAL

(LEVITT-PICKMAN) Directed and Written by Michel Drach; Photography, Yann Le Masson, William Lubtchansky; Music, Jean Manuel De Scarano, Jacques Monty; A Violons Associates Ltd. Presentation; In black and white, and color; Not rated; 110 minutes; December release.

CAST

Michel's Wife/Mother	Marie-Josee Nat
Michel	Jean-Louis Trintignant
Grandmother	Gabrielle Doulcet
Michel Drach	Himself
Michel as a boy	David Drach
Michel's Brother	Christian Rist
Michel's Sister	Nathalie Roussel

Left: Marie-Josee Nat

Marie-Josee Nat, David Drach

Nathalie Roussel, Jean-Louis Trintignant

Marie-Josee Nat, David Drach

EMMANUELLE

(COLUMBIA) Producer, Yves Rousset-Rouard; Director, Just Jaeckin; Screenplay, Jean-Louis Richard; Based on novel by Emmanuelle Arsan; Photography, Richard Suzuki; Editor, Claudine Bouchet; In Eastmancolor; Rated X; 105 minutes; December release.

CAST

Emmanuelle	Sylvia Kristel
Mario	Alain Cuny
Jean	Daniel Sarky
Bee	Marika Green
Ariane	Jeanne Colletin
Marie-Ange	Christine Boisson

Right: Sylvia Kristel, Alain Cuny

Jeanne Colletin, Sylvia Kristel
Above: Alain Cuny, Sylvia Kristel

Marika Green, Sylvia Kristel
Above: Christine Boisson, Daniel Sarkey,
Sylvia Kristel

STAVISKY

(CINEMATION) Executive Producers, Alexandre Mnouchkine, George Dancigers; Director, Alain Resnais; Screenplay, Jorge Semprun; Photography, Sacha Vierny; Editor, Albert Jurgenson; Music, Stephen Sondheim; A Production of Ariane Films/Cerita Films/Euro International; In color; Rated PG; 117 minutes; December release.

CAST

Alexandre Stavisky	Jean Paul Belmondo
Arlette Stavisky	Anny Duperey
Baron Raoul	Charles Boyer
Borelli	Francois Perier
Montalvo	Roberto Bisacca
Dr. Mezy	Claude Rich
Bonny	Michel Lonsdale
Henriet	Gigi Balista

Right: Jean Paul Belmondo

Francois Perier, Jean Paul Belmondo, Charles Boyer

THE MAN WITH THE GOLDEN GUN

(UNITED ARTISTS) Producers, Albert R. Broccoli, Harry Saltzman; Director, Guy Hamilton; Screenplay, Richard Maibaum, Tom Mankiewicz; Music, John Barry; Lyrics, Don Black; Associate Producer, Charles Orme; Photography, Ted Moore, Ossie Morris; Designer, Peter Murton; Art Directors, John Graysmark, Peter Lamont; Editor, Roy Poulton; In color; Rated PG; 125 minutes; December release.

CAST

James Bond	Roger Moore
Scaramanga	Christopher Lee
Mary Goodnight	Britt Ekland
Andrea	Maud Adams
Nick Nack	Herve Villechaize
J. W. Pepper	Clifton James
Hip	Soon Taik Oh
Hai Fat	Richard Loo
Rodney	Marc Lawrence
"M"	Bernard Lee
Miss Moneypenny	Lois Maxwell
Lazar	Marne Maitland
"Q"	Desmond Llewellyn
Colthorpe	James Cossins
Chula	Chan Yiu Lam
Saida	Carmen Sautoy
Frazier	Gerald James
Naval Lieutenant	Michael Osborne
Communications Officer	Michael Fleming

Left: Roger Moore

Roger Moore, Britt Ekland, Herve Villachaize

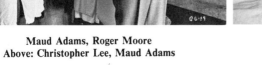

Maud Adams, Roger Moore
Above: Christopher Lee, Maud Adams

Roger Moore, Britt Ekland
Above: Christopher Lee, Roger Moore   191

Max von Sydow, Dominique Sanda

STEPPENWOLF

(D/R FILMS) Executive Producer, Peter J. Sprague; Producers, Melvin Fishman, Richard Herland; Direction and Screenplay, Fred Haines; Photography, Tom Pinter; Editor, Irving Lerner; Art Director, Leo Karen; Choreographer, Ray Bosier; Costumes, Else Heckman; Associate Producer, Thilo Theilen; Music, George Gruntz; Assistant Directors, Renato Romano, Ernst Bertschi, Gabria Belloni; In color; Rated R; 105 minutes; December release.

CAST

Harry	Max von Sydow
Hermine	Dominique Sanda
Pablo	Pierre Clementi
Maria	Carla Romanelli
Aztec	Roy Bosier
Geothe	Alfred Baillou
Gustav	Niels-Peter Rudolph
Franz	Helmut Furnbacher
Loering	Charles Regnier
Hefte	Eduard Linkers
Dora	Sylvia Reize
Rosa	Judith Mellics
Frau Hefte	Helen Hesse

Dominique Sanda, Carla Romanelli
Above: Pierre Clementi

Max von Sydow, Pierre Clementi
Above: Max von Sydow

**Tetsuro Tamba
in "The Human Revolution"**

**Tsung Hua
in "Sacred Knives of Vengeance"**

THE HUMAN REVOLUTION (Toho) Executive Producer, Tomoyuki Tanaka; Director, Toshio Masuda; Story, Daisaku Ikeda; Screenplay, Shinobu Hashimoto; Photography, Rokuro Nishigaki; Music, Akira Ifukube; A Shinano Kikaku Production; Presented by NSA Productions; In Color; Rated G; 160 minutes; January release. CAST: Tetsuro Tamba (Josei), Michiyo Aratama (Ikue)

CRY OF THE WILD (National Board of Canada) Director-Photographer, Bill Mason; 90 minutes; January release. A documentary on the Canadian wilds and the Mason family.

DEMONS (Radim) Produced, Directed, Written by Toshio Matsumoto; Based on play by Nanboku Tsuruya; Photography, Tatsuo Suzuki; In black and white; 135 minutes; Not rated; January release. CAST: Katsuo Nakamura (Gengo), Yasuko Sanjo (Koman), Juro Kara (Sango), Masao Imafuki (Hachiemon)

RAZOR IN THE FLESH (Ronin) Director, Braz Chedlak; Screenplay, Plinio Marcos, Fernando Ferreira, Emiliano Queiroz; From play by Plinio Marcos; Photography, Helio Silva; Editor, Rafael Valverde; A Magnus Films Production; In black and white; Not rated; 95 minutes; January release. CAST: Jece Valadao (Vado), Glauce Rocha (Neuza), Emiliano Queirez (Veludo)

MR. SUPERINVISIBLE (K-Tel International) A co-production of Edo Cinema, Carsten Productions, Dia Productions; In Technicolor; Rated G; 90 minutes; January release. CAST: Dean Jones, Gastone Moschin, Ingeborg Schoener, Peter Carsten

THUNDERFIST (Artisan) In Technicolor; Rated PG; No other credits available; January release.

FRANKENSTEIN'S BLOODY TERROR (Independent International) Director, Henry L. Egan; In Eastmancolor; Rated PG; 83 minutes; January release. CAST: Paul Naschy (Count), Diana Zura (Countess), Michael Manza (Rudolph), Julian Ugarte (Mikelhov), Rossanna Yanni (Wandessa)

THE SACRED KNIVES OF VENGEANCE (Warner Bros.) Producer, Run Run Shaw; Director, Chu Yuan; Screenplay, Kuo Chia; Photography, Wu Cho-hua; Art Director, Chen Ching Shen; Editor, Chiang Hsing-Lung; Music, Chen Yung-shu; Assistant Directors, Ku Chen, Chang Chi-pei; In Technicolor; Rated R; 94 minutes; January release. CAST: Chin Han (Ma I), Wang Ping (Yu Chiao), Tsung Hua (Hsieh Chun), Ku Feng (Ruffian), Ching Miao (Wang), Yang Che Ching (Yun), Chiang Nan (Chiao), Cheng Lei (Kao), Li Hao (Jen)

BLACK BELT (Howard Mahler) In color; Rated PG; No other credits; January release.

THE BAMBOO BROTHERHOOD (Howard Mahler) In color; Rated R; No other credits; January release.

THE DEATH WHEELERS (Scotia International) Producer, Andrew Donally; Director, Don Sharp; Screenplay, Arnaud Dusseay; In Technicolor; Rated PG; No other credits available; January release. CAST: George Sanders, Beryl Reid, Nicky Henson, Mary Larkin, Roy Holder, Robert Hardy, Patrick Holt, Denis Gilmore.

FEARLESS FIGHTERS (Ellman Enterprises) Director, Wu Min-Hsiung; In Metrocolor; Rated R; No other details available; January release. CAST: Chang Ching, Yee Yuang, Chen Lieh

MISTRESS PAMELA (Fanfare) Producer-Director, Jim O'Connolly; Exeutive Producers, Julian Sacher, Michael Glass; In Eastmancolor; Rated R; No other details available; January release. CAST: Ann Michelle, Julian Barnes, Anna Quayle, Rosemary Dunham

TUPAMAROS! (Tricontinental) Director, Jan Lindqvist; Music, Numa Moraes, Daniel Viglietti; Animation, A. Weps; In color; 50 minutes; January release. A documentary on Uruguay's National Liberation Movement.

**Dean Jones
in "Mr. Superinvisible"**

"Tupamaros!"

"When the People Awake"

"Bamboo Gods and Iron Men"

WHEN THE PEOPLE AWAKE (Tricontinental) Anonymous; In color; 60 minutes; January release. A documentary on political events in Chile, beginning with Allende's investiture in 1970.

AROUND THE WORLD WITH FANNY HILL (Seaberg) Producer, Tore Sjoberg; Director, Mac Ahlberg; Screenplay, Albert G. Miller; Photography, Mikael Salomon; Editor, Ingemar Ejve; Art Director, P. A. Lundgren; Music, Georg Riedel; A Minerva International Films Production; In Consolidated Color; 92 minutes; Rated X; January release. CAST: Shirley Corrigan (Fanny), Gaby Fuchs (Monica), Peter Bonke (Roger), Bo Brundin (Peter), Peter Kuiper (Pomodori), Nico Wolferstatter (Victor), Karl-Heinz Windhorst (Policeman), Marie Ekorre (Anita), Gosta Pruzelius (Lawyer)

TEACH ME (Centaur) In color; Rated X; 75 minutes; January release; Starring Christine Schuberth (Josephine), Peter Planer (Ferdinand). No other details available.

MAN OF IRON (Bardene International) Producer, Run Run Shaw; Director, Chang Cheh; Screenplay, I. Kuang, Chang Cheh; Photography, Juan Ting-pang; Editor, Kuo Tin-hung; In DeLuxe Color; Rated R; 92 minutes; January release. CAST: Chen Kuan-tai, Ching Li, Wang Chung

HORROR EXPRESS (Scotia International) Director, Eugenio Martin; Photography, Alejandro Ullea; Story and Screenplay, Arnaud D'Usseau; In Eastmancolor; Rated R; January Release. CAST: Christopher Lee (Prof. Alex Caxton), Peter Cushing (Dr. Wells), Telly Savalas (Capt. Kazan), Alberto de Mendoza (Inspector)

THE BLOCKHOUSE (Cannon) Producer, Anthony Rufas Isaacs, Edgar M. Bronfman, Jr.; Director, Clive Rees; Screenplay, Clive Rees, John Gould; Based on novel by Jean Paul Ciebert; Photography, Keith Goddard; Editor, Peter Gold; Music, Stanley Myers; In Panavision and Eastmancolor; 93 minutes; January release. CAST: Peter Sellers (Roquet), Charles Aznavour (Visconti), Per Oscarsson (Lund), Peter Vaughan (Aufret), Jeremy Kemp (Grabinski), Leon Lissek (Kozhek), Nicholas Jones (Kramer), Aldred Lynch (Larshen)

RAMPART OF DESIRE (Allied Artists) Producers, Robert and Raymond Hakim; Director, Guy Casaril; Screenplay, Guy Casaril, Francoise Mallet-Joret; From book by Miss Mallet-Joret; Photography, Andreas Winding; Editor, Louisette Hautecoeur; Music, Michel Delpech, Roland Vincent; In Eastmancolor; Rated R; 90 minutes; January release. CAST: Nicole Courcel (Tamara), Anicee Alvina (Helene), Vanentino Venantini (Max), Jean Martin (Rene), Harry Max (Grandfather), Ginette Leclerc (Nina), Yvonne Clech (Mrs. Perier)

HOLY MOUNTAIN (ABKCO) Direction, Screenplay, Music, Alexandro Jodorowsky; Photography, Rafael Corkidi; Editor, Frederic Landeros; In Techniscope and Technicolor; 126 minutes; January release. CAST: Alexandro Jodorowsky (Master), Horacio Salinas (Christ Figure), Ramona Saunders (Disciple)

CANTERBURY TALES (United Artists) Producer, Albert Grimaldi; Direction and Screenplay, Pier Paolo Pasolini; Based on Chaucer's "Canterbury Tales"; Photography, Tonino Delli Colli; Art Director, Dante Ferretti; Costumes, Danilo Donati; In Technicolor; 111 minutes; January release. CAST: Hugh Griffith, Ninetto Davoli, Franco Citti, Laura Betti, Josephine Chaplin

MARTA (GGP) Producer, Jose Frade; Director, Jose Antonio Nieves Conde; Screenplay, Juan Jose Alonso Millan, Lopez Aranda; Jose Antonio Nieves Conde; Based on story by Juan Jose Alonso Millan; Photography, Ennio Guarnierri; Music, Piero Piccione; Art Director, Roman Calatayud; Editor, Maruja Soriano; In Eastmancolor; Rated R; 100 minutes; January release. CAST: Marisa Mell (Marta), Jesus Puente (Don Carlos), Jorge Rigaud (Arturo), Howard Ross (Luis), Isa Miranda (Elena), Melida Quiroga (Dona Clara)

THE CHINESE PROFESSIONALS (National General) Producer, Raymond Chow; Director, Wang Tu; In Technicolor; Rated R; No other details available; January release; Starring Wang Yu

"Teach Me"

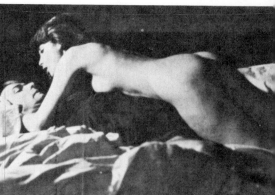

"Around the World with Fanny Hill"

"Bamboo Gods and Iron Men"

"Blood on the Sun"

BAMBOO GODS AND IRON MEN (American International)
Producer, Cirio H. Santiago; Director, Cesar Gallardo; Story and
Screenplay, Kenneth Metcalfe, Joseph Zucherro; Music, Tito Sotto;
Photography, Felipe J. Sacdalan; Editor, Gervacio Santos; Assistant
Director, Jun Amazan; Associate Director, Jum Gallardo; Art Di-
rector, Ben Otico; In Movielab Color; Rated R; 96 minutes; January
release. CAST: James Iglehart (Calvin), Shirley Washington (Mrs.
Jefferson), Chiquito (Charley), Marissa Delgado, Eddie Garcia, Ken
Metcalfe, Joe Zucherro, Michael Boyet, Robert Rivera, Zubas Her-
rero, Leo Martinez, Benny Pestano, Steve Alcarado, Roert Picate,
Boy Picate, Tony Uy

WHEN WOMEN PLAYED DING DONG (Paragon) An Emondo
Amati presentation; In color; Rated R; January release; Starring,
Nadia Cassini, Antonio Sabato

KUNG FU QUEEN (Aquarius) Alternate title "The Queen Boxer";
In color; Rated R; No other credits available; January release; Starring Judy Lee.

THE LION HAS SEVEN HEADS (New Yorker) Producers,
Claude Antoine, Gianni Barcelloni; Director, Glauber Rocha;
Screenplay, Glauber Rocha, Gianni Amico; In color; Not rated; 103
minutes; February release. CAST: Rada Rassimov, Gabriele Tinti,
Jean Pierre Leaud, Giulio Brogi, Carvana, Rene Koldhoffer

DEATH BY HANGING (Grove Press) Producer, Sozosha; Director, Nagisa Oshima; Screenplay, Tsutomu Tamura, Mamoru Sasaki,
Michinori Fukao, Nagisa Oshima; Editor, Sucko Shiraishi; Photography, Yasuhiro Yoshioka; Music, Hikaru Hayashi; Not rated; 117
minutes; February release. CAST: Yun-Do Yun (R), Kei Sato (Exe-
cution Chief), Fumio Watanabe (Education Officer), Toshiro Ishido
(Chaplain), Masao Adachi (Security Officer), Mutsuhro Toura
(Doctor), Akiko Koyama (Girl)

BLOOD ON THE SUN (Centaur) Producers, Sun Shing Yuan,
Wong Wen Yuan, Wu Ke; Directors, Sun Shing Yuan, Song Ting
Mei; English Version, James Hong; In color and Cinemascope; Not
rated; 81 minutes; February release. CAST: Chang Ching Ching,
Tieng Peng, Yu Yuan, Yang Hsiao Ping

ILLUSIONS OF A LADY (Variety) Produced, Directed, and Writ-
ten by Jonas Middleton; Photography, Charles Slavonvich; Editors,
Marizo Zaurman, Arion Ober, Vern Carlson; Art Director, Sandy
Harvey; In Movielab Color; Rated X; 70 minutes; February release.
CAST: Andrea True (Dr. Miranda Woolf), Michelle Magazine
(Trala), Martine Gay (Leslie), Mary Madigan (Lorie), Davy Jones
(Robin), Jamie Gillis (Stuart), Mike Jeffery (Howard)

A REASON TO LIVE, A REASON TO DIE (K-Tel International)
Producer, Michael Billingsley; Director, Tonino Valerii; Story and
Screenplay, Tonino Valerii, Ernesto Gastaldi; Music, Riz Orolani; A
Heritage Enterprises Production; In color; Rated PG; 92 minutes;
February release. CAST: James Coburn (Col. Pembroke), Telly
Savalas (Maj. Ward), Bud Spencer (Eli), Ralph Goodwin (Sgt.
Brent), Joseph Mitchell (Ballard), Robert Burton (Donald), William
Spofford (Ted), Guy Ranson (Will), Joe Pollini (Halfbreed), Allan
Leroy (Confederate Sergeant)

TALL FISHING TALES (Promotional Films) Produced, Directed,
and Photographed by Alfred Peterson; Screenplay, Buz Fawcett;
Underwater Photography, Jim Mitchell; An Alfred Kron Production; In color; Not rated; 105 minutes; February release. CAST:
Steve Cannon, Steve Edstrom, Joe McFarland, David Anders

WAREHOUSE (Ronin) Producer, Daiei; Director, Yasuzo
Masumura; Screenplay, Yoshio Shirasaka; Based on story by Ranpo
Edogawa; In color; Not rated; 86 minutes; February release. CAST:
Ei ji Funakoshi (Michio), Mako Midori (Aki), Noriko Sengoku
(Shino)

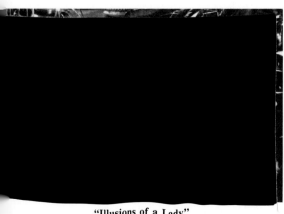

"Illusions of a Lady"

James Coburn (C) in "A Reason to Live,
A Reason to Die!"

Aiko Koyama (C)
in "The Ceremony"

Laura Antonelli, Alessandro Momo
in "Malizia"

THE CEREMONY (New Yorker) Director, Nagisa Oshima; Screenplay, Nagisa Oshima, Tsutomu Tamura, Toichiro Narushima; Editor, Keichiro Uracka; Music, Toru Takemitsu; Art Direction, Jusho Toda; In color; 122 minutes; Not rated; February release. CAST: Kenzo Kawarazaki (Masuo), Atsuo Nakamura (Terumichi), Aiko Koyama (Setsuko), Kei Sato (Kazuomi), Kiyoshi Tsuchiya (Tadashi)

ZARDOZ (20th Century-Fox) Produced, Directed, and Written by John Boorman; Associate Producer, Charles Orme; Assistant Director, Simon Relph; Continuity, Jean Skinner; Photography, Geoffrey Unsworth; Photography, Peter MacDonald; Designer, Anthony Pratt; Costumes, Christel Kruse Boorman; Editor, John Merritt; Music, David Munrow; In Panavision and DeLuxe Color; Rated R; 104 minutes; February release. CAST: Sean Connery (Zed), Charlotte Rampling (Consuella), Sara Kestelman (May), John Alderton (Friend), Sally Ann Newton (Avalow), Niall Buggy (Zardoz/Arthur), Bosco Hogan (George), Jessica Swift (Apathetic), Bairbre Dowling (Star), Christopher Casson (Scientist), Reginald Jarman (Death)

THE GODFATHERS OF HONG KONG (Cannon) In color; Rated R; No other credits available; February release

HATCHET FOR A HONEYMOON (GGP) Director, Mario Bava; In Eastmancolor; Rated R; 83 minutes; No other details available; February release. CAST: Stephen Forsyth, Dagmar Lassander

FANGS OF THE LIVING DEAD (Europix International) In Eastmancolor; Rated PG; No other credits available; February release; Starring Anita Ekberg, John Hamilton

HOUSE OF THE MISSING GIRLS (VIP) Presented by Jack H. Harris; In color, Rated R; No other credits available; February release; Starring Anna Gael

TRAITORS (Tricontinental) Producer, William Susman; Directed, Written and Acted by members of the Grupo de la Base; Not rated; 114 minutes; February release.

MALIZIA (Paramount) Producer, Silvio Clementelli; Director, Salvatore Samperi; Photography, Vittorio Storaro; Designer, Ezio Altieri; Editor, Sergio Montanari; Music, Fred Bongusto; Story, Salvatore Samperi; Screenplay, Ottavio Jemma, Salvatore Samperi, Alessandro Parenzo; Assistant Director, Gianluigi Calderone; In Technicolor; Rated R; 98 minutes; February release. CAST: Laura Antonelli (Angela), Turi Ferro (Don Ignazio), Alessandro Momo (Nino), Tina Aumont (Luciana), Lilla Brignone (Nonna), Pino Caruso (Don Cirillo), Angela Luce (Widow Carallo), Gianluigi Chirizzi (Antonio), Massimiliano Filoni (Enzino), Stefano Amato (Porcello), Grazia Di Marza (Adelina)

NEITHER THE SEA NOR THE SAND (International Amusement Corp.) Executive Producers, Tony Tenser, Peter J. Thompson; Co-Producers, Jack Smith, Peter Fetterman; Director, Fred Burnley; Screenplay, Gordon Honeycombe from his novel; Additional Dialogue, Rosemary Davies; Music, Nachum Heiman; Photography, David Muir; Art Director, Michael Bastow; Editor, Norman Wanstall; Assistant Director, Derek Whitehurst; In Eastmancolor; Rated R; 110 minutes; February release. CAST: Susan Hampshire (Anna), Michael Petrovitch (Hugh), Frank Finlay (George), Michael Craze (Collie), Jack Lambert (Dr. Irving), David Garth (MacKay), Betty Duncan (Mrs. MacKay), Anthony Booth (Delamare)

THE HONG KONG CONNECTION (Cannon) In color; Rated R; No other credits Available; February release.

AFRICA UNCENSORED (Trans American) Directors, Angelo Castiglioni, Guido Guerrasio; In Technicolor; March release. A documentary on bizarre rituals of primitive tribes in Africa.

DRACULA'S GREAT LOVE (International Amusements) Director, Javier Aguirre; In color; Rated R; No other credits available; March release. CAST: Paul Naschy, Haydee Politoff, Rossanna Yanni

LOVE IN 3-D (Dimension) In technicolor; Rated X; March release; No other credits available. CAST: Ingrid Steeger, Evelyn Reese, Christina Lindberg

Sean Connery, Charlotte Rampling
in "Zardoz"

Sean Connery
in "Zardoz"

"Bordello"

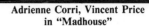

Adrienne Corri, Vincent Price
in "Madhouse"

BORDELLO (Cambist) Producers, Cone Amore Productions, Anders Sandberg; Director, Ole Ege; English version produced and edited by Lane Carroll; In color; Rated X; 90 minutes; March release. CAST: Lonnie Feddersen, Ulla Ege, Sune Piilgaard, Gotha Andersen, James Morrison, Allan North

VALERIE AND HER WEEK OF WONDERS (Janus) Director, Jaromil Jires; Photography, Jan Curik; Editor, Josef Valusiak; Music, Lubos, Fiser; Art Director, Jan Oliva; Associate Directors, Eliska Stibrova, Ota Koval; Art Designer, Ester Krumbachova; Costumes, Eva Lackingerova; Screenplay, Ester Krumbachova, Jaromil Jires; Based on story by Vitezslav Mezval; In color; Not rated; 75 minutes; March release. CAST: Jaroslava Schallerova, Helena Anyzova, Petr Kopriva, Jirf Prymek, Jan Klusak, Libuse Komancova, Karel Engel, Alena Stojakova, Otto Hradecky, Martin Wielgus, Jirina Machalicka, Michaela Kosova, Zdenka Kovarova, Bedriska Chalupska

EXORCISM'S DAUGHTER (Howard Mahler) Direction and Screenplay, Rafael Morena Alba; In Eastmancolor; Rated R; 93 minutes; March release. CAST: Amelia Gade, Francisco Rabal, Espartaco Santoni

KILL KILL KILL (Cinerama) Producers, Alexander and Ilya Salkind; Direction and Screenplay, Roman Gary; Photography, Edmond Richard; Editor, Robert Dwyre; In Eastmancolor; Rated R; 102 minutes; March release. CAST: Jean Seberg (Emily), James Mason (Alan), Stephen Boyd (Killian), Curt Jurgens (Chief), Daniel Emilfork (Inspector), Henri Garcin (Lawyer)

POPSY POP (Cannon) Title changed to "The Butterfly Affair"; Director, Jean Herman; Screenplay, Henri Charriere, Jean Herman; Photography, Jean-Jacques Tarbes; Editor, Helene Plemianikoff; In Eastmancolor; 100 minutes; March release. CAST: Stanley Baker (Silva), Claudia Cardinale (Popsy), Henri Charriere (Marco), Marc Mazza (Heavy), Georges Aminet (Priest), Ginette Leclerc (Madame)

MADHOUSE (American International) Executive Producer, Samuel Z. Arkoff; Producers, Max J. Rosenberg, Milton Subotsky; Associate Producer, John Dark; Director, Jim Clark; Screenplay, Greg Morrison; Adaptation, Ken Levison; Based on Novel "Devilday" by Angus Hall; Photography, Ray Parslow; Editor, Clive Smith; Art Director, Tony Curtis; Music, Douglas Gamley; In Movielab Color; Rated PG; 89 minutes; March release. CAST: Vincent Price (Paul), Peter Cushing (Herbert), Robert Quarry (Quayle), Adrienne Corri (Faye), Natasha Pyne (Julia), Michael Parkinson (TV interviewer), Linda Hayden (Elizabeth), Barry Dennen (Blount), Ellis Dayle (Alfred), Catherine Willmer (Louise), John Garrie (Harper), Ian Thompson (Bradshaw), Jenny Lee Wright (Carol), Julie Crosthwaite (Ellen), Peter Halliday (Psychiatrist)

FIRST CHARGE OF THE MACHETE (Tricontinental) Producer, Miguel Mendoza; Director, Manuel Octavio Gomez; Screenplay, Julio Garcia Espinosa, Alfredo de Cueto, Jorge Herrera, Manuel Octavio Gomez; Photography, Jorge Herrera; Editor, Nelson Rodriguez; Music, Leo Brower, Pablo Milanes; In Spanish with English subtitles; In black and white; No rating; 84 minutes; March release. CAST: Rigoberto Aguila, Idalia Andreus, Miguel Benavides, Carlos Bermudez, Luis Carreres, Jose M. Catineira, Aida Conde, Rene de la Cruz, Aramis Delgado, Raul Eguren, Roger Ferrer, Eugenio Hernandez, Daniel Jordan, Gabriel Lopez, Miguel Lucern, Adolfo Llaurado, Julian Martinez, Luis M. Martinez Casado, Eduardo Moure, Miguel Navarro, Frank Negro, Eslinda Nunez, Alfredo Perojo, Raul Pomares, Jose Antonio Rodriguez, Felipe Santos, Juan Troya, Omar Valdes, Julio Vega, Ana Vinas

KUNG FU, THE PUNCH OF DEATH (Lana) In color; Rated R; No other credits available; March release.

CAMPUS SWINGERS (Hemisphere) Producer, Wolf C. Hartwig; Director, Ernst Hofbauer; In Eastmancolor; Rated R; March Release. CAST: Ingred Steeger, Margrit Sigel, Evelyn Traeger

LIBIDO (United International) Director, Max Pecas; In color; Rated X; March release; No other credits available. CAST: Sandra Julien, Janine Reynaud, Patric Verde, Allen Hitier

"Valerie and Her Week of Wonders"

"First Charge of the Machete"

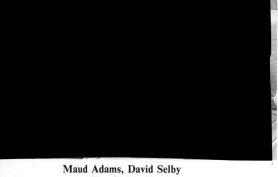

Maud Adams, David Selby
in "The Girl in Blue"

Paula Kelly, Isaac Hayes, Lino Ventura
in "Three Tough Guys"

THE GIRL IN BLUE (Cinerama) Producer-Director, George Kaczender; Executive Producer, DAL Productions; Screenplay, Douglas Bowie; Photography, Miklos Lente; Music, Neil Chotem; Art Director, Wolf Kroeger; Assistant Director, Scott Maitland; In Panavision and Eastmancolor; March release. CAST: David Selby (Scott), Maud Adams (Paula/Tracy), Gay Rowan (Bonnie), William Osler (Prof. Bamberger), Diane Dewey (Holly), Michael Kirby (Kippie), Walter Wakefield (Old Man), Don Arioli (Sidewalk Artist), Valda Dalton (Bingo Woman), Guy Martin (Policeman), Michel Maillot (Good Humour Man), Hanka Poznanska (Flower Woman), George Robertson (Tennis Pro), Elsa Pickthorne (Georgette), Donald Ewer (Les), Marilyn Lazar-Medicoff (Melody), Terry Haig (Blair), Maryann Joffe (Cindy), Jimmy Thompson (Ferry Driver), James McGee (Gas Attendant), Marjorie Pauch (Cherry), Don MacIntyre (Gil), Robin Ward (Traf), Christiane Robinson (Holly's Sister), Lee McGrath (Kippie's Brother), Jennifer Gilbert (Jennie), John Gilbert (Jim), Aubert Pallascio (Young Ferry Driver), Bronwen Mantel (Nurse), Basil Fitzgibbon (Executive), Dee Myles (Blonde in MG), Rosemary Dixon (Girl in lobby), Claude Ravenelle (Janitor), Violet Bussey (Holly's mother), Don Arres (Binocular man), Danny Carloni (Waiter), Margriet Zwarts (Hitchhiker), Danny Freedman (Gas Attendant)

FOTOGRAFIA (Hunnia) Director, Pal Zolnay; Screenplay, Pal Zolnay, Orsolya Szekely; Photography, Elemer Ragalyi; Editor, Maria Szecsenyi; Music, Ferenc Sebo; In black and white; Not rated; 82 minutes; March release. CAST: Istvan Iglodi, Mark Zalan, Ferenc Sebo

CHINESE HERCULES (Bryanston) Producer, Peter Poon; Director, Choy Tak; A Hong Kong Kai Fa Film Co. Production; In color; Rated R; March release; Starring Yang Sze

BLOOD (Bryanston) Producer, Walter Kent; Direction and Screenplay, Andy Milligan; Rated R; In color; 74 minutes; March release. CAST: Allan Berendt, Hope Stransbury, Eve Crosby, Patti Gaul, Pamela Adams

THREE TOUGH GUYS (Paramount) Director, Duccio Tessari; Music and Lyrics, Isaac Hayes; Story and Screenplay, Luciano Vincenzoni, Nicola Badalucco; Photography, Aldo Tonti; Art Director, Francesco Bronzi; Editors, Mario Morra, Richard Marks; Assistant Director, Gianni Cozzi; A Dino De Laurentiis Presentation; In Technicolor; Rated PG; 92 minutes; March release. CAST: Lino Ventura (Father Charlie), Isaac Hayes (Lee), Fred Williamson (Joe), Paula Kelly (Fay), William Berger (Capt. Ryan), Luciano Salce (Bishop), Vittorio Sanipoli (Mike), Jacques Herlin (Tequila), Jess Hahn (Bartender), Lorella De Luca (Anne), Thurman E. Scott (Tony), Mario Erpichini (Gene), Guido Leontini (Sgt. Sam), Joel Cory (Truckdriver), Dutchell Smith (Streetwalker), Ira Rogers (Lou), Margot Novick (Prostitute), Tommy Brubaker (Hood), Buddy Stein (Cab Driver), Max Klevin (Huge Man), Walt Scott (Petralia's Man), Frank Grimaldi (Blinky), Emanuele Spatafora (Joe Bell), Hans Jung Bluth (Mechanic)

SONNY AND JED (K-Tel) Producer, Roberto Loyola; Director, Sergio Carbucci; Music, Ennio Morricone; In Technicolor; Rated R; 87 minutes; March release. CAST: Thomas Milian (Jed), Susan George (Sonny), Telly Savalas (Franciscus), Rossana Ranni, Laura Betti

MEMORIES OF HELEN (New Yorker) Producer, Mapa Ltda, Julio Bressana, Julio Graber; Director, David Neves; Screenplay, David Neves, P. E. Sales Gomes; Photography, David Zingg; In color, black and white; Not rated; March release. CAST: Rosa Maria Pena (Helen), Adriana Prietro, Arduino Colassanti, Joel Barcelos, Aurea Campos, Mair Tavares, Humberto Mauro, Neyla Tavares

THE MOTHER AND THE WHORE (New Yorker) Executive Producer, Pierre Cottrell; Direction and Screenplay, Jean Eustache; Photography, Pierre Lhomme; Editors, Jean Eustache, Denise de Casabianca; Costumes, Catherine; In black and white; Not rated; 215 minutes; March release. CAST: Bernadette Lafont (Maria),

Jean-Pierre Leaud (Alexandre), Francoise Lebrun (Veronika), Isabelle Weingarten (Gilberte), Jacques Renard, Jean-Noel Picq, Jessa Darrieux, Marinka Matuszewski, Genevieve Mnich, Berthe Grandval

Thomas Milian, Susan George
in "Sonny and Jed"

Jean-Pierre Leaud, Francoise Lebrun, Bernadette
Lafont in "The Mother and the Whore"

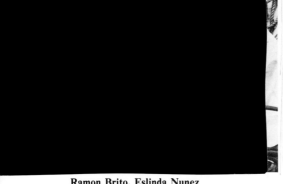

**Ramon Brito, Eslinda Nunez
in "Lucia"**

**Aldo Sassi (L), Yves Beneyton (C)
in "In the Name of the Father"**

LUCIA (Tricontinental) Director, Humberto Solas; Screenplay, Humberto Solas, Julio Garcia Espinosa, Nelson Rodriguez; Photography, Jorge Herrera; Editor, Nelson Rodriguez; Music, Leo Brouwer; Art Directors, Pedro Garcia Espinosa, Roberto Miqueli; Costumes, Maria Elena Molinet; Costumes, Maria Elena Molinet; Assistant Directors, Inger Seeland, Maria Ramirez, Jose G. Aguilar; Song, Joseito Fernandez; In black and white; Spanish with English subtitles; Not rated; 160 minutes; March release. CAST: Raquel Revuelta (Lucia 1895), Eduardo Moure (Rafael), Eslinda Nunez (Lucia 1933), Ramon Brito (Aldo), Adela Legra (Lucia 1960), Adolfo Llaurado (Tomas)

LIGHTNING SWORDS OF DEATH (Columbia) Executive Producer, Shintaro Katsu; Director, Kenji Misumi; Screenplay, Kazuo Koike; Story, Kazuo Koike, Goyu Kojima; A Katsu Production in cooperation with Toho Co.; Rated R; In color; 83 minutes; March release. CAST: Tom Wakayama (Itto), Goh Kato, Yuko Hama

THE RAGMAN'S DAUGHTER (Independent) Producers, Harold Becker, Souter Harris; Director, Harold Becker; Screenplay, Alan Sillitoe; Based on his story; Editor, Antony Gibbs; Photography, Michael Seresin; Music, Kenny Clayton; Not classified; In color; 94 minutes; March release. CAST: Simon Rouse (Tony), Victoria Tennant (Doris), Patrick O'Connell (Tony at 35), Leslie Sands (Doris' Father), Rita Howard (Doris' Mother), Brenda Peters (Tony's Mother), Brian Murphy (Tony's Father), Jane Wood (Older Tony's Wife)

CHINESE HERCULES (Bryanston) Producer, Peter Poon; Director, Choy Tak; In color; Rated R; 90 minutes; March release; No other details available. CAST: Chen Wei Min, Chiang Fan, Fang Yeh, Yang Sze, Li Tien Ying, Yuan Feng, Chin Ti, Liang Tin, Fah Kiuh, Wang Chug Tsung

THE RED TRAIN Produced, Directed, Written by Peter Ammann; Photography, Jimmy Glasberg; Editor, Jacques Morzier; 90 minutes; March release. A Swiss documentary about capitalism.

MONTREAL MAIN Produced, Directed, Written by Frank Vitale; In color; Not rated; March release. No other details available

IN THE NAME OF THE FATHER (New Yorker) Producer, Franco Cristaldi; Directed and Written by Marco Bellocchio; Photography, Franco di Giacomo; Editor, Franco Artalli; Music, Nicola Piovani; Not rated; 107 minutes; March release. CAST: Yves Beneyton (Angelo), Renato Scarpa (Vice Rector), Aldo Sassi (Franco), Laura Betti (Franco's Mother), Lou Castel (Salvatore)

BUT WHERE IS DANIEL VAX? Producer, William L. Gross; Directed and Written by Avram Heffner; Photography, Amnon Salomon; Editor, Jacques Erlich; In color; Not rated; 95 minutes; March release. CAST: Lior Yaeni, Michael Lipkin, Esther Zevko, Yael Heffner, Zivit Abramson

ALL NUDITY SHALL BE PUNISHED Producer, Paulo Porto; Direction and Screenplay, Arnaldo Jabor; Based on play by Nelson Rodriques; Photography, Lauro Escorel; Editor, Rafael Justo Valverde; Not rated; 102 minutes; March release. CAST: Paulo Porto (Herculano), Darlene Gloria (Geni), Paulo Sacks (Serginho), Paulo Pereiro (Patricio)

IN THE DEVIL'S GARDEN (Hemisphere) Formerly titled "Assault"; Producer, Peter Rogers; Director, Sidney Hayers; Screenplay, John Kruse; From novel "The Ravine" by Kendal Young; Photography, Ken Hodges; Art Director, Lionel Couch; Editor, Tony Palk; Costumes, Courtenay Elliott; Music, Eric Rogers; Assistant Director, Stuart Freeman; In Panavision and Color; Rated R; 90 minutes; April release. CAST: Suzy Kendall (Julie), Frank Finlay (Velyan), Freddie Jones (Reporter), James Laurenson (Greg), Leslie-Anne Down (Tessa), Tony Beckley (Leslie), Anthony Ainley (Bartell), Dilys Hamlett (Mrs. Sanford), James Cosmo (Beale), Patrick Jordan (Milton), Alan Cuthbertson (Coroner), Anabel Littledale (Susan), Tom Chatto (Doctor), Kit Taylor, Jan Butlin, William Hoyland, John Swindells, Jill Cary, David Essex, Valerie Shute, John Stone, Siobhan Quinlan, Marianne Stone, Janet Lynn

"In Memory of Helen"

**Tomisaburo Wakayama
in "Lightning Swords of Death"**

Calvin Lockhart
in "The Beast Must Die"

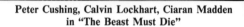

Peter Cushing, Calvin Lockhart, Ciaran Madden
in "The Beast Must Die"

BLOOD FINGERS (Sands) In color; Rated R; No other credits available; April release. CAST: Alan Tang, King Chan

IF I HAD A MILLION RUBIES (Celebrity Concert) Produced, Directed and Written by Mikhail Shveitser; Based on novel "The Golden Calf" by Ilf & Petrov; Photography, Sergei Poluyanov; Music, Georgy Firtich; Art Director, Abram Friedin; Assistant Directors, M. Amiradjibi, A. Yablochkin; A Mosfilm Production in black and white; Not rated; 95 minutes; April release. CAST: Sergei Yursky (Ostap), Leonid Kuraviev (Shura), Zinovi Gerdt (Mikhail), Yevgeny Yevstigneev (Alexander), Svetlana Starikova (Zosya)

I, MONSTER (Cannon) Producers, Max J. Rosenberg, Milton Subotsky; Director, Stephen Weeks; An Amicus Production; In color; Rated PG; April release. CAST: Christopher Lee (Marlowe), Peter Cushing (Utterson), Mike Raven (Enfield), Richard Hurndall (Lanyan), George Merritt (Poole), Kenneth J. Warren (Dean), Susan Jameson (Diane)

THE BEAST MUST DIE (Cinerama) Producers, Max J. Rosenberg, Milton Subotsky; Associate Producer, John Dark; Director, Paul Annett; Screenplay, Michael Winder; Photography, Jack Hildyard; Art Director, John Stoll; Assistant Director, Richard Jenkins; Editor, Peter Tanner; Music, Douglas Gamley; Executive Producer, Robert Greenberg; An Amicus Production; In Color; Rated PG; 93 minutes; April release. CAST: Calvin Lockhart (Tom), Peter Cushing (Dr. Lundgren), Charles Gray (Bennington), Anton Diffring (Pavel), Marlene Clark (Caroline), Ciaran Madden (Davina), Tom Chadbon (Paul), Michael Gambon (Jarmokowski), Sam Mansaray (Butler), Andrew Lodge (Pilot), Carol Bohun, Eric Carte (Hunters)

STREET GANGS OF HONG KONG (Cinerama) Producer, Runme Shaw; Directors, Chang Cheh, Kuei Chih-Hung; Photography, Yu Chi; Music, Chen Yung-Yu; In color; Rated R; 100 minutes; April release. CAST: Wang Chung (Shen), Lily Li (Huang), Pei Ti (Teng), Lu Ti (Father), Tung Lin (Lan), Fan Mei Sheng (Ta), Wang Kuang Yu (Iron Pipe), Shih Tien (Handicapped), Shen Lao (Chao)

SON OF DRACULA (Cinemation) Producer, Ringo Starr; Director, Freddie Francis; Music, Harry Nilsson; Screenplay, Jay Fairbank; In color; Rated PG; 90 minutes; April release. CAST: Harry Nilsson (Count Down), Ringo Starr (Merlin), Dennis Price (Van) Freddie Jones (Dr. Frankenstein), Suzanna Leigh (Girl), Peter Frampton, Keith Moon, John Bonham (Musicians)

NURSES REPORT (Hemisphere) Director, Walter Brothers; In color; Rated X; April release. CAST: Doris Arden, Karin Heske, Ingrid Steeger

THE BLOOD SPATTERED BRIDE (Europix International) Direction and Screenplay, Vicente Aranda; In Eastmancolor; Rated R, April release. CAST: Simon Andrew, Maribel Martin, Alexandra Bastedo, Dean Selmier

THE SEX THIEF (International Amusement) Producers, Michael Style, Teddy White; Director, Martin Campbell; Photography Grenville Middleton; Assistant Director, David Bracknell; Art Director, Anthony Noble; Editor, Rex Graves; Screenplay, Edward Hyde; Music, Mike Vickers; An Ocarina/Drumbeat/Rainbow Production; In color; Rated X; 85 minutes; April release. CAST: Jenny Westbrook (Emily), David Warbeck (Grant), Henry Rayner (Constable), Gerald Taylor (Herbert), Michael Armstrong (Sgt. Plinth) Terence Edmond (Ins. Smith), Diane Keen (Judy), Christopher Neil (Guy), Harvey Hall (Jacobi), Gloria Walker (Angie), Christopher Biggins (Porky), Christopher Mitchell (Wesleydale), Eric Deacon (Crabshaw), Susan Glanville (Florinda), Linda Coombes (Jezebel) David Landor (Guido), James Aubrey (Reporter), David Pugh (Reporter), Brenda Rae (Salesgirl), Anthony May (Barman), Derek Martin (Doorman), Val Penny (Stripper), Dave Carter (Jeweller) Neville Barber (Auctioneer), Michael Hannah (Chauffeur), Carlotta Barrow (Waitress), Veronica Doran (Meter Attendant)

THE STRANGER'S GUNDOWN (Cohen) Producers, Herman Cohen, Anthony Steffen, Teodoro Corra; Directed and Written by Sergio Garroni; Photography, Gino Santini; Music, Mancuso; In color; Rated PG; April release. CAST: Not available.

Wang Chung
in "Street Gangs of Hong Kong"

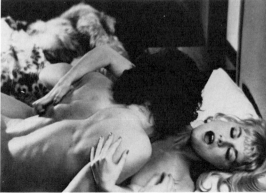

David Warbeck, Linda Coombes
in "The Sex Thief"

Gila Almagor, Ophir Shalhin
in "The House on Chelouche Street"

Gila Almagor
in "The House on Chelouche Street"

THE HOUSE ON CHELOUCHE STREET (Productions Unlimited) Producer, Menahem Golan; Director, Moshe Mizrahi; Executive Producer, Yoram Globus; Editor, Dov Hoenig; Art Director, Zuli Sander; Photography, Adam Greenberg; Screenplay, Moshe Mizrahi, Rachel Fabien; In Widescreen and Eastmancolor; English subtitles; Rated PG; 115 minutes; April release. CAST: Gila Almagor (Clara), Shai Ophir (Sami), Yosseph Shiloah (Nissam), Michal Bat-Adam (Sonia), Avner Hizkiahou (Halfon)

SANSHIRO SUGATA (Toho) Directed and Written by Akira Kurosawa; Story, Tsueno Tomita; Not rated; 80 minutes; April release. CAST: Susumu Fujita (Sugata), Jenjiro Okochi (Hansuke), Yukiyo Todoroki (Sayo), Yoshio Kosugi (Saburo)

BLACK HOLIDAY (New Yorker) Director, Marco Leto; Screenplay, Marco Leto, Lino Del Fra, Cecilia Mangini; Photography, Giuseppe Blacobino; Music, Egisto Macchi; In black and white; Not rated; 110 minutes; April release. CAST: Adalberto Maria Meril (Prof. Rossini), Adolfo Celli (Police Commissioner), John Steiner (Scagnetti), Milena Vukotic (Mrs. Rossini), Biagio Pelligra (Masprodonato)

THE JACKAL OF NAHUELTORO (Tricontinental) Directed and Written by Miguel Littin; Photography, Hector Rios; Music, Sergio Ortega; Not rated 95 minutes; April release. CAST: Nelson Villagra (Jorge), Shenda Roman (Rosa), Luis Melo (Mayor), Marcelo Romo (Reporter), Hector Noguera (Chaplain)

OVER NIGHT Produced, Directed, and Written by Karin Thome; Based on idea by Max Zihlmann; Photography, Martin Schaefer, Achim Lenz; Not rated; 85 minutes; April release. CAST: Werner Enzel (Frist), Karin Thome (Laura), Rudolf Thome (Panzer)

ORDINARY TENDERNESS Producer, Paul Larose; Director, Jacques Leduc; Screenplay, Robert Tremblay; Photography, Alain Dostle; Editor, Pierre Bernier; Not rated; 82 minutes; April release. CAST: Esther Auger (Esther), Jocelyn Berube (Jocelyn), Luce Guilleault (Bernadette)

SLIPSTREAM (Pacific Rim Films) Producer, James Margellos; Director, David Acomba; Screenplay, William Fruet; Story, David Acomba; Photography, Marc Champion; Editor, Tony Lower; Music, Brian Ahern, Van Morrison, Eric Clapton; In Bellevue-Pathe Color; Not rated; 92 minutes; April release. CAST: Luke Askew (Mike), Patti Oatman (Kathy), Eli Rill (Alec), Scott Hylands (Terry), Danny Friedman (Hitch)

THE GOLDEN VOYAGE OF SINBAD (Columbia) Producers, Charles H. Schneer, Ray Harryhausen; Director, Gordon Hessler; Photography, Ted Moore; Screenplay, Brian Clemens; Art Director, Fernando Gonzalez; Editor, Roy Watts; Music, Miklos Rozsa; Designer, John Stoll; Assistant Director, Miguel A. Gil, Jr.; In color; Rated G; 105 minutes; April release. CAST: John Phillip Law (Sinbad), Caroline Munro (Margiana), Tom Baker (Koura), Douglas Wilmer (Vizier), Martin Shaw (Rachid), Gregoire Aslan (Hakim), Kurt Christian (Haroun), Takis Emmanuel (Achmed), John D. Garfield (Abdul), Aldo Sambrell (Omar)

'TIS PITY SHE'S A WHORE (International) Producer, Silvio Clementelli; Director, Giuseppe Patroni Griffi; Screenplay, Patroni Griffi, Alfio Valdarnini, Carlo Carunchio; Based on play by John Ford; Photography, Vittorio Storaro; Music, Ennio Morricone; In color; Rated R; 91 minutes; April release. CAST: Charlotte Rampling, Oliver Tobias, Fabio Testi, Antonio Falsi, Rick Battaglia, Angela Luce, Rino Imperio

ZATOICHI'S CONSPIRACY (Toho) Producers, Shintaro Katsu, Nishioica Kozen; Director, Kimiyoshi Yasuda; Story, Kan Shimozawa; Photography, Shozo Honda; Music, Akira Ifukube; In color; Not rated; 90 minutes; April release. CAST: Shintaro Katsu (Zatoichi), Eiji Okada (Shinbei), Kei Sato (Bailiff), Takashi Shimura (Sakubel), Yukie Toake (Omiyo)

DAYS OF 36 Producer, George Papalios; Directed and Written by Theo Angelopoulos; Editor, V. Syropoulos; 110 minutes; Not rated; April release. CAST: George Kiritsis (Deputy), Tharos Grammenos (Convict)

**Iain Ross, Paul Ssali
in "Two Men of Karamoja"**

**Miou-Miou, Patrick Dewaere
in "Going Places"**

THE DEVIL'S NIGHTMARE (Hemisphere) Director, Jean Brismee; In color; Rated R; No other credits available; April release. CAST: Erica Blanc, Jean Servais, Daniel Emilfork, Lucien Raimbourg

TWO MEN OF KARAMOJA (Tomorrow Entertainment) Producers, Natalie R. Jones, Eugene S. Jones; Director, Eugene S. Jones; Photography, Tony Mander; Music, Charles Randolph Grean; Editor, Stephen Milne; ESJ Production; A Jones/Howard Limited Presentation; In color; Rated PG; 102 minutes; May release. A documentary about cultural conflict in Uganda.

GOING PLACES (Cinema 5) Producer, Paul Claudon; Director, Bertrand Blier; Screenplay, Bertrand Blier, Philippe Dumarcay; Based on novel by Bertrand Blier; Photography, Bruno Nuyten; Editor, Kenout Peltier; Subtitles, Nina Levin, Brooke Leveque; Music, Stephane Grappelli; Rated R; 117 minutes; May release. CAST: Gerard Depardieu (Jean-Claude), Patrick Dewaere (Pierrot), Miou-Miou (Marie-Ange), Jeanne Moreau (Jeanne), Jacques Chailieux (Jacques), Michel Peurilon (Surgeon), Brigitte Fossey (Young mother), Isabelle Huppert (Jacqueline), Christiane Muller (Jacqueline's mother), Christian Alers (Jacqueline's father), Dominique Davray (Ursula), Jacques Rispal (Beautician), Marco Perrin (Warden), Gerard Boucaron (Garage owner), Michel Pilorge (Market manager)

DARK PLACES (Cinerama) Producer, James Hannah, Jr.; Director, Don Sharp; Screenplay, Ed Brennan, Joseph Van Winkle; Photography, Ernest Steward; Music, Wilfred Josephs; Editor, Teddy Darvas; Art Director, Geoffrey Tozer; Assistant Director, Barry Langley; In Eastmancolor; Rated PG; 91 minutes; May release. CAST: Christopher Lee (Dr. Mandeville), Joan Collins (Sarah), Robert Hardy (Edward/Andrew), Herbert Lom (Prescott), Jane Birkin (Alta), Carleton Hobbs (Old Marr), Jennifer Thanisch (Jessica), Michael McVey (Francis), Jean Marsh (Victoria), Martin Boddey (Police Sgt.), Roy Evans (Baxter), John Glyn Jones (Bank Manager), John Levene (Doctor), Barry Linehan (Gatekeeper), Linda Gray (Woman on hill), Lysandre de-la-Haye, Earl Rhodes (Children on hill)

TRAIL OF BLOOD Part I; Director Ikehiro; In color; Not rated; May release; No other details available. CAST: Yoshiro Harada

THE AMBITIOUS (Toho) A Nakamura Production; Director, Daisuke Ito; In black and white; Not rated; 120 minutes; May release. CAST: Toshiro Mifune, Taisuya Nakadai, Kinnosuke Nakamura

ITALIAN GRAFFITI (K-Tel International) Producer, Luciano Catenacci; Direction and Screenplay, Alfio Caltabiano; Photography, Guglielmo Mancori; Music, Guido and Maurizio de Angelis; In color; Rated PG; 86 minutes; May release. CAST: Pino Colizzi, Alf Thunder, Christa Linder, Ornella Muti, Luciano Catenacci, Tano Cimarosa

THEATER OF LIFE (Shochiku) Producers, Yoshiji Mishima, Yoshitaro Nomura; Director, Tai Kato; Screenplay, Yoshitaro Nomura, Haruhiko Mimura, Tai Kato; Story, Shiro Ozaki; Photography, Keiji Maruyama; Editor, Shizu Ohsawa; Not rated 166 minutes; May release. CAST: Muga Takewaki (Hyokichi), Jiro Tamiya (Kira), Hideki Takahashi (Hishakaku), Tetsuya Watari (Miyagawa), Hisaya Morishige (Hyotaro Aonari), Keiko Tsushima (Omine), Yoshiko Kayama (Osode), Mitsuko Baisho (Otoyo)

CHARULATA, THE LONELY WIFE (New Times) Directed and Written by Satyajit Ray; Story, Rabindranath Tagore; Not rated; 102 minutes; May release. CAST: Sailen Mukherjee (Charulata), Madhabi Mukherjee (Bhupati), Soumitra Chatterjee (Amal)

THE MINOR'S WIFE (Cambist) Producer, Gunter Otto; Direction and Screenplay, Franz Marischka; Based on novel by Hans Henning Claer; Photography, Gunter Otto; Costumes, Herta Deininger; English version Produced and Edited by Lane Carroll; In Eastmancolor; Rated X; May release. CAST: Michel Jacot, Anne Graf, Walter Kraus, Elke Boltenhagen, Birgit Bergen, Manuela Wittmann, Andre Eismann, Rinaldo Talamonti

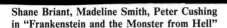
Shane Briant, Madeline Smith, Peter Cushing
in "Frankenstein and the Monster from Hell"

Omar Sharif in "The Mysterious Island
of Captain Nemo"

FRANKENSTEIN AND THE MONSTER FROM HELL (Paramount) Producer, Roy Skeggs; Director, Terence Fisher; Screenplay, John Elder; Photography, Brian Probyn; Editor, James Needs; Music, James Bernard; A Hammer Production; In color; Rated R; 93 minutes; June release. CAST: Peter Cushing (Frankenstein), Shane Briant (Simon), Madeline Smith (Sarah), Dave Prowse (Monster)

CAPTAIN KRONOS: VAMPIRE HUNTER (Paramount) Producers, Albert Fennell, Brian Clemens; Direction and Screenplay, Brian Clemens; Photography, Ian Wilson; Music, Laurie Johnson; Editor, James Needs; A Hammer Production; In color; Rated R; 91 minutes; June release. CAST: Horst Janson (Capt. Kronos), John Carson (Dr. Marcus), Shane Briant (Paul), Caroline Munro (Carla), John Cater (Ghost)

KUNG FU MAMA (Crown International) Director, Chien Lung; In color; Rated R; June release. CAST: Wang Yu, Asien Chin-Chu, Chang Ching Ching, Tzu Lang, Kang Kai

THEY CALL HER ONE EYE (American International) Executive Producer, Bo A. Vibenius; Director, Alex Fridolinski; Screenplay, Alex Fridolinski, Bo A. Vibenius; A Cruel Picture; United Producers Presentation; In Movielab Color; Rated R; 89 minutes; June release. CAST: Christina Lindberg (Frigga), Heinz Hopf (Tony)

CRAZE (Warner Bros.) Producer, Herman Cohen; Executive Producer, Gustave Berne; Director, Freddie Francis; Screenplay, Aben Kandel, Herman Cohen; Based on novel "Infernal Idol" by Henry Seymour; Photography, John Wilcox; Art Director, George Provis; Editor, Henry Richardson; Music, John Scott; Assistant Director, Peter Saunders; A Harbor Productions Presentation; In Technicolor; Rated R; 96 minutes; June release. CAST: Jack Palance (Neal), Diana Dors (Dolly), Jule Ege (Helena), Edith Evans (Aunt Louise), Hugh Griffith (Solicitor), Trevor Howard (Supt. Bellamy), Michael Jayston (Det. Sgt. Wall), Suzy Kendall (Sally), Martin Potter (Ronnie), Percy Herbert (Det. Russet), David Warbeck (Det. Wilson), Kathleen Byron (Muriel), Venecia Day (Dancer), Marianne Stone (Barmaid), Dean Harris (Ronnie's Friend)

THE MYSTERIOUS ISLAND OF CAPTAIN NEMO (Cinerama) Producer, Jacques Bar; Directors, Juan Antonio Bardem, Henri Colpi; Screenplay, Jacques Champreux, Juan Antonio Bardem; Assistant Directors, Jean-Claude Garcia, Jose Puyol; Photography, Enzo Serafin, Guy Delecluze, Julio Ortaz; Music, Gianni Ferrio; Editors, Paul Cayatte, Aurore Camp, Frederique Michaud; Designers, Cubero y Galicia, Philippe Ancellin; Costumes, Leon Revuelta, Peris Hermanos; A Cite Films Presentation; In color; Rated PG; 96 minutes; June release. CAST: Omar Sharif (Nemo), Philippe Nicaud (Spilett), Gerard Tichy (Smith), Jess Hann (Pencroff), Rafael Bardem (Herbert), Ambroise M'Bia, Gabriele Tinti (Ayrton), Vidal Molina (Harvey), Rick Bataglia (Finch)

PIPPI IN THE SOUTH SEAS (G. G. Communications) Producers, Allan Eckelund, Ernst Liesenhoff; Director, Olle Hellbom; Screenplay, Astrid Lindgren from her books; Music, Georg Riedel; Designer, Leif Nilsson; Photography, Kalle Bergholm; In Movielab Color; Rated G; 99 minutes; June release. CAST: Inger Nilsson (Pippi), Maria Persson (Annika), Par Sundberg (Tommy), Beppe Wolgers (Longstocking), Martin Ljund (Knife-Jocke), Jarl Borssen (Blood-Svente), Alfred Schieske (Innkeeper), Wolfgang Volz (Oscar), Nikolaus Schilling (Kalle), Tor Isedal (Franco), Hakan Serner (Pedro), Ollegard Welton (Mrs. Zettergren), Frederik Olsson (Zettergren), Staffan Hallerstam (Marco)

WOMAN OF THE GANGES Producer, O. R. T. F.; Directed, and Written by Marguerite Duras; Not rated; 90 minutes; June release; No other details available. CAST: Catherine Sellers, Dionys Mascolo, Nicole Hiss

BEDROOM MAGIC (Sherpix) A Palladium Film; In Eastmancolor; Rated X; June release; starring Anne Grete

THE MANDARIN MAGICIAN (Howard Mahler) Produced by Sun Gold Films; Presented by Howard Lin; In color; Rated R; June Release; Starring Larry Li, Bruce Ma

BED BUNNIES (Harnell) Direction and Screenplay, Ilja Von Arnutroff; In color; Rated X; June release. CAST: Morena Landen, Dagmar Conrad, Barbara Nicolei, Rena Bergen, Bianca Herr

Jack Palance, Martin Potter
in "Craze"

"Pippi in the South Seas"

"Promised Lands"

Raf Vallone (C)
in "Terror in 2A"

THE GOLDEN CALF (Celebrity Concert Corp.) Produced, Directed, and Written by Mikhail Shveitser; Based on novel by Ilf and Petrov; English version, Zeon Prochnik; Photography, Sergei Paluyanov; Music, Georgy Firtich; Art Director, Abram Freidin; A Mosfilm Production; EYR Presentation; Not rated; 95 minutes; June release. CAST: Sergei Yursky (Cast Bender), Zinovi Gerdt (Panitovsky), Leonid Kuratev (Shura), Yevgeny Yevstignev (Koreiko), Nikolai Boyorsky (Adam), Svetlana Starikova (Zosya)

HOODLUM SOLDIER (Altura) Producer, Masaichi Nagata; Director, Yasuzo Masumura; Screenplay, Ryuzo Kikushima; Story, Yorlyoshi Arima; Photography, Setsuo Kobayashi; A Daiei Production; In black and white; Not rated; 103 minutes; June release. CAST: Shintaro Katsu (Kisaburo), Takahiro Tamura (Arita), Keiko Awaii (Otomaru), Eiko Taki (Midori), Kikio Narita (MP)

BECAUSE OF THE CATS (International Co-Productions) Director, Fons Rademakers; Screenplay, Hugo Claus; From Nicholas Freeling novel; Photography, Eduard Van der Enden; Art Director, Jean-Paul Vroom; Editor, Poi Aarde; Assistant Director, Lili Rademakers; A Cine-Vog release; In Eastmancolor; Rated R; June release. CAST: Bryan Marshall (Van der Valk), Alexandra Stewart (Feodora), Alex Van Rooyen (Carnavalet), Leo Bayers (Uncle), Martin Van Zundert (Brinkman), George Baker (Inspector), Lilliane Vincent (Mrs. Kleft)

COLD SWEAT (Emerson) Producer, Robert Dorfmann; Director, Terence Young; Screenplay, Shimon Wincelberg, Albert Simonin; From book by Richard Matteson; Photography, Jean Rabier; Music, Michel Magne; A Corona Fair Film Production; In Eastmancolor; Rated PG; June release. CAST: Charles Bronson (Joe), Liv Ullman (Fabienne), James Mason (Rosso), Jill Ireland (Moira), Jean Topart (Katonga), Michael Constanti

COUNT DRACULA (Crystal) Director, Jesus Franco; Photography, Manuel Marino; Music, Bruno Nicolai; In Panavision and Eastmancolor; Rated PG; 100 minutes; July release. CAST: Christopher Lee, Herbert Lom, Klaus Kinsky, Soledad Miranda, Maria Rohm, Fred Williams, Jack Taylor, Paul Muller

TERROR IN 2A (Productions Unlimited) In Eastman color; 92 minutes; No other details available; July release. CAST: Raf Vallone, John Scanlon, Angelo Infanti, Karin Schubert

PROMISED LANDS (New Yorker) Producer, Nicole Stephane; Associate Producers, Nadine Haim, Alex Massis; Director, Susan Sontag; Photography, Jeri Sopanen; Assistant Director, David Rieff; Editors, Annie Chevallay, Florence Bocquet; In color; 87 minutes; July release. A documentary on Israel during the recent war.

MY NAME IS NOBODY (Universal) Producer, Claudio Mancini; Executive Producer, Fulvio Morsella; Screenplay, Ernesto Gastaldi; Story, Fulvio Morsella, Ernesto Gastaldi; Director, Tonino Valerii; Photography, Giuseppe Ruzzolini, Armando Mannuzzi; Art Director, Cianni Polidori; Music, Ennio Morricone; Editor, Nino Baragli; Costumes, Vera Marzot; Assistant Director, Stefano Rolla; An Italo-German-French Co-Production; In Panavision and Technicolor; A Sergio Leone/MCA Presentation; Rated PG; 115 minutes; July release. CAST: Terence Hill (Nobody), Henry Fonda (Jack), Jean Martin (Sullivan), Piero Lulli (Sheriff), Leo Gordon (Red), R. G. Armstrong (Honest John), Neil Summers (Westerner), Steve Kanaly (Barber), Geoffrey Lewis (Scape)

THE HEIRS (New Yorker) Producer, Jarbas Barbosa; Director, Carlos Diegues; Executive Producer, Jose Oliosi; Associate Producers, Luis Carlos Barreto, Carlos Diegues; Screenplay, Carlos Diegues; Photography, Dib Lutfi; Editor, Eduardo Escorel; Art Director, Luis Carlos Ripper; Costumes, Fernando Bede; Music, H. Villa-Lobos; in Eastmancolor; Not rated; 110 minutes; July release. CAST: Sergio Cardoso (Jorge), Odette Lara (Eugenia), Mario Lago (Joaquim), Paulo Porto (Medeiros), Isabel Ribeiro (Rachel), Andre Gouvela (Ramos), Grande Otelo (Popular Leader), Jean-Pierre Leaud (Frenchman)

THE HERO (Trans-World) Producer, R. D. Bansal; Directed and Written by Satyajit Ray; Not rated; 119 minutes; July release. CAST: Uttam Kumar (Arindam), Sharmila Tagora (Aditi), Raniit Sen (Haren Bose)

Terence Hill, Henry Fonda
in "My Name Is Nobody"

Jean-Pierre Leaud
in "The Heirs"

Marcel Marceau (in dual role)
in "Shanks"

Janis Joplin in "Janis"

SHANKS (Paramount) Producer, Steven North; Director, William Castle; Screenplay, Ranald Graham; Photography, Joe Biroc; Music, Alex North; Designer, Boris Leven; Editor, David Berlatsky; Choreography, Marcel Marceau; Costumes, Guy Verhille; Associate Producer, Sheldon Schrager; Assistant Directors, Sheldon Schrager, Val Raset, Martin Walters; In Movielab Color; Rated PG; 93 minutes; October release. CAST: Marcel Marceau (Malcolm Shanks/Old Walker), Tsilla Chelton (Mrs. Barton), Philippe Clay (Barton), Cindy Eilbacher (Celia), Helena Kallianiotes (Mata Hari), Larry Bishop (Napoleon), Don Calfa (Einstein), Biff Manard (Goliath), Mondo (Genghis Khan), Read Morgan (Policeman), William Castle (Grocer), Phil Adams (Beethoven), Lara Wing (Little Girl)

BLACK CHRISTMAS (Ambassador) Executive Producer, Findlay Quinn; Producer-Director, Bob Clark; Co-Producer, Gerry Arbeid; Associate Producer, Richard Schouten; Screenplay, Roy Moore; Music, Carl Zittrer; Photography, Reg Morris; Art Director, Karen Bromley; Editor, Stan Cole; An August Film Production; In color; Rated R; 93 minutes; October release. CAST: Olivia Hussey (Jess), Keir Dullea (Peter), Margot Kidder (Barb), Andrea Martin (Phyl), John Saxon (Lt. Fuller), Marian Waldman (Mrs. Mac), Art Hindle (Chris), Lynne Griffin (Clare), James Edmonds (Harrison)

THE WIDOW COUDERC (H. G. Entertainment) Producer, Raymond Danon; Director, Pierre Granier-Deferre; Screenplay, Pierre Granier-Deferre, Pascal Jardin; Adapted from novel by George Simeon; Photography, Walter Wottitz; Music, Phillipe Sarde; A Co-Production of Lira Films and Pegaso Films; Not rated; 92 minutes; October release. CAST: Alain Delon (Jean), Simone Signoret (La Veuve Couderc), Ottavia Piccolo (Felicie)

ALVIN PURPLE (Sands) Producer-Director, Tim Burstall; Screenplay, Alan Hopgood; Photography, John Seale; Music, Brian Cadd; A Bi-Jay Films Presentation; In color; Rated R; 92 minutes; October release. CAST: Graeme Blundell (Alvin Purple), George Whaley (Dr. McBurney), Penne Hackforth-Jones (Dr. Liz Sort), Elli Maclure (Tina), Noel Ferrier (Judge), Jill Foster (Mrs. Horwood)

JANIS (Universal Studios) Executive Producer, F. R. Crawley; Directed and Edited by Howard Alk, Seaton Findlay; Coordinator, Paul Harris; In color, black and white; Rated R; 96 minutes; October release. A documentary on Janis Joplin.

THE HOUSE THAT VANISHED (American International) Director, Joseph Larraz; A Hallmark Production; In color; Rated R; 95 minutes; October release. CAST: Andrea Allan, Karl Lanchbury, Judy Matheson

FEAR IN THE NIGHT (International Co-Productions) Producer-Director, Jimmy Sangster; A Hammer Film; Executive Producer, Michael Carreras; In color; Rated R; October release. CAST: Joan Collins, Ralph Bates, Peter Cushing, Judy Geeson

HINDERED Produced and Directed by Steve Dwoskin; In color; Not rated; No other details available; November release. CAST: Steve Dwoskin, Carola Regnier

CONFESSIONS OF A POLICE CAPTAIN (Avco Embassy) Producers, Bruno Turchetto, Mario Montanari; Director, Damiano Damiani; Screenplay, Damiano Damiani, Salvatore Laurani; Photography, Claudio Ragona; Music, Riz Ortolani; Editor, Antonio Siciliano; Set and Costumes, Umberto Turco; A Euro International Film; Explorer Film '58 Production; A Joseph E. Levine Presentation; In Technicolor; Rated R; 90 minutes; November release. CAST: Martin Balsam (Bonavia), Franco Nero (Traini), Marilu' Tolo (Serena), Claudio Gora (Attorney), Arturo Dominici (Canestraro), Michele Gammino (Himself), Luciano Lorcas (Dubrosio), Giancarlo Prete (Rizzo), Adolfo Lastretti (LiPuma)

BEAUTIFUL PEOPLE (Warner Bros.) Produced, Directed, Written, Filmed, and Edited by Jamie Uys; Assisted by Sue Burman; Executive Producer, Boet Troskie; Narrator, Paddy O'Byrne; Post-Production Director, Gordon Zahler; Music Editors, Jamie Uys, Theodore Roberts; Animation, Caroline Burls, Hettie Uys, Peggy Currie; In Technicolor; 92 minutes; November release. A documentary on wild life in Africa.

Marilu' Tolo, Martin Balsam
in "Confessions of a Police Captain"

"Beautiful People"

211

Angela Covello, Carla Brait
in "Torso"

Suzy Kendall, Tina Aumont
in "Torso"

TORSO (Joseph Brenner) Producer, Carlo Ponti; Director, Sergio Martino; Screenplay, E. Gastaldi, S. Martino; Photography, Giancarlo Ferrando; In Technicolor; Rated R; 90 minutes; November release. CAST: Suzy Kendall (Jane), Tina Aumont (Dani), Luc Merenda (Roberto), John Richardson (Franz), Roberto Bisacco (Stefano), Angela Covello (Katia), Carla Brait (Ursula), Cristina Airoldi (Carol), Patricia Adiutori (Flo)

LE TRIO INFERNAL (Levitt-Pickman) Producers, Raymond Danon, Jacques Dorfmann; Director, Francis Girod; Screenplay, Francis Girod, Jacques Rouffio; Based on novel by Solange Fasquelle; Music, Ennio Morricone; Photography, Andrea Winding; In Color; Not rated; 106 minutes; November release. CAST: Romy Schneider (Philomene), Michel Piccoli (George), Mascha Gomska (Catherine), Andrea Ferreol (Noemie), Monica Fiorentini (Magali), Hubert Deschamps (Chambon)

SIMABADDHA Producers, Bharat Shamsher, Jang Bahadur Rana; Direction, Screenplay, and Music by Satyajit Ray; Not rated; 112 minutes; November release. Starring Baru Chanda and Sharmila Tagore

THE NADA GANG (New Line) Executive Producer, Andre Genoves; Director, Claude Chabral; Screenplay, Claude Chabral, Jean-Patrick Manchette; Based on book by Mr. Manchette; Photography, Jean Rabier; Not rated; 110 minutes; November release. CAST: Fabio Testi (Diaz), Mariangela Melato (Cash), Maurice Garrel (Epaulard), Michel Duchaussoy (Treuffais), Michel Aumont (Goemond)

THE ALIENIST (New Yorker) Produced, Directed, and Written by Nelson Pereira dos Santos; Based on story by Machado de Assis; Photography, Dib Lutfi; Editor, Rafael Valverde; Music, Guicherme Magalhaes Vaz; Not rated; 88 minutes; November release. CAST: Nildo Parente (Priest), Isabel Ribeiro (Dona Evarista), Arduino Colasanti (Husband), Leila Dintz (Druggist's wife)

ROCCO PAPALEO (Rumson) Producers, Pio Angeletti, Adriano De Micheli; Director, Ettore Scola; Screenplay, Ruggero Maccari, Ettore Scola; Photography, Claudio Cirillo; Art Director, Luciano Ricceri; Editor, Ruggero Mastroianni; Music, Armando Trovaioli; In Eastmancolor; Rated R; 120 minutes; November release. CAST: Marcello Mastroianni (Rocco), Lauren Hutton (Jenny)

SHOCK (New Line) Direction and Screenplay, Alain Jessua; Photography, Jacques Robinson; Editor, Helene Plemmianikov; Art Director, Yannis Kokos; In Eastmancolor; 90 minutes; November release. CAST: Alain Delon (Devilers), Annie Girardot (Helene), Robert Hirsch (Gerome), Michel Duchaussoy (Bernard), Jean-Francois Calve (Gassin)

UP POMPEII (MGM-EMI) Producer, Ned Sherrin; Director, Bob Kellett; Screenplay, Sid Colin; From idea by Talbot Rothwell; Photography, Ian Wilson; Art Director, Sean Flannery; Editor, Al Geil; Costumes, Penny Lowe; Assistant Director, Allan James; Title Song music and lyrics, Ken Howard, Alan Blaikley; In Eastmancolor; Rated R; 90 minutes; November release. CAST: Frankie Howerd (Lucio), Patrick Cargill (Nero), Michael Hordern (Ludicrus), Barbara Murray (Ammonia), Lance Percival (Bilius), Bill Fraser (Prosperus), Adrienne Posta (Scrubba), Julie Ege (Voluptua), Bernard Bresslaw (Gorgo), Royce Mills (Nausius), Madeline Smith (Erotica), Rita Webb (Cassandra), Ian Trigger (Odius), Aubrey Woods (Villanus), Hugh Paddick (Priest), Laraine Humphreys (Flavia), Roy Hudd (M. C.), George Woodridge (Fat Bather), Andrea Lloyd (Dolly), Derek Griffiths (Steam Slave)

THE STREET FIGHTER (New Line) Director, S. Ozawa; Fight Direction, Ken Kamaza, M. Suzuki, Reginald Jones; Photography, Ken Tsukakoshi; In Actionscope and Eastmancolor; Rated X; 90 minutes; November release. CAST: Sonny Chiba (Terry), Gerald Yamada (Rat Nose), Doris Nakajima, Tony Setera

THE WEREWOLF VS. THE VAMPIRE WOMAN (Ellman Enterprises) Director, Leon Klimovsky; Screenplay, Jacinto Molina, Hans Munkell; A Plata Films and Intent International Picture; In Eastmancolor; Rated R; November release. CAST: Paul Naschy, Gaby Fuchs, Barbara Cappell, Patty Sheppard

"The Infernal Trio"

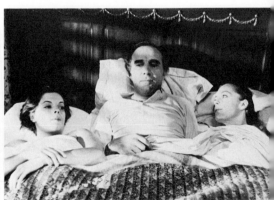

Mascha Gomska, Michel Piccoli, Romy Schneider
in "The Infernal Trio"

Anouk Aimee

Edward Albert

Jane Alexander

Michael Ansara

Elizabeth Ashley

BIOGRAPHICAL DATA

(Name, real name, place and date of birth, school attended)

ABBOTT, JOHN: London, June 5, 1905.

ABEL, WALTER: St. Paul, Minn., June 6, 1898, AADA.

ADAMS, EDIE: (Elizabeth Edith Enke) Kingston, Pa., Apr. 16, 1931. Juilliard, Columbia.

ADAMS, JULIE: (Betty May) Waterloo, Iowa, Oct. 17, 1928. Little Rock Jr. College.

ADAMS, MAUD: (Maud Wikstrom) Lulea, Sweden.

ADDAMS, DAWN: Felixstowe, Suffolk, Eng., Sept. 21, 1930. RADA.

ADRIAN, IRIS: (Iris Adrian Hostetter) Los Angeles, May 29, 1913.

AGAR, JOHN: Chicago, Jan. 31, 1921.

AHERNE, BRIAN: Worcestershire, Eng., May 2, 1902. Malvern College, U. of London.

AHN, PHILIP: Los Angeles, Mar. 29, 1911. U. of Calif.

AIMEE, ANOUK: Paris, Apr. 27, 1934. Bauer-Therond.

ALBERGHETTI, ANNA MARIA: Pesaro, Italy, May 15, 1936.

ALBERT, EDDIE: (Eddie Albert Heimberger) Rock Island, Ill, Apr. 22, 1908. U. of Minn.

ALBERT, EDWARD: Los Angeles, Feb. 20, 1951.

ALBERTSON, JACK: Rever, Mass.

ALBRIGHT, LOLA: Akron, Ohio, July 20, 1925.

ALDA, ALAN: NYC, Jan. 28, 1936, Fordham.

ALDA, ROBERT: (Alphonso D'Abruzzo) New York City, Feb. 26, 1914. NYU.

ALEJANDRO, MIGUEL: NYC, 1958.

ALEXANDER, JANE: Boston, Mass., Oct. 28, 1939, Sarah Lawrence.

ALLBRITTON, LOUISE: Oklahoma City, July 3, 1920. U. of Okla.

ALLEN, STEVE: New York City, Dec. 26, 1921.

ALLEN, WOODY: Brooklyn, Dec. 1, 1935.

ALLENTUCK, KATHERINE: NYC, Oct. 16, 1954: Calhoun.

ALLYSON, JUNE: (Ella Geisman) Westchester, N.Y., Oct. 7, 1923.

AMECHE, DON: (Dominic Amichi) Kenosha, Wisc., May 31, 1908.

AMES, ED: Boston, July 9, 1929.

AMES, LEON: (Leon Wycoff) Portland, Ind., Jan. 20, 1903.

AMOS, JOHN: Newark, NJ., Dec. 27, Bronx Com. Col.

ANDERSON, JUDITH: Adelaide, Australia, Feb. 10, 1898.

ANDERSON, MICHAEL, JR.: London, Eng., 1943.

ANDERSSON, BIBI: Stockholm, Nov. 11, 1935, Royal Dramatic Sch.

ANDES, KEITH: Ocean City, N.J., July 12, 1920. Temple U., Oxford.

ANDRESS, URSULA: Switz., Mar. 19, 1936.

ANDREWS, DANA: Collins, Miss., Jan. 1, 1912. Sam Houston College.

ANDREWS, EDWARD: Griffin, Ga., Oct. 9, 1914. U. VA.

ANDREWS, HARRY: Tonbridge, Kent, Eng., Nov. 10, 1911.

ANDREWS, JULIE: (Julia Elizabeth Wells) Surrey, Eng. Oct. 1, 1935.

ANGEL, HEATHER: Oxford, Eng., Feb. 9, 1909. Wycombe Abbey School.

ANN-MARGRET: (Olsson) Valsjobyn, Sweden, Apr. 28, 1941. Northwestern U.

ANSARA, MICHAEL: Lowell, Mass., Apr. 15, 1922. Pasadena Playhouse.

ANTHONY, TONY: Clarksburg, W. Va., Oct 16, 1937. Carnegie Techn.

ARCHER, JOHN: (Ralph Bowman) Osceola, Neb., May 8, 1915. U. of S. Calif.

ARDEN, EVE: (Eunice Quedens) Mill Valley, Calif., Apr. 30, 1912.

ARKIN, ALAN: NYC, Mar. 26, 1934. LACC.

ARLEN, RICHARD: Charlottesville, VA., Sept. 1, 1900. St. Thomas College.

ARNAZ, DESI: Santiago, Cuba, Mar. 2, 1917, Colegio de Dolores.

ARNAZ, DESI, JR.: Los Angeles, 1953.

ARNESS, JAMES: (Aurness) Minneapolis, Minn., May 26, 1923. Beloit College.

ARTHUR, BEATRICE: (Frankel) NYC, May 13, 1926, New School.

ARTHUR, JEAN: NYC, Oct. 17, 1908.

ARTHUR, ROBERT: (Robert Arthaud) Aberdeen, Wash., June 18. U. of Wash.

ASHLEY, ELIZABETH: Ocala, Fla., Aug. 30, 1939.

ASTAIRE, FRED: (Fred Austerlitz) Omaha, Neb., May 10, 1899.

ASTIN, JOHN: Baltimore, Md., Mar. 30, 1930, UMinn.

ASTOR, MARY: (Lucile V. Langhanke) Quincy, Ill., May 3, 1906. Kenwood-Loring School.

ATHERTON, WILLIAM: New Haven, Conn., July 30, 1947, Carnegie Tech.

ATTENBOROUGH, RICHARD: Cambridge, Eng., Aug. 29, 1923. RADA.

AUBERJONOIS, RENE: NYC, June 1, 1940, Carnegie.

AUGER, CLAUDINE: Paris, Apr. 26, Dramatic Cons.

AULIN, EWA: Stockholm, Sweden, Feb. 14, 1950.

AUMONT, JEAN PIERRE: Paris, Jan. 5, 1913. French Nat'l School of Drama.

AUTRY, GENE: Tioga, Texas, Sept. 29, 1907.

AVALON, FRANKIE: (Francis Thomas Avallone) Philadelphia, Sept. 18, 1940.

AYLMER, FELIX: Corsham, Eng., Feb. 21, 1889. Oxford.

AYRES, LEW: Minneapolis, Minn., Dec. 28, 1908.

AZNAVOUR, CHARLES: (Varenagh Aznourian) Paris, May 22, 1924.

BACALL, LAUREN: (Betty Perske) NYC, Sept. 16, 1924. AADA.

BACKUS, JIM: Cleveland, Ohio, Feb. 25, 1913. AADA.

BADDELEY, HERMIONE: Shropshire, Eng., Nov. 13, 1908. Margaret Morris School.

BAILEY, PEARL: Newport News, Va., March 29, 1918.

BAIN, BARBARA: Chicago, Sept. 13, 1934. U. Ill.

Warren Beatty   **Candice Bergen**   **Robert Blake**   **Joan Blondell**   **Dirk Bogarde**

BAKER, CARROLL: Johnstown, Pa., May 28, 1931. St. Petersburg Jr. College.

BAKER, DIANE: Hollywood, Calif, Feb. 25, USC

BAKER, STANLEY: Glamorgan, Wales, Feb. 28, 1928.

BALABAN, ROBERT: Chicago, Aug. 16, 1945, Colgate.

BALIN, INA: Brooklyn, Nov. 12, 1937. NYU.

BALL, LUCILLE: Jamestown, N.Y., Aug. 6, 1911. Chatauqua Musical Inst.

BALSAM, MARTIN: NYC Nov. 4, 1919. Actors Studio.

BANCROFT, ANNE: (Anna Maria Italiano) Bronx, N.Y., Sept. 17, 1931. AADA.

BANNEN, IAN: Airdrie, Scot., June 29, 1928.

BARDOT, BRIGITTE: Paris, Sept. 28, 1934.

BARRIE, WENDY: London, May 8, 1919.

BARRON, KEITH: Mexborough, Eng., Aug. 8, 1936. Sheffield Playhouse.

BARRY, DONALD: (Donald Barry de Acosta) Houston, Tex. Texas School of Mines.

BARRY, GENE: (Eugene Klass) NYC, June 14, 1921.

BARRYMORE, JOHN BLYTH: Beverly Hills, Calif., June 4, 1932. St. John's Military Academy.

BARTHOLOMEW, FREDDIE: London, Mar. 28, 1924.

BASEHART, RICHARD: Zanesville, Ohio, Aug. 31, 1914.

BATES, ALAN: Allestree, Derbyshire, Eng., Feb. 17, 1934. RADA.

BAXTER, ALAN: East Cleveland, Ohio, Nov. 19, 1911. Williams U.

BAXTER, ANNE: Michigan City, Ind., May 7, 1923, Ervine School of Drama.

BAXTER, KEITH: South Wales, Apr. 29, 1933, RADA.

BEAL, JOHN: (J. Alexander Bliedung) Joplin, Mo., Aug. 13, 1909. Pa. U.

BEATTY, ROBERT: Hamilton, Ont., Can., Oct. 19, 1909. U. of Toronto.

BEATTY, WARREN: Richmond, Virginia, March 30, 1937.

BEERY, NOAH, JR.: NYC, Aug. 10, 1916. Harvard Military Academy.

BELAFONTE, HARRY: NYC, Mar. 1, 1927.

BELASCO, LEON: Odessa, Russia, Oct. 11, 1902.

BEL GEDDES, BARBARA: NYC, Oct. 31, 1922.

BELL, TOM: Liverpool, Eng., 1932.

BELLAMY, RALPH: Chicago, June 17, 1905.

BELMONDO, JEAN PAUL: Paris, Apr. 9, 1933.

BENEDICT, DIRK: Montana, 1945, Whitman Col.

BENJAMIN, RICHARD: NYC, May 22, 1938, Northwestern U.

BENNETT, BRUCE: (Herman Brix) Tacoma, Wash., U. of Wash.

BENNETT, JILL: Penang, Malay, Dec. 24, 1931.

BENNETT, JOAN: Palisades, N.J., Feb. 27, 1910. St. Margaret's School.

BENSON, ROBBY: Dallas, Tex., Jan. 21, 1956.

BERENSON, MARISSA: NYC, 1947.

BERGEN, CANDICE: Los Angeles, May. 8, 1946.

BERGEN, EDGAR: Chicago, Feb. 16, 1903. Northwestern U.

BERGEN, POLLY: Knoxville, Tenn., July 14, 1930. Compton Jr. College.

BERGER, HELMUT: Salzburg, Aus., 1945.

BERGER, WILLIAM: Austria, Jan. 20, 1928, Columbia.

BERGERAC, JACQUES: Biarritz, France, May 26, 1927. Paris U.

BERGMAN, INGRID: Stockholm, Sweden, Aug. 29, 1915. Royal Dramatic Theatre School.

BERLE, MILTON: (Milton Berlinger) NYC, July 12, 1908. Professional Children's School.

BERLIN, JEANNIE: Los Angeles, Nov. 1, 1949.

BERLINGER, WARREN: Brooklyn, Aug. 31, 1937. Columbia.

BEST, JAMES: Corydon, Ind., July 26, 1926.

BETTGER, LYLE: Philadelphia, Feb. 13, 1915. AADA.

BETZ, CARL: Pittsburgh, Mar. 9. Duquesne, Carnegie Tech.

BEYMER, RICHARD: Avoca, Iowa, Feb. 21, 1939.

BIKEL, THEODORE: Vienna, May 2, 1924. RADA.

BISHOP, JOEY: (Joseph Abraham Gottlieb) Bronx, N.Y., Feb. 3, 1918.

BISHOP, JULIE: (formerly Jacqueline Wells) Denver, Colo., Aug. 30, 1917. Westlake School.

BISSET, JACQUELINE: Waybridge, Eng., Sept. 13, 1944.

BIXBY, BILL: San Francisco, Jan. 22, 1934. U. Cal.

BLACK, KAREN: (Ziegler) Park Ridge, Ill., July 1, 1942. Northwestern.

BLAINE, VIVIAN: (Vivian Stapleton) Newark, N.J., Nov. 21, 1924.

BLAIR, BETSY: (Betsy Boger) NYC, Dec. 11.

BLAIR, JANET: (Martha Jane Lafferty) Blair, Pa., Apr. 23, 1921.

BLAKE, AMANDA: (Beverly Louise Neill) Buffalo, N.Y., Feb. 20.

BLAKE, ROBERT: (Michael Gubitosi) Nutley, N.J., Sept. 18, 1933.

BLAKELY, SUSAN: Frankfurt, Germany 1950. U. Tex.

BLONDELL, JOAN: NYC, Aug. 30, 1909.

BLOOM, CLAIRE: London, Feb. 15, 1931. Badminton School.

BLYTHE, ANN. Mt. Kisco, N.Y., Aug. 16, 1928. New Wayburn Dramatic School.

BOGARDE, DIRK: London, Mar. 28, 1921. Glasgow & Univ. College.

BOLGER, RAY: Dorchester, Mass., Jan. 10, 1906.

BOND, DEREK: Glasgow, Scot., Jan. 26, 1920. Askes School.

BONDI, BEULAH: Chicago, May 3, 1892.

BOONE, PAT: Jacksonville, Fla., June 1, 1934. Columbia U.

BOONE, RICHARD: Los Angeles. June 18, 1917, Stanford U.

BOOTH, SHIRLEY: (Thelma Ford) NYC, Aug. 30, 1907.

BORGNINE, ERNEST: (Borgnino) Hamden, Conn., Jan. 24, 1918. Randall School.

BOTTOMS, TIMOTHY: Santa Barbara, Ca., Aug. 30, 1951.

BOWKER, JUDI: Shawford, Eng., Apr. 6, 1954.

BOWMAN, LEE: Cincinnati, Dec. 28, 1914. AADA.

BOYD, STEPHEN: (William Miller) Belfast, Ire., July 4, 1928.

BOYER, CHARLES: Figeac, France, Aug. 28, 1899. Sorbonne U.

BOYLE, PETER: Philadelphia, Pa., 1937, LaSalle Col.

BRACKEN, EDDIE: NYC, Feb. 7, 1920. Professional Children's School.

BRADY, SCOTT: (Jerry Tierney) Brooklyn, Sept. 13, 1924. Bliss-Hayden Dramatic School.

BRAND, NEVILLE: Kewanee, Ill., Aug. 13, 1921.

Jocelyn Brando   Jim Brown   Diahann Carroll   Dyan Cannon

BRANDO, JOCELYN: San Francisco, Nov. 18, 1919. Lake Forest College. AADA.

BRANDO, MARLON: Omaha, Neb., Apr. 3, 1924. New School of Social Research.

BRASSELLE, KEEFE: Elyria, Ohio, Feb. 7.

BRAZZI, ROSSANO: Bologna, Italy, 1916. U. of Florence.

BRENT, GEORGE: Dublin, Ire., Mar. 15, 1904. Dublin U.

BRENT, ROMNEY: (Romulo Larralde) Saltillo, Mex., Jan. 26, 1902.

BRIAN, DAVID: NYC, Aug. 5, 1914. CCNY.

BRIDGES, BEAU: Los Angeles, Dec. 9, 1941. UCLA.

BRIDGES, JEFF: Los Angeles, Dec. 4, 1949.

BRIDGES, LLOYD: San Leandro, Calif., Jan. 15, 1913.

BRITT, MAY: (Maybritt Wilkins) Sweden, March 22, 1936.

BRODIE, STEVE: (Johnny Stevens) Eldorado, Kan., Nov. 25, 1919.

BROMFIELD, JOHN: (Farron Bromfield) South Bend, Ind., June 11, 1922. St. Mary's College.

BRONSON, CHARLES: (Buchinsky) Ehrenfield, Pa., Nov. 3, 1922.

BROOKS, GERALDINE: (Geraldine Stroock) NYC, Oct. 29, 1925. AADA.

BROWN, BARRY: San Jose, Cal., Apr. 19, 1951, LACC.

BROWN, JAMES: Desdemona, Tex., Mar. 22, 1920. Baylor U.

BROWN, JIM: Manhasset, L.I., N.Y., Feb. 17, 1935 Syracuse U.

BROWN, TOM: NYC, Jan. 6, 1913. Professional Children's School.

BROWNE, CORAL: Melbourne, Aust., July 23, 1913.

BRUCE, VIRGINIA: Minneapolis, Sept. 29, 1910.

BRYNNER, YUL: Sakhalin Island, Japan, July 11, 1915.

BUCHHOLZ, HORST: Berlin, Ger., Dec. 4, 1933. Ludwig Dramatic School.

BUETEL, JACK: Dallas, Tex., Sept. 5, 1917.

BUJOLD, GENEVIEVE: Montreal, Can., July 1, 1942.

BURKE, PAUL: New Orleans, July 21, 1926. Pasadena Playhouse.

BURNETT, CAROL: San Antonio, Tex., Apr. 26, 1933. UCLA.

BURNS, CATHERINE: NYC, Sept. 25, 1945, AADA.

BURNS, GEORGE: (Nathan Birnbaum) NYC, Jan. 20, 1896.

BURR, RAYMOND: New Westminster, B.C., Can., May 21, 1917. Stanford, U. of Cal., Columbia.

BURSTYN, ELLEN: (Edna Rae Gillooly) Detroit, Mich., 1932.

BURTON, RICHARD (Richard Jenkins) Pontrhydyfen, S. Wales, Nov. 10, 1925. Oxford.

BUTTONS, RED: (Aaron Chwatt) NYC, Feb. 5, 1919.

BUZZI, RUTH: Wequetequock, R.I., July 24, 1936. Pasadena Playhouse.

BYGRAVES, MAX: London, Oct. 16, 1922. St. Joseph's School.

BYRNES, EDD: NYC, July 30, 1933. Haaren High.

CAAN, JAMES: Bronx, NY, Mar. 26, 1939.

CABOT, SUSAN: Boston, July 6, 1927.

CAESAR, SID: Yonkers, N.Y., Sept. 8, 1922.

CAGNEY, JAMES: NYC, July 1, 1904. Columbia.

CAGNEY, JEANNE: NYC, Mar. 25, 1919. Hunter.

CAINE, MICHAEL: (Maurice Michelwhite) London, Mar. 14, 1933.

CALHOUN, RORY: (Francis Timothy Durgin) Los Angeles, Aug. 8, 1923.

CALLAN, MICHAEL: (Martin Calinieff) Philadelphia, Nov. 22, 1935.

CALVERT, PHYLLIS: London, Feb. 18, 1917. Margaret Morris School.

CALVET, CORRINE: (Corrine Dibos) Paris, Apr. 30. U. Of Paris.

CAMBRIDGE, GODFREY: NYC, Feb. 26, 1933. CCNY.

CAMERON, ROD: (Rod Cox) Calgary, Alberta, Can., Dec. 7, 1912.

CAMPBELL, GLEN: Delight, Ark. Apr. 22, 1935.

CANALE, GIANNA MARIA: Reggio Calabria, Italy, Sept. 12.

CANNON, DYAN: (Samille Diane Friesen) Jan. 4, 1929, Tacoma, Wash.

CANOVA, JUDY: Jacksonville, Fla., Nov. 20, 1916.

CAPERS, VIRGINIA: Sumter, SC, 1925, Juilliard.

CAPUCINE: (Germaine Lefebvre) Toulon, France, Jan. 6, 1935.

CARDINALE, CLAUDIA: Tunis, N. Africa, Apr. 15, 1939; College Paul Cambon.

CAREY, HARRY, JR.: Saugus, Calif., May 16, Black Fox Military Academy.

CAREY, MACDONALD: Sioux City, Iowa, Mar. 15, 1913. U. of Wisc., U. of Iowa.

CAREY, PHILIP: Hackensack, N.J., July 15, 1925. U. of Miami.

CARMICHAEL, HOAGY: Bloomington, Ind., Nov. 22, 1899. Ind. U.

CARMICHAEL, IAN: Hull, Eng., June 18, 1920. Scarborough College.

CARNE, JUDY: (Joyce Botterill) Northampton, Eng., 1939. Bush-Davis Theatre School.

CARNEY, ART: Mt. Vernon, N.Y., Nov. 4, 1918.

CARON, LESLIE: Paris, July 1, 1931. Nat'l Conservatory, Paris.

CARR, VIKKI: (Florence Cardona) July 19, 1942. San Fermando Col.

CARRADINE, DAVID: Hollywood, Dec. 8, 1936. San Francisco State.

CARRADINE, JOHN: NYC, Feb. 5, 1906.

CARREL, DANY: Tourane, Indochina, Sept. 20, 1936. Marseilles Cons.

CARROLL, DIAHANN: (Johnson) NYC, July 17, 1935. NYU.

CARROLL, JOHN: (Julian LaFaye) New Orleans.

CARROLL, MADELEINE: West Bromwich, Eng., Feb. 26, 1906. Birmingham U.

CARROLL, PAT: Shreveport, La., May 5, 1927. Catholic U.

CARSON, JOHN DAVID: 1951, Calif. Valley Col.

CARSON, JOHNNY: Corning, Iowa, Oct. 23, 1925. U. of Neb.

CARSTEN, PETER: (Ransenthaler) Weissenberg, Bavaria, Apr. 30, 1929; Munich Akademie for Actors.

CASH, ROSALIND: Atlantic City, NJ, Dec. 31, 1938, CCNY.

CASON, BARBARA: Memphis, Tenn., Nov. 15, 1933, UIowa.

CASS, PEGGY: (Mary Margaret) Boston, May 21, 1925.

CASSAVETES, JOHN: NYC, Dec. 9, 1929. Colgate College, Academy of Dramatic Arts.

CASSEL, JEAN-PIERRE: Paris, 1932.

CASSIDY, DAVID: NYC, Apr. 12, 1950.

CASSIDY, JOANNA: Camden, NJ, 1944, Syracuse U.

Gower Champion   James Coco   Linda Cristal   Alex Cord

CASTELLANO, RICHARD: Bronx, NY, Sept. 3, 1934.

CAULFIELD, JOAN: Orange, N.J., June 1. Columbia U.

CAVANI, LILIANA: Bologna, Italy, Jan. 12, 1937; UBologna.

CELI, ADOLFO: Sicily, July 27, 1922, Rome Academy.

CHAKIRIS, GEORGE: Norwood, O., Sept. 16, 1933.

CHAMBERLAIN, RICHARD: Beverly Hills, Cal., March 31, 1935. Pomona.

CHAMPION, GOWER: Geneva, Ill., June 22, 1921.

CHAMPION, MARGE: Los Angeles, Sept. 2, 1926.

CHANNING, CAROL: Seattle, Jan. 31, 1921. Bennington.

CHAPLIN, CHARLES: London, Apr. 16, 1889.

CHAPLIN, GERALDINE: Santa Monica, Cal. July 31, 1944. Royal Ballet.

CHAPLIN, SYDNEY: Los Angeles, Mar. 31, 1926. Lawrenceville.

CHARISSE, CYD: (Tula Ellice Finklea) Amarillo, Tex., Mar. 3, 1923. Hollywood Professional School.

CHASE, ILKA: NYC, Apr. 8, 1905.

CHER: (Cheryl La Piere) 1946.

CHIARI, WALTER: Verona, Italy, 1930.

CHRISTIAN, LINDA: (Blanca Rosa Welter) Tampico, Mex., Nov. 13, 1923.

CHRISTIE, JULIE: Chukua, Assam, India, Apr. 14, 1941.

CHRISTOPHER, JORDAN: Youngstown, O., Oct. 23, 1940. Kent State.

CHURCHILL, SARAH: London, Oct. 7, 1916.

CILENTO, DIANE: Queensland, Australia, Oct. 5, 1933. AADA.

CLARK, DANA: NYC, Feb. 18, 1915. Cornell, Johns Hopkins U.

CLARK, DICK: Mt. Vernon, N.Y., Nov. 30, 1929, Syracuse University.

CLARK, PETULA: Epsom England, Nov. 15, 1932.

CLARK, MAE: Philadelphia, Aug. 16, 1910.

CLEMENTS, STANLEY: Long Island, N.Y., July 16, 1926.

CLOONEY, ROSEMARY: Maysville Ky., May 23, 1928.

COBB, LEE J.: NYC, Dec. 8, 1911. CCNY.

COBURN, JAMES: Laurel, Neb., Aug. 31, 1928. LACC.

COCA, IMOGENE: Philadelphia, Nov. 18, 1908.

COCO, JAMES: NYC, Mar. 21, 1929.

CODY, KATHLEEN: Bronx, NY, Oct. 30, 1953.

COLBERT, CLAUDETTE: (Claudette Chauchoin) Paris, Sept. 13, 1907. Art Students League.

COLE, GEORGE: London, Apr. 22, 1925.

COLLINS, JOAN: London, May 23, 1933. Francis Holland School.

COMER, ANJANETTE: Dawson, Tex., Aug. 7, 1942. Baylor, Tex. U.

CONANT, OLIVER: NYC, Nov. 15, 1955; Dalton.

CONNERY, SEAN: Edinburgh, Scot. Aug. 25, 1930.

CONNORS, CHUCK: (Kevin Joseph Connors) Brooklyn, Apr. 10, 1924. Seton Hall College.

CONRAD, WILLIAM: Louisville, Ky., Sept. 27, 1920.

CONTE, RICHARD: (Nicholas Conte) NYC, Mar. 24, 1914. Neighborhood Playhouse.

COOGAN, JACKIE: Los Angeles, Oct. 25, 1914. Villanova College.

COOK, ELISHA, JR.: San Francisco, Dec. 26, 1907. St. Albans.

COOPER, BEN: Hartford, Conn., Sept. 30. Columbia U.

COOPER, JACKIE: Los Angeles, Sept. 15, 1921.

COOTE, ROBERT: London, Feb. 4, 1909. Hurstpierpont College.

CORBY, ELLEN: (Hansen) Racine, Wisc., June 13, 1914.

CORCORAN, DONNA: Quincy, Mass., Sept. 29.

CORD, ALEX: (Viespi) Floral Park, L.I., Aug. 3, 1931. NYU, Actors Studio.

CORDAY, MARA: (Marilyn Watts) Santa Monica, Calif., Jan. 3, 1932.

COREY, JEFF: NYC, Aug. 10, 1914. Fagin School.

CORRI, ADRIENNE: Glasgow, Scot., Nov. 13, 1933. RADA.

CORTESA, VALENTINA: Milan, Italy, Jan. 1, 1925.

COSBY, BILL: Philadelphia, 1937. Temple U.

COTTEN, JOSEPH: Petersburg, Va., May 13, 1905.

COURTENAY, TOM: Hull, Eng., Feb. 25, 1937. RADA.

CORLAN, ANTHONY: Cork City, Ire., May 9, 1947; Birmingham School of Dramatic Arts.

COURTLAND, JEROME: Knoxville, Tenn., Dec. 27, 1926.

CRABBE, BUSTER (LARRY): (Clarence Linden) Oakland, Calif., U. of S. Cal.

CRAIG, JAMES: (James H. Meador) Nashville, Tenn., Feb. 4, 1912. Rice Inst.

CRAIG, MICHAEL: India in 1929.

CRAIN, JEANNE: Barstow, Cal., May 25, 1925.

CRANE, BOB: Waterbury, Conn., July 13.

CRAWFORD, BRODERICK: Philadelphia, Dec. 9, 1911.

CRAWFORD, JOAN: (Billie Cassin) San Antonio, Tex., Mar. 23, 1908.

CRENNA, RICHARD: Los Angeles, Nov. 30, 1927. USC.

CRISTAL, LINDA: (Victoria Moya) Buenos Aires, 1935.

CROSBY, BING: (Harry Lillith Crosby) Tacoma, Wash., May 2, 1904. Gonzaga College.

CROWLEY, PAT: Olyphant, Pa., Sept. 17, 1933.

CULLUM, JOHN: Knoxville, Tenn., Mar. 2, 1930, UTenn.

CULP, ROBERT: Oakland, Calif., Aug. 16, 1930. U. Wash.

CULVER, CALVIN: Canandaigua, NY, 1943.

CUMMINGS, CONSTANCE: Seattle, Wash., May 15, 1910.

CUMMINGS, ROBERT: Joplin, Mo., June 9, 1910. Carnegie Tech.

CUMMINS, PEGGY: Prestatyn, N. Wales, Dec. 18, 1926. Alexandra School.

CURTIS, KEENE: Salt Lake City, U., Feb. 15, 1925, U. Utah.

CURTIS, TONY: (Bernard Schwartz) NYC, June 3, 1925.

CUSHING, PETER: Kenley, Surrey, Eng., May 26, 1913.

DAHL, ARLENE: Minneapolis, Aug. 11, 1927. U. Minn.

DALLESANDRO, JOE: Pensacola, Fla., Dec. 31, 1948.

DALTON, TIMOTHY: Wales, 1945; RADA.

DAMONE, VIC: (Vito Farinola) Brooklyn, June 12, 1928.

DANIELS, WILLIAM: Bklyn, Mar. 31, 1927. Northwestern.

DANNER, BLYTHE: Philadelphia, Pa., Bard Col.

DANO, ROYAL: NYC, Nov. 16, 1922, NYU.

DANTE, MICHAEL: (Ralph Vitti) Stamford, Conn., 1935. U Miami.

DANTINE, HELMUT: Vienna, Oct. 7, 1918. U. Calif.

DANTON, RAY: NYC, Sept. 19, 1931. Carnegie Tech.

DARBY, KIM: (Deborah Zerby) North Hollywood, Cal., July 8, 1948.

Doris Day

Sammy Davis, Jr.

Catherine Deneuve

Michael Douglas

Agneta Eckemyr

DARCEL, DENISE: (Denise Billecard) Paris, Sept. 8, 1925. U. Dijon.
DARREN, JAMES: Philadelphia, June 8, 1936. Stella Adler School.
DARRIEUX, DANIELLE: Bordeaux, France, May 1, 1917. Lycee LaTour.
DA SILVA, HOWARD: Cleveland, Ohio, May 4, 1909. Carnegie Tech.
DAUPHIN, CLAUDE: Crobeil, France, Aug. 19, 1903. Beaux Arts School.
DAVIDSON, JOHN: Pittsburgh, Dec. 13, 1941. Denison U.
DAVIES, RUPERT: Liverpool, Eng., 1916.
DAVIS, BETTE: Lowell, Mass., Apr. 5, 1908. John Murray Anderson Dramatic School.
DAVIS, OSSIE: Cogdell, Ga., Dec. 18, 1917. Howard U.
DAVIS, SAMMY, JR.: NYC, Dec. 8, 1925.
DAY, DENNIS: (Eugene Dennis McNulty) NYC, May 21, 1917. Manhattan College.
DAY, DORIS: (Doris Kappelhoff) Cincinnati, Apr. 3, 1924.
DAY, LARAINE: (Johnson) Roosevelt, Utah, Oct. 13, 1920.
DAYAN, ASSEF: Israel, 1945. U. Jerusalem.
DEAN, JIMMY: Plainview, Tex., Aug. 10, 1928.
DE CARLO, YVONNE: (Peggy Yvonne Middleton) Vancouver, B.C., Can., Sept. 1, 1924. Vancouver School of Drama.
DEE, FRANCES: Los Angeles, Nov. 26, 1907. Chicago U.
DEE, JOEY: (Joseph Di Nicola) Passaic, N.J., June 11, 1940. Patterson State College.
DEE, RUBY: Cleveland, O., Oct. 27, Hunter Col.
DEE, SANDRA: (Alexandra Zuck) Bayonne, N.J., Apr. 23, 1942.
DE FORE, DON: Cedar Rapids, Iowa, Aug. 25, 1917. U. Iowa.
DE HAVEN, GLORIA: Los Angeles, July 23, 1925.
DE HAVILLAND, OLIVIA: Tokyo, Japan, July 1, 1916. Notre Dame Convent School.
DELL, GABRIEL: Barbados, BWI, Oct. 7, 1930.
DELON, ALAIN: Sceaux, Fr., Nov. 8, 1935.
DEL RIO, DOLORES: (Dolores Ansunsolo) Durango, Mex., Aug. 3, 1905. St. Joseph's Convent.
DE NIRO, ROBERT: NYC, Aug. 17, 1943, Stella Adler.

DENISON, MICHAEL: Doncaster, York, Eng., Nov. 1, 1915. Oxford.
DENEUVE, CATHERINE: Paris, Oct. 22, 1943.
DENNIS, SANDY: Hastings, Neb., Apr. 27, 1937. Actors Studio.
DEREK, JOHN: Hollywood, Aug. 12, 1926.
DERN, BRUCE: Chicago, June 4, 1936, UPa.
DEVINE, ANDY: Flagstaff, Ariz., Oct. 7, 1905. Ariz. State College.
DEWHURST, COLLEEN: Montreal, June 3, 1926, Lawrence U.
DEXTER, ANTHONY: (Walter Reinhold Alfred Fleischmann) Talmadge, Neb., Jan. 19, 1919. U. Iowa.
DHIEGH, KHIGH: New Jersey 1910.
DICKINSON, ANGIE: Kulm, N. Dak., Sept. 30, 1932. Glendale College.
DIETRICH, MARLENE: (Maria Magdalene von Losch) Berlin, Ger., Dec. 27, 1904. Berlin Music Academy.
DIFFRING, ANTON: Loblenz, Ger. Berlin Dramatic Art School.
DILLER, PHYLLIS: Lima, O., July 17, 1917. Bluffton College.
DILLMAN, BRADFORD: San Francisco, Apr. 14, 1930.
DOBSON, TAMARA: Baltimore, Md., 1947, Md. Inst. of Art.
DOMERGUE, FAITH: New Orleans, June 16, 1925.
DONAHUE, TROY: (Merle Johnson) NYC, Jan. 27, 1937. Columbia U.
DONNELL, JEFF: (Jean Donnell) South Windham, Me., July 10, 1921. Yale Drama School.
DONNELLY, RUTH: Trenton, N.J., May 17, 1896.
DORS, DIANA: Swindon, Wilshire, Eng., Oct. 23, 1931. London Academy of Music.
D'ORSAY, FIFI: Montreal, Can., Apr. 16, 1904.
DOUGLAS, KIRK: Amsterdam, N.Y., Dec. 9, 1916. St. Lawrence U.
DOUGLAS, MELVYN: (Melvyn Hesselberg) Macon, Ga., Apr. 5, 1901.
DOUGLAS, MICHAEL: Hollywood, Sept. 25, 1944, U. Cal.
DOWN, LESLEY ANN: London, Mar. 17, 1954.
DRAKE, BETSY: Paris, Sept. 11, 1923.

DRAKE, CHARLES: (Charles Rupert) NYC, Oct. 2, 1914. Nichols College.
DREW, ELLEN: (formerly Terry Ray) Kansas City, Mo., Nov. 23, 1915.
DREYFUSS, RICHARD: Brooklyn, NY, 1948.
DRIVAS, ROBERT: Chicago, Oct. 7, 1938. U. Chi.
DRU, JOANNE: (Joanne LaCock) Logan, W. Va., Jan. 31, 1923. John Robert Powers School.
DUFF, HOWARD: Bremerton, Wash., Nov. 24, 1917.
DUKE, PATTY: NYC, Dec. 14, 1946.
DULLEA, KEIR: Cleveland, N.J., May 30, 1936. Neighborhood Playhouse, SF State Col.
DUNAWAY, FAYE: Bascom, Fla., Jan, 14, 1941. Fla. U.
DUNCAN, SANDY: Henderson, Tex., Feb. 20, 1946; Len Morris Col.
DUNNE, IRENE: Louisville, Ky., Dec. 20, 1904. Chicago College of Music.
DUNNOCK, MILDRED: Baltimore, Jan. 25, 1906. Johns Hopkins and Columbia U.
DURANTE, JIMMY: NYC, Feb. 10, 1893.
DURNING, CHARLES: Highland Falls, NY, Feb. 28, 1933, NYU.
DUVALL, ROBERT: San Diego, Cal., 1930, Principia Col.
DVORAK, ANN: (Ann McKim) NYC, Aug. 2, 1912.
EASTON, ROBERT: Milwaukee, Nov. 23, 1930. U. of Texas.
EASTWOOD, CLINT: San Francisco, May 31, 1930 LACC.
EATON, SHIRLEY: London, 1937. Aida Foster School.
ECKEMYR, AGNETA: Karlsborg, Swed., July 2. Actors Studio.
EDEN, BARBARA: (Moorhead) Tucson, Ariz., 1934.
EDWARDS, VINCE: NYC, July 9, 1928. AADA.
EGAN, RICHARD: San Francisco, July 29, 1923. Stanford U.
EGGAR, SAMANTHA: London, Mar. 5, 1939.
EKBERG, ANITA: Malmo, Sweden, Sept. 29, 1931.
ELLIOTT, DENHOLM: London, May 31, 1922. Malvern College.
ELSOM, ISOBEL: Cambridge, Eng., Mar. 15, 1894.
ELY, RON: (Ronald Pierce) Hereford, Tex. June 21, 1938.

Richard Erdman	Edith Evans	James Farentino	Mitzi Gaynor	Vincent Gardenia

EMERSON, FAYE: Elizabeth, La., July 8, 1917. San Diego State College.

ENSERRO, MICHAEL: Soldier, Pa., Oct. 5, 1918. Allegheny Col.

ERDMAN, RICHARD: Enid, Okla., June 1, 1925.

ERICKSON, LEIF: Alameda, Calif., Oct. 27, 1911. U. of Calif.

ERICSON, JOHN: Dusseldorf, Ger., Sept. 25, 1926. AADA.

ESMOND, CARL: Vienna, June 14, 1906. U. of Vienna.

EVANS, DALE: (Francis Smith) Uvalde, Texas, Oct. 31, 1912.

EVANS, EDITH: London, Feb. 8, 1888.

EVANS, GENE: Holbrook, Ariz., July 11, 1922.

EVANS, MAURICE: Dorchester, Eng., June 3, 1901.

EVERETT, CHAD: (Ray Cramton) South Bend, Ind., June 11, 1936.

EWELL, TOM: (Yewell Tompkins) Owensboro, Ky., Apr. 29, 1909. U. of Wisc.

FABARES SHELLEY: Los Angeles, Jan. 19, 1944.

FABIAN: (Fabian Forte) Philadelphia, Feb. 6, 1940.

FABRAY, NANETTE: (Ruby Nanette Fabares) San Diego, Oct. 27, 1920.

FAIRBANKS, DOUGLAS JR.: NYC, Dec. 9, 1909, Collegiate School.

FALK, PETER: NYC, Sept. 16, 1927, New School.

FARENTINO, JAMES: Brooklyn, Feb. 24, 1938.

FARR, FELICIA: Westchester, N.Y., Oct. 4, 1932. Penn State College.

FARRELL, CHARLES: Onset Bay, Mass., Aug. 9, 1901. Boston U.

FARROW, MIA: Los Angeles, Feb. 9, 1945.

FAULKNER, GRAHAM: London, Sept. 26, 1947, Webber-Douglas Acad.

FAYE, ALICE: (Ann Leppert) NYC, May 5, 1915.

FELDON, BARBARA: (Hall) Pittsburgh, Mar. 12, 1941. Carnegie Tech.

FELLOWS, EDITH: Boston, May 20, 1923.

FERRER, JOSE: Santurce, P.R., Jan. 8, 1912. Princeton U.

FERRER, MEL: Elberon, N.J., Aug. 25, 1917. Princeton U.

FERRIS, BARBARA: London 1943.

FERZETTI, GABRIELE: Italy 1927; Rome Acad. of Drama.

FIELD, SALLY: Pasadena, Cal., Nov. 6, 1946.

FIGUEROA, RUBEN: NYC 1958.

FINCH, PETER: London, Sept. 28, 1916.

FINNEY, ALBERT: Salford, Lancashire, Eng., May 9, 1936. RADA.

FISHER, EDDIE: Philadelphia, Aug. 10, 1928.

FITZGERALD, GERALDINE: Dublin, Ire., Nov. 28, 1914. Dublin Art School.

FLEMING, RHONDA: (Marilyn Louis) Los Angeles, Aug. 10, 1922.

FLEMYNG, ROBERT: Liverpool, Eng., Jan. 3, 1912. Haileybury College.

FOCH, NINA: Leyden, Holland, Apr. 20, 1924.

FONDA, HENRY: Grand Island, Neb., May 16, 1905. Minn. U.

FONDA, JANE: NYC, Dec. 21, 1937. Vassar.

FONDA, PETER: NYC, Feb. 23, 1939. U. of Omaha.

FONTAINE, JOAN: Tokyo, Japan, Oct. 22, 1917.

FORD, GLENN: (Gwyllyn Samuel Newton Ford) Quebec, Can., May 1, 1916.

FORD, PAUL: Baltimore, Nov. 2, 1901. Dartmouth.

FOREST, MARK: (Lou Degni) Brooklyn, Jan. 1933.

FORREST, STEVE: Huntsville, Tex., Sept. 29. UCLA.

FORSTER, ROBERT: (Foster, Jr.) Rochester, N.Y., July 13, 1941. Rochester U.

FORSYTHE, JOHN: Penn's Grove, N.J., Jan. 29, 1918.

FOX, EDWARD: London, 1937, RADA.

FOX, JAMES: London, 1939.

FRANCIS, CONNIE: (Constance Franconero) Newark, N.J., Dec. 12, 1938.

FRANCIOSA, ANTHONY: NYC, Oct. 25, 1928.

FRANCIS, ANNE: Ossining, N.Y., Sept. 16.

FRANCIS, ARLENE: (Arlene Kazanjian) Boston, Oct. 20, 1908. Finch School.

FRANCISCUS, JAMES: Clayton, Mo., Jan. 31, 1934, Yale.

FRANCKS, DON: Vancouver, Can., Feb. 28, 1932.

FRANZ, ARTHUR: Perth Amboy, N.J., Feb. 29, 1920. Blue Ridge College.

FRANZ, EDUARD: Milwaukee, Wisc., Oct. 31, 1902.

FRAZIER, SHEILA: NYC, 1949.

FREEMAN, AL, JR.: San Antonio, Texas, 1934. CCLA.

FREEMAN, MONA: Baltimore, Md., June 9, 1926.

FREY, LEONARD: Brooklyn, Sept. 4, 1938, Neighborhood Playhouse.

FURNEAUX, YVONNE: Lille, France, 1928. Oxford U.

GABEL, MARTIN: Philadelphia, June 19, 1912. AADA.

GABIN, JEAN: Villette, France, May 17, 1904.

GABOR, EVA: Budapest, Hungary, Feb. 11, 1925.

GABOR, ZSA ZSA: (Sari Gabor) Budapest, Hungary, Feb. 6, 1923.

GAM, RITA: Pittsburgh, Pa., Apr. 2, 1928.

GARBER, VICTOR: Montreal, Can., Mar. 16, 1949.

GARBO, GRETA: (Greta Gustafson) Stockholm, Sweden, Sept. 18, 1906.

GARDENIA, VINCENT: Naples, Italy, Jan. 7, 1922.

GARDINER, REGINALD: Wimbledon, Eng., Feb. 1903. RADA.

GARDNER, AVA: Smithfield, N.C., Dec. 24, 1922. Atlantic Christian College.

GARFIELD, ALLEN: Newark, N.J., Nov. 22, 1939. Actors Studio.

GARNER, JAMES: (James Baumgarner) Norman, Okla., Apr. 7, 1928. Okla. U.

GARNER, PEGGY ANN: Canton, Ohio, Feb. 3, 1932.

GARR, TERI: Lakewood, Ohio, 1952.

GARRETT, BETTY: St. Joseph, Mo., May 23, 1919. Annie Wright Seminary.

GARRISON, SEAN: NYC, Oct. 19, 1937.

GARSON, GREER: Ireland, Sept. 29, 1908.

GASSMAN, VITTORIO: Genoa, Italy, Sept. 1, 1922. Rome Academy of Dramatic Art.

GAVIN, JOHN: Los Angeles, Apr. 8, 1935. Stanford U.

GAYNOR, JANET: Philadelphia, Oct. 6, 1906.

GAYNOR, MITZI: (Francesca Marlene Von Gerber) Chicago, Sept. 4, 1930.

GAZZARA, BEN: NYC, Aug. 28, 1930.

GEER, WILL: Frankfort, Ind., Mar. 9, 1902, Columbia.

GEESON, JUDY: Arundel, Eng., Sept. 10, 1948, Corona.

Chief Dan George   **Julie Gholson**   **Charles Grodin**   **Elizabeth Hartman**   **David Hartman**

GENN, LEO: London, Aug. 9, 1905. Cambridge.

GEORGE, CHIEF DAN: (Geswanouth Slaholt) North Vancouver, Can., June 24, 1899.

GHOLSON, JULIE: Birmingham, Ala., June 4, 1958.

GIANNINI, GIANCARLO: Spezia, Italy, Aug. 1, 1942; Rome Acad. of Drama.

GIELGUD, JOHN: London, Apr. 14, 1904. RADA.

GILLIAM, DAVID: Vancouver, Can.

GILLMORE, MARGALO: London, May 31, 1897. AADA.

GILMORE, VIRGINIA: (Sherman Poole) Del Monte, Calif., July 26, 1919. U. of Calif.

GINGOLD, HERMIONE: London, Dec. 9, 1897.

GISH, LILLIAN: Springfield, Ohio, Oct. 14, 1896.

GLEASON, JACKIE: Brooklyn, Feb. 26, 1916.

GODDARD, PAULETTE: (Levy) Great Neck, N.Y., June 3, 1911.

GONZALES-GONZALEZ, PEDRO: Aguilares, Tex., Dec. 21, 1926.

GORDON, GALE: (Aldrich) NYC, Feb. 2, 1906.

GORDON, RUTH: (Jones) Wollaston, Mass., Oct. 30, 1896. AADA.

GORING, MARIUS: Newport, Isle of Wright; 1912; Cambridge; Old Vic.

GORMAN, CLIFF: Jamaica, NY, Oct. 13, 1936, NYU.

GOULD, ELLIOTT: (Goldstein); Bklyn, Aug. 29, 1938. Columbia U.

GOULET, ROBERT: Lawrence, Mass., Nov. 26, 1933. Edmonton School.

GRAHAME, GLORIA: (Gloria Grahame Hallward) Los Angeles, Nov. 28, 1929.

GRANGER, FARLEY: San Jose, Calif., July 1, 1925.

GRANGER, STEWART: (James Stewart) London, May 6, 1913. Webber-Douglas School of Acting.

GRANT, CARY: (Archibald Alexander Leach) Bristol, Eng., Jan. 18, 1904.

GRANT, KATHRYN: (Olive Grandstaff) Houston, Tex., Nov. 25, 1933. UCLA.

GRANT, LEE: NYC, Oct. 31, 1929, Juilliard.

GRANVILLE, BONITA: NYC, Feb. 2, 1923.

GRAVES, PETER: (Aurness) Minneapolis, Mar. 18, 1926. U. of Minn.

GRAY, COLEEN: (Doris Jensen) Staplehurst, Neb., Oct. 23, 1922. Hamline U.

GRAYSON, KATHRYN: (Zelma Hedrick) Winston-Salem, N.C., Feb. 9, 1923.

GREENE, LORNE: Ottawa, Can., Feb. 12, 1915.

GREENE, RICHARD: Plymouth, Eng., Aug. 25, 1918. Cardinal Vaughn School.

GREENWOOD, JOAN: London, 1919. RADA.

GREER, JANE: Washington, D.C., Sept. 9, 1924.

GREER, MICHAEL: Galesburg, Ill., Apr. 20, 1943.

GREY, JOEL: (Katz) Cleveland, O., Apr. 11, 1932.

GREY, VIRGINIA: Los Angeles, Mar. 22, 1923.

GRIEM, HELMUT: Hamburg, Ger. UHamburg.

GRIFFITH, ANDY: Mt. Airy, N.C., June 1, 1926. U.N.C.

GRIFFITH, HUGH: Marian Glas, Anglesey, N. Wales, May 30, 1912.

GRIMES, GARY: San Francisco, June 2, 1955.

GRIMES, TAMMY: Lynn, Mass., Jan. 30, 1934, Stephens Col.

GRIZZARD, GEORGE: Roanoke Rapids, N.C., Apr. 1, 1928. U.N.C.

GRODIN, CHARLES: Pittsburgh, Pa., Apr. 21, 1935.

GUARDINO, HARRY: Brooklyn, Dec. 23, 1925, Haaren High.

GUINNESS, ALEC: London, Apr. 2, 1914. Pembroke Lodge School.

GWILLIM, DAVID: Plymouth, Eng., Dec. 15, 1948, RADA.

HACKETT, BUDDY: (Leonard Hacker) Brooklyn, Aug. 31, 1924.

HACKETT, JOAN: NYC, May 1, Actors Studio.

HACKMAN, GENE: San Bernardino, Jan. 30, 1931.

HADDON, DALE: Montreal, Can., May 26, 1949, Neighborhood Playhouse.

HALE, BARBARA: DeKalb, Ill., Apr. 18, 1922. Chicago Academy of Fine Arts.

HAMILTON, GEORGE: Memphis, Tenn., Aug. 12, 1939. Hackley School.

HAMILTON, MARGARET: Cleveland, Ohio, Dec. 9, 1902. Hathaway-Brown School.

HAMILTON, NEIL: Lynn, Mass., Sept. 9, 1899.

HAMPSHIRE, SUSAN: London, May 12, 1941.

HARDIN, TY: (Orison Whipple Hungerford II) NYC, 1930.

HARDING, ANN: (Dorothy Walton Gatley) Fort Sam Houston, Texas, Aug. 17, 1904.

HARRINGTON, PAT: NYC, Aug. 13, 1929, Fordham U.

HARRIS, BARBARA: (Sandra Markowitz) Evanston, Ill., 1937.

HARRIS, JULIE: Grosse Pointe, Mich., Dec. 2, 1925. Yale Drama School.

HARRIS, RICHARD: Limerick, Ire., Oct. 1, 1930. London Acad.

HARRIS, ROSEMARY: Ashby, Eng., Sept. 19, 1930. RADA

HARRISON, NOEL: London, Jan. 29, 1936.

HARRISON, REX: Huyton, Cheshire, Eng., Mar. 5, 1908.

HARTMAN, DAVID: Pawtucket, RI., May 19. Duke U.

HARTMAN, ELIZABETH: Youngstown, O., Dec. 23, 1941. Carnegie Tech.

HAVER, JUNE: Rock Island, Ill., June 10, 1926.

HAVOC, JUNE: (June Hovick) Seattle, Wash., Nov. 8, 1916.

HAWN, GOLDIE: Washington, DC, Nov. 21, 1945.

HAYDEN, LINDA: Stanmore, Eng., Aida Foster School.

HAYDEN, STERLING: (John Hamilton) Montclair, N.J., March 26, 1916.

HAYES, HELEN: (Helen Brown) Washington, D.C., Oct. 10, 1900. Sacred Heart Convent.

HAYES, MARGARET: (Maggie) Baltimore, Dec. 5, 1925.

HAYWARD, SUSAN: (Edythe Marrener) Brooklyn, June 30, 1919.

HAYWORTH, RITA: (Margarita Cansino) NYC, Oct. 17, 1919.

HEATHERTON, JOEY: NYC, Sept. 14, 1944.

HECKART, EILEEN: Columbus, Ohio, Mar. 29, 1919. Ohio State U.

HEDISON, DAVID: Providence, R.I., May 20, 1929. Brown U.

HEMMINGS, DAVID: Guilford, Eng.; Nov. 18, 1938.

HENDERSON, MARCIA: Andover, Mass., July 22, 1932. AADA.

HENDRIX, WANDA: Jacksonville, Fla., Nov. 3, 1928.

221

Buck Henry   Gayle Hunnicutt   Ken Howard   Glynis Johns   Page Johnson

HENDRY, GLORIA: Jacksonville, Fla., 1949.

HENREID, PAUL: Trieste, Jan. 10, 1908.

HENRY, BUCK: (Zuckerman) NYC, 1931; Dartmouth.

HEPBURN, AUDREY: Brussels, Belgium, May 4, 1929.

HEPBURN, KATHARINE: Hartford, Conn., Nov. 8, 1909. Bryn Mawr.

HESTON, CHARLTON: Evanston, Ill., Oct. 4, 1924. Northwestern U.

HEYWOOD, ANNE: (Violet Pretty) Birmingham, Eng., Dec. 11, 1933.

HICKMAN, DARRYL: Hollywood, Cal., July 28, 1931. Loyola U.

HICKMAN, DWAYNE: Los Angeles, May 18, 1934. Loyola.

HILL, STEVEN: Seattle, Wash., Feb. 24, 1922. U. Wash.

HILL, TERENCE: (Mario Giotti) Venice, Italy, 1941, URome.

HILLER, WENDY: Bramhall, Cheshire, Eng., Aug. 15, 1912. Winceby House School.

HOFFMAN, DUSTIN: Los Angeles, Aug. 8, 1937. Pasadena Playhouse.

HOLBROOK, HAL: (Harold) Cleveland, O., Feb. 17, 1925. Denison.

HOLDEN, WILLIAM: O'Fallon, Ill., Apr. 17, 1918. Pasadena Jr. Coll.

HOLLIMAN, EARL: Tennesas Swamp, Delhi, La., Sept. 11, UCLA.

HOLLOWAY, STANLEY: London, Oct. 1, 1890.

HOLM, CELESTE: NYC, Apr. 29, 1919.

HOMEIER, SKIP: (George Vincent Homeier) Chicago, Oct. 5, 1930. UCLA.

HOMOLKA, OSCAR: Vienna, Aug. 12, 1898. Vienna Dramatic Academy.

HOOKS, ROBERT: Washington, D.C., Apr. 18, 1937. Temple.

HOPE, BOB: London, May 26, 1904.

HOPPER, DENNIS: Dodge City, Kan., May 17, 1936.

HORNE, LENA: Brooklyn, June 30, 1917.

HORTON, ROBERT: Los Angeles, July 29, 1924. UCLA.

HOUGHTON, KATHARINE: Hartford, Conn., Mar. 10, 1945. Sarah Lawrence.

HOUSER, JERRY: Los Angeles, July 14, 1952; Valley Jr. Col.

HOUSEMAN, JOHN: Bucharest, Sept. 22, 1902.

HOWARD, KEN: El Centro, Cal., Mar. 28, 1944, Yale.

HOWARD, RON: Duncan, Okla., Mar. 1, 1954.

HOWARD, RONALD: Norwood, Eng., Apr. 7, 1918. Jesus College.

HOWARD, TREVOR: Kent, Eng., Sept. 29, 1916. RADA.

HOWES, SALLY ANN: London, July 20, 1934.

HUDSON, ROCK: (Roy Scherer Fitzgerald) Winnetka, Ill., Nov. 17, 1925.

HUGHES, BARNARD: Bedford Hills, NY, July 16, 1915, Manhattan Col.

HUNNICUTT, ARTHUR: Gravelly, Ark., Feb. 17, 1911. Ark. State.

HUNNICUT, GAYLE: Ft. Worth, Tex., Feb. 6, 1943. UCLA.

HUNT, MARSHA: Chicago, Oct. 17, 1917.

HUNTER, IAN: Cape Town, S.A., June 13, 1900. St. Andrew's College.

HUNTER, KIM: (Janet Cole) Detroit, Nov. 12, 1922.

HUNTER, TAB: (Arthur Galien) NYC, July 11, 1931.

HUSSEY, RUTH: Providence, R.I., Oct. 30, 1917. U. of Mich.

HUSTON, JOHN: Nevada, Mo., Aug. 5, 1906.

HUTTON, BETTY: (Betty Thornberg) Battle Creek, Mich., Feb. 26, 1921.

HUTTON, LAUREN: (Mary): Charleston, S.C., Nov. 17, 1943. Newcomb Col.

HUTTON, ROBERT: (Winne) Kingston, N.Y., June 11, 1920. Blair Academy.

HYDE-WHITE, WILFRID: Gloucestershire, Eng., May 13, 1903. RADA.

HYER, MARTHA: Fort Worth, Tex., Aug. 10, 1930. Northwestern U.

IRELAND, JOHN: Vancouver, B.C., Can., Jan. 30, 1915.

IVES, BURL: Hunt Township, Ill., June 14, 1909. Charleston Ill. Teachers College.

JACKSON, ANNE: Alleghany, Pa., Sept. 3, 1926. Neighborhood Playhouse.

JACKSON, GLENDA: Hoylake, Cheshire, Eng., May 9, 1936. RADA.

JACOBI, LOU: Toronto, Can., Dec. 28, 1913.

JACOBY, SCOTT: Chicago, Nov. 19, 1956.

JAECKEL, RICHARD: Long Beach, N.Y., Oct. 10, 1926.

JAFFE, SAM: NYC, Mar. 8, 1898.

JAGGER, DEAN: Lima, Ohio, Nov. 7, 1903. Wabash College.

JANSSEN, DAVID: (David Meyer) Naponee, Neb., Mar. 27, 1930.

JARMAN, CLAUDE, JR.: Nashville, Tenn., Sept. 27, 1934.

JASON, RICK: NYC, May 21, 1926. AADA.

JEAN, GLORIA: (Gloria Jean Schoonover) Buffalo, N.Y. Apr. 14, 1928.

JEFFREYS, ANNE: (Carmichael) Goldsboro, N.C., Jan. 26, 1923. Anderson College.

JEFFRIES, LIONEL: London, 1927, RADA.

JERGENS, ADELE: Brooklyn, Nov. 26, 1922.

JESSEL, GEORGE: NYC, Apr. 3, 1898.

JOHNS, GLYNIS: Durban, S. Africa, Oct. 5, 1923.

JOHNSON, CELIA: Richmond, Surrey, Eng., Dec. 18, 1908. RADA.

JOHNSON, PAGE: Welch, W. Va., Aug. 25, 1930. Ithaca.

JOHNSON, RAFER: Hillsboro, Tex., Aug. 18, 1935. UCLA.

JOHNSON, RICHARD: Essex, Eng., 1927. RADA.

JOHNSON, VAN: Newport, R.I., Aug. 28, 1916.

JONES, CAROLYN: Amarillo, Tex., Apr. 28, 1933.

JONES, CHRISTOPHER: Jackson, Tenn., Aug. 18, 1941, Actors Studio.

JONES, DEAN: Morgan County, Ala., Jan. 25, 1936. Ashburn College.

JONES, JACK: Bel-Air, Calif., Jan. 14, 1938.

JONES, JAMES EARL: Arkabutla, Miss., Jan 17, 1931. U. Mich.

JONES, JENNIFER: (Phyllis Isley) Tulsa, Okla., Mar. 2, 1919. AADA.

JONES, SHIRLEY: Smithton, Pa., March 31, 1934.

JONES, TOM: (Thomas Jones Woodward) Pontypridd, Wales, June 7, 1940.

JORDAN, RICHARD: NYC, July 19, 1938, Harvard.

JORY, VICTOR: Dawson City, Can., Nov. 28, 1902, CalU.

| Diane Keaton | Aron Kincaid | Shirley Knight | Burt Lancaster | Angela Lansbury |

JOURDAN, LOUIS: Marseilles, France, June 18, 1921.

JURADO, KATY: (Maria Christina Jurado Garcia) Guadalajara, Mex., 1927.

KAHN, MADELINE: Boston, Mass., Sept. 29, 1942, Hofstra U.

KANE, CAROL: Cleveland, O., 1952.

KASZNAR, KURT: Vienna, Aug. 12, 1913. Gymnasium, Vienna.

KAUFMANN, CHRISTINE: Lansdorf, Graz, Austria, Jan. 11, 1945.

KAYE, DANNY: (David Daniel Kominski) Brooklyn, Jan. 18, 1913.

KAYE, STUBBY: NYC, Nov. 11, 1918.

KEACH, STACY: Savannah, Ga., June 2, 1941; UCal., Yale.

KEATON, DIANE: (Hall) Los Angeles, Ca., Jan. 5, 1946. Neighborhood Playhouse.

KEDROVA, LILA: Greece, 1918.

KEEL, HOWARD: (Harold Keel) Gillespie, Ill., Apr. 13, 1919.

KEELER, RUBY: (Ethel) Halifax, N.S. Aug. 25, 1909.

KEITH, BRIAN: Bayonne, N.J., Nov. 14, 1921.

KELLERMAN, SALLY: Long Beach, Cal., June 2, 1938; Actors Studio West.

KELLY, GENE: Pittsburgh, Aug. 23, 1912. U. of Pittsburgh.

KELLY, GRACE: Philadelphia, Nov. 12, 1929. AADA.

KELLY, JACK: Astoria, N.Y., Sept. 16, 1927. UCLA.

KELLY, NANCY: Lowell, Mass., Mar. 25, 1921. Bentley School.

KEMP, JEREMY: Chesterfield, Eng., 1935, Central Sch.

KENNEDY, ARTHUR: Worcester, Mass., Feb. 17, 1914. Carnegie Tech.

KENNEDY, GEORGE: NYC, Feb. 18, 1925.

KERR, DEBORAH: Helensburg, Scot., Sept. 30, 1921. Smale Ballet School.

KERR, JOHN: Nov. 15, 1931. Harvard and Columbia.

KIDDER, MARGOT: Yellow Knife, Can., Oct. 17, 1948; UBC.

KILEY, RICHARD: Chicago, Mar. 31, 1922. Loyola.

KINCAID, ARON: (Norman Neale Williams III) Los Angeles, June 15, 1943. UCLA.

KING, ALAN: (Irwin Kniberg) Brooklyn, Dec. 26, 1927.

KITT, EARTHA: North, S.C., Jan. 26, 1928.

KLEMPERER, WERNER: Cologne, Mar. 22, 1920.

KNIGHT, ESMOND: East Sheen, Eng., May 4, 1906.

KNIGHT, SHIRLEY: Goessel, Kan., July 5. Wichita U.

KNOWLES, PATRIC: (Reginald Lawrence Knowles) Horsforth, Eng., Nov. 11, 1911.

KNOX, ALEXANDER: Strathroy, Ont., Can., Jan. 16, 1907.

KNOX, ELYSE: Hartford, Conn., Dec. 14, 1917. Traphagen School.

KOHNER, SUSAN: Los Angeles, Nov. 11, 1936. U. of Calif.

KORVIN, CHARLES: (Geza Korvin Darpathi) Czechoslovakia, Nov. 21. Sorbonne.

KOSLECK, MARTIN: Barkotzen, Ger., Mar. 24, 1914. Max Reinhardt School.

KOTTO, YAPHET: NYC, Nov. 15, 1937.

KREUGER, KURT: St. Moritz, Switz., July 23, 1917. U. of London.

KRUGER, HARDY: Berlin, Ger., April. 12, 1928.

KUNTSMANN, DORIS: Hamburg, 1944.

KWAN, NANCY: Hong Kong, May 19, 1939. Royal Ballet.

LACY, JERRY: Sioux City, I., Mar. 27, 1936, LACC.

LAMARR, HEDY: (Hedwig Kiesler) Vienna, Sept. 11, 1915.

LAMAS, FERNANDO: Buenos Aires, Jan. 9, 1920.

LAMB, GIL: Minneapolis, June 14, 1906. U. of Minn.

LAMOUR, DOROTHY: Dec. 10, 1914. Spence School.

LANCASTER, BURT: NYC, Nov. 2, 1913. NYU.

LANCHESTER, ELSA: (Elsa Sullivan) London, Oct. 28, 1902.

LANDON, MICHAEL: (Eugene Orowitz) Collingswood, N.J., 1936.

LANE, ABBE: Brooklyn, Dec. 14, 1935.

LANGAN, GLENN: Denver, Colo., July 8, 1917.

LANGE, HOPE: Redding Ridge, Conn., Nov. 28, 1933. Reed College.

LANGTON, PAUL: Salt Lake City, Apr. 17, 1913. Travers School of Theatre.

LANSBURY, ANGELA: London, Oct. 16, 1925. London Academy of Music.

LANSING, ROBERT: (Brown) San Diego, Cal., June 5.

LASSER, LOUISE: NYC. Brandeis U.

LAURIE, PIPER: (Rosetta Jacobs) Detroit, Jan. 22, 1932.

LAW, JOHN PHILLIP: Hollywood, Sept. 7, 1937. Neighborhood Playhouse., UHawaii.

LAWFORD, PETER: London, Sept. 7, 1923.

LAWRENCE, BARBARA: Carnegie, Okla., Feb. 24, 1930. UCLA.

LAWRENCE, CAROL: (Laraia) Melrose Park, Ill., Sept. 5, 1935.

LAWSON, LEIGH: Atherston, Eng., July 21, 1945, RADA.

LEACHMAN, CLORIS: Des Moines, Iowa, Apr. 30, 1930. Northwestern U.

LEDERER, FRANCIS: Karlin, Prague, Czechoslovakia, Nov. 6, 1906.

LEE, CHRISTOPHER: London, May 27, 1922. Wellington College.

LEE, MICHELE: (Dusiak) Los Angeles, June 24, 1942. LACC.

LEIBMAN, RON: NYC, Oct. 11, 1937, Ohio Wesleyan.

LEIGH, JANET: (Jeanette Helen Morrison) Merced, Calif., July 6, 1927. College of Pacific.

LEIGHTON, MARGARET: Barnt Green, Worcestershire, Eng., Feb. 26, 1922. Church of England Col.

LEMBECK, HARVEY: Brooklyn, Apr. 15, 1923. U. of Ala.

LEMMON, JACK: Boston, Feb. 8, 1925. Harvard.

LENZ, RICK: Springfield, Ill., Nov. 21, 1939. U. Mich.

LEONARD, SHELDON: (Bershad) NYC, Feb. 22, 1907, Syracuse U.

LEROY, PHILIPPE: Paris, Oct. 15, 1930; UParis.

LESLIE, BETHEL: NYC, Aug. 3, 1929. Breaney School.

LESLIE, JOAN: (Joan Brodell) Detroit, Jan. 26, 1925. St. Benedict's.

LESTER, MARK: Oxford, Eng., July 11, 1958.

LETTIERI, AL: NYC, Feb. 24, Actors Studio.

LEVENE, SAM: NYC, 1907.

LEWIS, JERRY: Newark, N.J., Mar. 16, 1926.

LIGON, TOM: New Orleans, La., Sept. 10, 1945.

LILLIE, BEATRICE: Toronto, Can., May 29, 1898.

LINCOLN, ABBEY: (Anna Marie Woolridge) Chicago, Aug. 6, 1930.

223

Gina Lollobrigida   Jacques Marin   Marsha Mason   Peter McEnery   Elaine May

LINDFORS, VIVECA: Uppsala, Sweden, Dec. 29, 1920. Stockholm Royal Dramatic School.

LISI, VIRNA: Rome, 1938.

LITTLE, CLEAVON: Chickasha, Okla., June 1, 1939, San Diego State.

LIVESEY, ROGER: Barry, Wales, June 25, 1906. Westminster School.

LOCKE, SONDRA: Shelbyville, Tenn., 1947.

LOCKHART, JUNE: NYC, June 15, 1925. Westlake School.

LOCKWOOD, GARY: Van Nuys, Cal., 1937.

LOCKWOOD, MARGARET: Karachi, Pakistan, Sept. 15, 1916. RADA.

LOLLOBRIGIDA, GINA: Subiaco, Italy, 1928. Rome Academy of Fine Arts.

LOM, HERBERT: Prague, Czechoslovakia, 1917. Prague U.

LONDON, JULIE: (Julie Peck) Santa Rosa, Calif., Sept. 26, 1926.

LOPEZ, PERRY: NYC, July 22, 1931. NYU.

LORD, JACK: (John Joseph Ryan) NYC, Dec. 30, 1928. NYU.

LOREN, SOPHIA: (Sofia Scicolone) Rome, Italy, Sept. 20, 1934.

LOUISE, TINA: (Blacker) NYC, Feb. 11, 1934. Miami U.

LOVELACE, LINDA: Bryan, Tex., 1952.

LOY, MYRNA: (Myrna Williams) Helena, Mont., Aug. 2, 1905. Westlake School.

LUND, JOHN: Rochester, N.Y., Feb. 6, 1913.

LUNDIGAN, WILLIAM: Syracuse, N.Y., June 12, 1914. Syracuse U.

LUPINO, IDA: London, Feb. 4, 1918. RADA.

LYNDE, PAUL: Mt. Vernon, Ohio, June 13, 1926. Northwestern U.

LYNLEY, CAROL: (Jones) NYC, Feb. 13, 1942.

LYNN, JEFFREY: Auburn, Mass., 1910. Bates College.

LYON, SUE: Davenport, Iowa, July 10, 1946.

LYONS, ROBERT F.: Albany, N.Y.; AADA.

MacARTHUR, JAMES: Los Angeles, Dec. 8, 1937. Harvard.

MacGINNIS, NIALL: Dublin, Ire., Mar. 29, 1913. Dublin U.

MacGRAW, ALI: NYC, Apr. 1, 1939, Wellesley.

MacLAINE, SHIRLEY: (Beatty) Richmond, Va., Apr. 24, 1934.

MacMAHON, ALINE: McKeesport, Pa., May 3, 1899. Barnard College.

MacMURRAY, FRED: Kankakee, Ill., Aug. 30, 1908. Carroll College.

MACNEE, PATRICK: London, Feb. 1922.

MacRAE, GORDON: East Orange, N.J., Mar. 12, 1921.

MADISON, GUY: (Robert Moseley) Bakersfield, Calif., Jan. 19, 1922. Bakersfield Jr. College.

MAHARIS, GEORGE: Astoria, N.Y., Sept. 1, 1928. Actors Studio.

MAHONEY, JOCK: (Jacques O'-Mahoney) Chicago, Feb. 7, 1919. U. of Iowa.

MALDEN, KARL: (Malden Sekulovich) Gary, Ind., Mar. 22, 1914.

MALONE, DOROTHY: Chicago, Jan. 30, 1925. S. Methodist U.

MARAIS, JEAN: Cherbourg, France, Dec. 11, 1913. St. Germain.

MARCH, FREDRIC: (Frederick McIntyre Bickel) Racine, Wisc., Aug. 31, 1897. U. of Wisc.

MARGO: (Maria Marguerita Guadalupe Boldoay Castilla) Mexico City, May 10, 1918.

MARGOLIN, JANET: NYC, July 25, 1943. Walden School.

MARIN, JACQUES: Paris, Sept. 9, 1919. Conservatoire National.

MARLOWE, HUGH: (Hugh Hipple) Philadelphia, Jan. 30, 1914.

MARSHALL, BRENDA: (Ardis Anderson Gaines) Isle of Negros, P.I., Sept. 29, 1915. Texas State College.

MARSHALL, E. G.: Owatonna, Minn., June 18, 1910. U. of Minn.

MARSHALL, WILLIAM: Gary, Ind., Aug. 19, 1924. NYU.

MARTIN, DEAN: (Dino Crocetti) Steubenville, Ohio, June 17, 1917.

MARTIN, MARY: Weatherford, Tex., Dec. 1, 1914. Ward-Belmont School.

MARTIN, STROTHER: Kokomo, Ind., 1919, UMich.

MARTIN, TONY: (Alfred Norris) Oakland, Cal., Dec. 25, 1913. St. Mary's College.

MARVIN, LEE: NYC, Feb. 19, 1924.

MARX, GROUCHO: (Julius Marx) NYC, Oct. 2, 1895.

MASON, JAMES: Huddersfield, Yorkshire, Eng., May 15, 1909. Cambridge.

MASON, MARSHA: St. Louis, Mo., Apr. 3, 1942, Webster Col.

MASON, PAMELA: (Pamela Kellino) Westgate, Eng., Mar. 10, 1918.

MASSEN, OSA: Copenhagen, Den., Jan. 13, 1916.

MASSEY, DANIEL: London, Oct. 10, 1933. Eaton and King's Colleges.

MASSEY, RAYMOND: Toronto, Can., Aug. 30, 1896. Oxford.

MASTERSON, PETER: Angleton, Tex., June 1, 1934; Rice U.

MASTROIANNI, MARCELLO: Fontana Liri, Italy, Sept. 28, 1924.

MATTHAU, WALTER: (Matuschanskayasky) NYC, Oct. 1, 1920.

MATURE, VICTOR: Louisville, Ky., Jan. 29, 1916.

MAY, ELAINE: (Berlin) Philadelphia, Apr. 21, 1932.

MAYEHOFF, EDDIE: Baltimore, July 7, Yale.

McCALLUM, DAVID: Scotland, Sept. 19, 1933. Chapman Coll.

McCAMBRIDGE, MERCEDES: Jolliet, Ill., March 17, 1918, Mundelein College.

McCARTHY, KEVIN: Seattle, Wash., Feb. 15, 1914. Minn. U.

McCLORY, SEAN: Dublin, Ire., March 8, 1924. U. of Galway.

McCLURE, DOUG: Glendale, Calif., May 11, 1938. UCLA.

McCOWEN, ALEC: Tunbridge Wells, Eng., May 26, 1925, RADA.

McCREA, JOEL: Los Angeles, Nov. 5, 1905. Pomona College.

McDERMOTT, HUGH: Edinburgh, Scot., Mar. 20, 1908.

McDEVITT, RUTH: Coldwater, Mich., Sept. 13, 1895; AADA.

McDOWALL, RODDY: London, Sept. 17, 1928. St. Joseph's.

McDOWELL, MALCOLM: (Taylor) Leeds, Eng., June 13, 1943.

McENERY, PETER: Walsall, Eng., Feb. 21, 1940.

McGAVIN, DARREN: Spokane, Wash., May 7, 1922. College of Pacific.

McGIVER, JOHN: NYC, Nov. 5, 1915. Fordham, Columbia U.

McGUIRE, BIFF: New Haven, Conn., Oct. 25, 1926, Mass State Col.

McGUIRE, DOROTHY: Omaha, Neb., June 14, 1919.

McKAY, GARDNER: NYC, June 10, 1932. Cornell.

McKENNA, VIRGINIA: London, June 7, 1931.

McKUEN, ROD: Oakland, Cal., Apr. 29, 1933.

McLERIE, ALLYN ANN: Grand Mere, Can., Dec. 1, 1926.

McNAIR, BARBARA: Chicago, March 4, 1939. UCLA.

McNALLY, STEPHEN: (Horace McNally) NYC, July 29, Fordham U.

Cameron Mitchell

Barbara McNair

Richard Mulligan

Julie Newmar

Zero Mostel

McNAMARA, MAGGIE: NYC, June 18. St. Catherine.

McQUEEN, BUTTERFLY: Tampa, Fla., Jan. 8, 1911. UCLA.

McQUEEN, STEVE: Slater, Mo., Mar. 24, 1932.

MEADOWS, AUDREY: Wuchang, China, 1924. St. Margaret's.

MEADOWS, JAYNE: (formerly, Jayne Cotter) Wuchang, China, Sept. 27, 1923. St. Margaret's.

MEDFORD, KAY: (Maggie O'Regin) NYC, Sept. 14, 1920.

MEDWIN, MICHAEL: London, 1925. Instut Fischer.

MEEKER, RALPH: (Ralph Rathgeber) Minneapolis, Nov. 21, 1920. Northwestern U.

MELL, MARISA: Vienna, Austria, 1942.

MERCOURI, MELINA: Athens, Greece, Oct. 18, 1915.

MEREDITH, BURGESS: Cleveland, Ohio, Nov. 16, 1909. Amherst.

MEREDITH, LEE: (Judi Lee Sauls) Oct. 1947. AADA.

MERKEL, UNA: Covington, Ky., Dec. 10, 1903.

MERMAN, ETHEL: (Ethel Zimmerman) Astoria, N.Y., Jan. 16, 1909.

MERRILL, DINA: (Nedinia Hutton) NYC, Dec. 9, 1925. AADA.

MERRILL, GARY: Hartford, Conn., Aug. 2, 1915. Bowdoin, Trinity.

MICHELL, KEITH: Adelaide, Aus., Dec. 1, 1926.

MIFUNE, TOSHIRO: Tsingtao, China, Apr. 1, 1920.

MILES, SARAH: Ingatestone, Eng., Dec. 31, 1943.

MILES, SYLVIA: NYC, Sept. 9, 1932.

MILES, VERA: (Ralston) Boise City, Okla., Aug. 23, 1929, UCLA.

MILLAND, RAY: (Reginald Truscott-Jones) Neath, Wales, Jan. 3, 1908. King's College.

MILLER, ANN: (Lucille Ann Collier) Chireno, Tex., Apr. 12, 1919. Lawler Professional School.

MILLER, JASON: Long Island City, NY, Apr. 22, 1939, Catholic U.

MILLER, MARVIN: St. Louis, July 18, 1913. Washington U.

MILLS, HAYLEY: London, Apr. 18, 1946. Elmhurst School.

MILLS, JOHN: Suffolk, Eng., Feb. 22, 1908.

MILNER, MARTIN: Detroit, Mich., 1933.

MIMIEUX, YVETTE: Los Angeles, Jan. 8, 1941. Hollywood High.

MINEO, SAL: NYC, Jan. 10, 1939. Lodge School.

MINNELLI, LIZA: Los Angeles, Mar. 12, 1946.

MIRANDA, ISA: (Isabella Sampietro) Milan, Italy, July 5, 1917.

MITCHELL, CAMERON: Dalastown, Pa., Nov. 1918. N.Y. Theatre School.

MITCHELL, JAMES: Sacramento, Calif., Feb. 29, 1920. LACC.

MITCHUM, JAMES: Los Angeles, Cal., May 8, 1941.

MITCHUM, ROBERT: Bridgeport, Conn., Aug. 6, 1917.

MONTALBAN, RICARDO: Mexico City, Nov. 25, 1920.

MONTAND, YVES: (Yves Montand Livi) Mansummano, Tuscany, Oct. 13, 1921.

MONTGOMERY, BELINDA: Winnipeg, Can., July 23, 1950. •

MONTGOMERY, ELIZABETH: Los Angeles, Apr. 15, 1933. AADA.

MONTGOMERY, GEORGE: (George Letz) Brady, Mont., Aug. 29, 1916. U. of Mont.

MONTGOMERY, ROBERT: (Henry, Jr.) Beacon, N.Y., May 21, 1904.

MOOR, BILL: Toledo, O., July 13, 1931, Northwestern.

MOORE, CONSTANCE: Sioux City, Iowa, Jan. 18, 1922.

MOORE, DICK: Los Angeles, Sept. 12, 1925.

MOORE, KIERON: County Cork, Ire., 1925. St. Mary's College.

MOORE, MARY TYLER: Brooklyn, Dec. 29, 1937.

MOORE, ROGER: London, Oct. 14, 1927. RADA.

MOORE, TERRY: (Helen Koford) Los Angeles, Jan. 7, 1929.

MOORE, KENNETH: Gerrards Cross, Eng., Sept. 20, 1914. Victoria College.

MOREAU, JEANNE: Paris, Jan. 3, 1928.

MORENO, RITA: (Rosita Alverio) Humacao, P.R., Dec. 11, 1931.

MORGAN, DENNIS: (Stanley Morner) Prentice, Wisc., Dec. 10, 1920. Carroll College.

MORGAN, HARRY (HENRY): (Harry Bratsburg) Detroit, Apr. 10, 1915. U. of Chicago.

MORGAN, MICHELE: (Simone Roussel) Paris, Feb. 29, 1920. Paris Dramatic School.

MORIARTY, MICHAEL: Detroit, Mich., Apr. 5, 1941. Dartmouth.

MORISON, PATRICIA: NYC, 1919.

MORLEY, ROBERT: Wiltshire, Eng., May 26, 1908. RADA.

MORRIS, GREG: CLeveland, O., 1934. Ohio State.

MORRIS, HOWARD: NYC, Sept. 4, 1919, NYU.

MORROW, VIC: Bronx, N.Y., Feb. 14, 1932. Fla. Southern College.

MORSE, ROBERT: Newton, Mass., May 18, 1931.

MOSTEL, ZERO: Brooklyn, Feb. 28, 1915. CCNY.

MULLIGAN, RICHARD: NYC, Nov. 13, 1932.

MURPHY, GEORGE: New Haven, Conn., July 4, 1902. Yale.

MURRAY, DON: Hollywood, July 31, 1929. AADA.

MURRAY, KEN: (Don Court) NYC, July 14, 1903.

NADER, GEORGE: Pasadena, Calif., Oct. 19, 1921. Occidental College.

NAPIER, ALAN: Birmingham, Eng., Jan. 7, 1903. Birmingham University.

NATWICK, MILDRED: Baltimore, June 19, 1908. Bryn Mawr.

NAUGHTON, JAMES: Middletown, Conn., Dec. 6, 1945, Yale.

NEAL, PATRICIA: Packard, Ky., Jan. 20, 1926. Northwestern U.

NEFF, HILDEGARDE: (Hildegard Knef) Ulm, Ger., Dec. 28, 1925. Berlin Art Academy.

NELSON, BARRY: (Robert Nielsen) Oakland, Cal., 1925.

NELSON, DAVID: NYC, Oct. 24, 1936. USC.

NELSON, GENE: (Gene Berg) Seattle, Wash., Mar. 24, 1920.

NELSON, HARRIET HILLIARD: (Peggy Lou Snyder) Des Moines, Iowa, July 18.

NELSON, LORI: (Dixie Kay Nelson) Santa Fe, N.M., Aug. 15, 1933.

NELSON, OZZIE: (Oswald) Jersey City, N.J., Mar. 20, 1907. Rutgers U.

NELSON, RICK: (Eric Hilliard Nelson) Teaneck, N.J., May 8, 1940.

NESBITT, CATHLEEN: Cheshire, Eng., Nov. 24, 1889. Victoria College.

NEWLEY, ANTHONY: Hackney, London, Sept. 21, 1931.

NEWMAN, BARRY: Boston, Ma., Mar. 26, 1938. Brandeis U.

NEWMAN, PAUL: Cleveland, Ohio, Jan. 26, 1925. Yale.

NEWMAN, SCOTT: NYC 1954; Washington Col.

NEWMAR, JULIE: (Newmeyer) Los Angeles, Aug. 16, 1935.

NICHOLS, MIKE: (Michael Igor Peschkowsky) Berlin, Nov. 1931. U. Chicago.

Sheree North	Don Nute	Tricia O'Neil	Christopher Plummer	Joanna Pettet

NICHOLSON, JACK: Neptune, N.J., Apr. 22, 1937.

NICOL, ALEX: Ossining, N.Y., Jan. 20, 1919. Actors Studio.

NIELSEN, LESLIE: Regina, Saskatchewan, Can., Feb. 11, 1926. Neighborhood Playhouse.

NIVEN, DAVID: Kirriemuir, Scot., Mar. 1, 1910. Sandhurst College.

NOLAN, LLOYD: San Francisco, Aug. 11, 1902. Stanford U.

NORRIS, CHRISTOPHER: NYC, Oct. 7, 1943; Lincoln Square Acad.

NORTH, HEATHER: Pasadena, Cal., Dec. 13, 1950; Actors Workshop.

NORTH, SHEREE: (Dawn Bethel) Los Angeles, Jan. 17, 1933. Hollywood High.

NOVAK, KIM: (Marilyn Novak) Chicago, Feb. 18, 1933. LACC.

NUGENT, ELLIOTT: Dover, Ohio, Sept. 20, 1900. Ohio State U.

NUTE, DON: Connellsville, Pa., Mar. 13, Denver U.

NUYEN, FRANCE: (Vannga) Marseilles, France, July 31, 1939. Beaux Arts School.

OATES, WARREN: Depoy, Ky., July 5, 1928.

OBERON, MERLE: (Estelle Merle O'Brien Thompson) Tasmania, Feb. 19, 1911.

O'BRIAN, HUGH: (Hugh J. Krampe) Rochester, N.Y., Apr. 19, 1928. Cincinnati U.

O'BRIEN, CLAY: Ray, Ariz., May 6, 1961.

O'BRIEN, EDMOND: NYC, Sept. 10, 1915. Fordham, Neighborhood Playhouse.

O'BRIEN, MARGARET: (Angela Maxine O'Brien) Los Angeles, Jan. 15, 1937.

O'BRIEN, PAT: Milwaukee, Nov. 11, 1899. Marquette U.

O'CONNELL, ARTHUR: NYC, Mar. 29, 1908. St. John's.

O'CONNOR, CARROLL: Bronx, N.Y., Aug. 2, 1925; Dublin National Univ.

O'CONNOR, DONALD: Chicago, Aug. 28, 1925.

O'CONNOR, GLYNNIS: NYC, Nov. 19, 1956, NYSU.

O'HARA, MAUREEN: (Maureen FitzSimons) Dublin, Ire., Aug. 17, 1921. Abbey School.

O'HERLIHY, DAN: Wexford, Ire., May 1, 1919. National U.

OLIVIER, LAURENCE: Dorking, Eng., May 22, 1907. Oxford.

OLSON, NANCY: Milwaukee, Wisc., July 14, UCLA.

O'NEAL, PATRICK: Ocala, Fla., Sept. 26, 1927. U. of Fla.

O'NEAL, RON: Utica, NY, Sept. 1, 1937, Ohio State.

O'NEAL, RYAN: Los Angeles, Apr. 20, 1941.

O'NEAL, TATUM: Los Angeles, Nov. 5, 1963.

O'NEIL, TRICIA: Shreveport, La., Mar. 11, 1945, Baylor U.

O'NEILL, JENNIFER: Rio de Janeiro, Feb. 20, 1949; Neighborhood Playhouse.

O'SULLIVAN, MAUREEN: Byle, Ire., May 17, 1911. Sacred Heart Convent.

O'TOOLE, PETER: Connemara, Ireland, Aug. 2, 1932. RADA.

OWEN, REGINALD: Wheathampstead, Eng., Aug. 5, 1887. Tree's Academy.

PACINO, AL: NYC, Apr. 25, 1940.

PAGE, GERALDINE: Kirksville, Mo., Nov. 22, 1924. Goodman School.

PAGET, DEBRA: (Debralee Griffin) Denver, Aug. 19, 1933.

PAIGE, JANIS: (Donna Mae Jaden) Tacoma, Wash., Sept. 16, 1922.

PALANCE, JACK: Lattimer, Pa., Feb. 18, 1920. U. N.C.

PALMER, BETSY: East Chicago, Ind., Nov. 1, 1929. DePaul U.

PALMER, GREGG: (Palmer Lee) San Francisco, Jan. 25, 1927. U. Utah.

PALMER, LILLI: Posen, Austria, May 24, 1914. Ilka Gruning School.

PALMER, MARIA: Vienna, Sept. 5, 1924. College de Bouffement.

PAPAS, IRENE: Chiliomodion, Greece, 1929.

PARKER, ELEANOR: Cedarville, Ohio, June 26, 1922. Pasadena Playhouse.

PARKER, FESS: Fort Worth, Tex., Aug. 16, 1927. USC.

PARKER, JEAN: (Mae Green) Deer Lodge, Mont., Aug. 11, 1918.

PARKER, SUZY: (Cecelia Parker) San Antonio, Tex. Oct. 28, 1933.

PARKER, WILLARD: (Worster Van Eps) NYC, Feb. 5, 1912.

PARKINS, BARBARA: Vancouver, Can., May 22, 1945.

PARSONS, ESTELLE: Lynn, Mass. Nov. 20, 1927. Boston U.

PATRICK, DENNIS: Philadelphia, Mar. 14, 1918.

PATRICK, NIGEL: London, May 2, 1913.

PATTERSON, LEE: Vancouver, Can., 1929. Ontario College of Art.

PAVAN, MARISA: (Marisa Pierangeli) Cagliari, Sardinia, June 19, 1932. Torquado Tasso College.

PEACH, MARY: Durban, S. Africa, 1934.

PEARSON, BEATRICE: Denison, Tex., July 27, 1920.

PECK, GREGORY: La Jolla, Calif., Apr. 5, 1916. U. of Calif.

PEPPARD, GEORGE: Detroit, Oct. 1, 1933. Carnegie Tech.

PERKINS, ANTHONY: NYC, Apr. 14, 1932. Rollins College.

PERREAU, GIGI: (Ghislaine) Los Angeles, Feb. 6, 1941.

PERRINE, VALERIE: Galveston, Tx., Sept. 3, 1946. UAriz.

PETERS, BERNADETTE: Jamaica, NY, Feb. 28, 1948.

PETERS, BROCK: NYC, July 2, 1927, CCNY.

PETERS, JEAN: (Elizabeth) Canton, Ohio, Oct. 15, 1926. Ohio State U.

PETTET, JOANNA: London, Nov. 16, 1944; Neighborhood Playhouse.

PHILLIPS, MACKENZIE: Hollywood, Ca. 1960.

PHILLIPS, MICHELLE: (Holly Gilliam) NJ, June 4, 1944.

PICERNI, PAUL: NYC, Dec. 1, 1922. Loyola U.

PICKENS, SLIM: (Louis Bert Lindley, Jr.) Kingsberg, Calif., June 29, 1919.

PICKFORD, MARY: (Gladys Mary Smith) Toronto, Can., Apr. 8, 1893.

PIDGEON, WALTER: East St. John, N.B., Can., Sept. 23, 1898.

PINE, PHILLIP: Hanford, Calif., July 16, 1925. Actors' Lab.

PLAYTEN, ALICE: NYC, Aug. 28, 1947, NYU.

PLEASENCE, DONALD: Workshop, Eng, Oct. 5, 1919. Sheffield School.

PLESHETTE, SUZANNE: NYC, Jan. 31, 1937. Syracuse U.

PLUMMER, CHRISTOPHER: Toronto, Can., Dec. 13, 1927.

PODESTA, ROSSANA: Tripoli, June 20, 1934.

POITIER, SIDNEY: Miami, Fla., Feb. 27, 1927.

POLITO, LINA: Naples, Italy, Aug. 11, 1954.

POLLARD, MICHAEL J.: Pacific, N.J., May 30, 1939.

PORTER, ERIC: London, Apr. 8, 1928, Wimbledon Col.

POWELL, ELEANOR: Springfield, Mass., Nov. 21, 1913.

POWELL, JANE: (Suzanne Burce) Portland, Ore., Apr. 1, 1929.

POWELL, WILLIAM: Pittsburgh, July 29, 1892. AADA.

POWERS, MALA: (Mary Ellen) San Francisco, Dec. 29, 1921. UCLA.

Richard Pryor   Charlotte Rampling   Michael Redgrave   Barbara Rush   Tony Roberts

PRENTISS, PAULA: (Paula Ragusa) San Antonio, Tex., Mar. 4, 1939. Northwestern U.

PRESLE, MICHELINE: (Micheline Chassagne) Paris, Aug. 22, 1922. Rouleau Drama School.

PRESLEY, ELVIS: Tupelo, Miss., Jan. 8, 1935.

PRESNELL, HARVE: Modesto, Calif., Sept. 14, 1933. USC.

PRESTON, ROBERT: (Robert Preston Meservey) Newton Highlands, Mass., June 8, 1913. Pasadena Playhouse.

PRICE, VINCENT: St. Louis, May 27, 1911. Yale.

PRINCE, WILLIAM: Nicholas, N.Y., Jan. 26, 1913. Cornell U.

PRINCIPAL, VICTORIA: Tokyo, Jan. 3, 1945. Dade Jr. Col.

PROVINE, DOROTHY: Deadwood, S.D., Jan. 20, 1937. U. of Wash.

PROWSE, JULIET: Bombay, India, Sept. 25, 1936.

PRYOR, RICHARD: Peoria, Ill., Dec. 1, 1940.

PURCELL, LEE: Cherry Point, N.C., 1947; Stephens.

PURCELL, NOEL: Dublin, Ire., Dec. 23, 1900. Irish Christian Brothers.

PURDOM, EDMUND: Welwyn Garden City, Eng., Dec. 19, St. Ignatius College.

QUAYLE, ANTHONY: Lancashire, Eng., Sept. 7, 1913. Old Vic School.

QUINN, ANTHONY: Chihuahua, Mex., Apr. 21, 1915.

RAFFERTY, FRANCES: Sioux City, Iowa, June 16, 1922. UCLA.

RAFT, GEORGE: NYC, 1903.

RAINES, ELLA: (Ella Wallace Rains Olds) Snoqualmie Falls, Wash., Aug. 6, 1921. U. of Wash.

RAMPLING, CHARLOTTE: Surmer, Eng., Feb. 5, 1946; UMadrid.

RAMSEY, LOGAN: Long Beach, Cal., Mar. 21, 1921; St. Joseph.

RANDALL, TONY: Tulsa, Okla., Feb. 26, 1920. Northwestern U.

RANDALL, RON: Sydney, Australia, Oct. 8, 1920. St. Mary's College.

RASULALA, THALMUS: (Jack Crowder) Miami, Fla., Nov. 15, 1939. U. Redlands.

RAY, ALDO: (Aldo DeRe) Pen Argyl, Pa. Sept. 25, 1926. UCLA.

RAYE, MARTHA: (Margie Yvonne Reed) Butte, Mont., Aug. 27 1916.

RAYMOND, GENE: (Raymond Guion) NYC, Aug. 13, 1908.

REAGAN, RONALD: Tampico, Ill., Feb. 6, 1911. Eureka College.

REASON, REX: Berlin, Ger,, Nov. 30, 1928. Pasadena Playhouse.

REDFORD, ROBERT: Santa Monica, Calif., Aug. 18, 1937. AADA.

REDGRAVE, CORIN: London, July 16, 1939.

REDGRAVE, LYNN: London, Mar. 8, 1943.

REDGRAVE, MICHAEL: Bristol, Eng., Mar. 20, 1908. Cambridge.

REDGRAVE, VANESSA: London, Jan. 30, 1937.

REDMAN, JOYCE: County Mayo, Ire., 1919. RADA.

REED, DONNA: (Donna Mullenger) Denison, Iowa, Jan. 27, 1921. LACC.

REED, OLIVER: Wimbledon, Eng., Feb. 13, 1938.

REED, REX: Ft. Worth, Tex., Oct. 2, 1939, LSU.

REEMS, HARRY: Bronx, NY, 1947. UPittsburgh.

REEVES, STEVE: Glasgow, Mont., Jan. 21, 1926.

REID, ELLIOTT: NYC, Jan. 16, 1920.

REINER, CARL: NYC, Mar. 20, 1922. Georgetown.

REINER, ROBERT: NYC, 1945, UCLA.

REMICK, LEE: Quincy, Mass., Dec. 14, 1935. Barnard College.

RETTIG, TOMMY: Jackson Heights, N.Y., Dec. 10, 1941.

REVILL, CLIVE: Wellington, NZ, Apr. 18, 1930.

REYNOLDS, BURT: West Palm Beach, Fla. Feb. 11, 1936. Fla. State U.

REYNOLDS, DEBBIE: (Mary Frances Reynolds) El Paso, Tex., Apr. 1, 1932.

REYNOLDS, MARJORIE: Buhl, Idaho, Aug. 12, 1921.

RHOADES, BARBARA: Poughkeepsie, N.Y., 1947.

RICH, IRENE: Buffalo, N.Y., Oct. 13, 1897. St. Margaret's School.

RICHARDS, JEFF: (Richard Mansfield Taylor) Portland, Ore., Nov. 1. USC.

RICHARDSON, RALPH: Cheltenham, Eng., Dec. 19, 1902.

RICKLES, DON: NYC, May 8, 1926. AADA.

RIGG, DIANA: Doncaster, Eng., July 20, 1938. RADA.

ROBARDS, JASON: Chicago, July 26, 1922. AADA.

ROBERTS, TONY: NYC, Oct. 22, 1939. Northwestern U.

ROBERTS, RACHEL: Llanelly, Wales, Sept. 20, 1927. RADA.

ROBERTS, RALPH: Salisbury, NC, Aug. 17, 1922. UNC.

ROBERTSON, CLIFF: La Jolla, Calif., Sept. 9, 1925. Antioch College.

ROBINSON, ROGER: Seattle, Wash., May 2, 1941; USCal.

ROBSON, FLORA: South Shields, Eng., Mar. 28, 1902. RADA.

ROCHESTER: (Eddie Anderson) Oakland, Calif., Sept. 18, 1905.

ROGERS, CHARLES "BUDDY": Olathe, Kan., Aug. 13, 1904. U. of Kan.

ROGERS, GINGER: (Virginia Katherine McMath) Independence, Mo., July 16, 1911.

ROGERS, ROY: (Leonard Slye) Cincinnati, Nov. 5, 1912.

ROGERS, WAYNE: Birmingham, Ala., Apr. 7, 1933. Princeton.

ROLAND, GILBERT: (Luis Antonio Damaso De Alonso) Juarez, Mex., Dec. 11, 1905.

ROMAN, RUTH: Boston, Dec. 23. Bishop Lee Dramatic School.

ROMERO, CESAR: NYC, Feb. 15, 1907. Collegiate School.

ROONEY, MICKEY: (Joe Yule, Jr.) Brooklyn, Sept. 23, 1920.

ROSS, DIANA: Detroit, Mich., Mar. 26, 1945.

ROSS, KATHARINE: Hollywood, Jan. 29, 1943.

ROTH, LILLIAN: Boston, Dec. 13, 1910.

ROUNDS, DAVID: Bronxville, NY, Oct. 9, 1938, Denison U.

ROUNDTREE, RICHARD: New Rochelle, N.Y., Sept. 7, 1942. Southern Ill.

ROWLANDS, GENA: Cambria, Wisc., June 19, 1936.

RULE, JANICE: Cincinnati, Aug. 15, 1931.

RUSH, BARBARA: Denver, Colo., Jan. 4. U. of Calif.

RUSSELL, JANE: Bemidji, Minn., June 21, 1921. Max Reinhardt School.

RUSSELL, JOHN: Los Angeles, Jan. 3, 1921. U. of Calif.

RUSSELL, KURT: Springfield, Mass., March 17, 1951.

RUSSELL, ROSALIND: Waterbury, Conn., June 4, 1911. AADA.

RUTHERFORD, ANN: Toronto, Can., 1924.

RUYMEN, AYN: Brooklyn, July 18, 1947, HB Studio.

SAINT, EVA MARIE: Newark, N.J., July 4, 1924. Bowling Green State U.

ST. JACQUES, RAYMOND: (James Arthur Johnson) Conn.

227

bara Hershey Seagull   Roy Scheider   Stella Stevens   Donald Sinden   Maureen Stapleton

ST. JOHN, BETTA: Hawthorne, Calif., Nov. 26, 1929.

ST. JOHN, JILL: (Jill Oppenheim) Los Angeles, Aug. 19, 1940.

SALT, JENNIFER: Los Angeles, Sept. 4, 1944. Sarah Lawrence Col.

SANDS, TOMMY: Chicago, Aug. 27, 1937.

SAN JUAN, OLGA: NYC, Mar. 16, 1927.

SARANDON, SUSAN: (Tomaling) NYC, Oct. 4, 1946. Catholic U.

SARGENT, RICHARD: (Richard Cox) Carmel, Cal., 1933. Stanford U.

SARRAZIN, MICHAEL: Quebec City, Can., May 22, 1940.

SAVALAS, TELLY: (Aristotle) Garden City, N.Y., Jan. 21, 1925. Columbia.

SAXON, JOHN: (Carmen Orrico) Brooklyn, Aug. 5, 1935.

SCHEIDER, ROY: Orange, N.J., Nov. 10, 1935, Franklin-Marshall.

SCHELL, MARIA: Vienna, Jan. 15, 1926.

SCHELL, MAXIMILIAN: Vienna, Dec. 8, 1930.

SCHNEIDER, MARIA: Paris, Mar. 27, 1952.

SCHNEIDER, ROMY: Vienna, Sept. 23, 1938.

SCOFIELD, PAUL: Hurstpierpoint, Eng., Jan. 21, 1922. London Mask Theatre School.

SCOTT, GEORGE C.: Wise, Va., Oct. 18, 1927. U. of Mo.

SCOTT, GORDON: (Gordon M. Werschkul) Portland, Ore., Aug. 3, 1927. Oregon U.

SCOTT, MARTHA: Jamesport, Mo., Sept. 22, 1914. U. of Mich.

SCOTT, RANDOLPH: Orange County, Va., Jan. 23, 1903. U. of N.C.

SEAGULL, BARBARA HERSHEY: (Herzstein) Hollywood, Feb. 5, 1948.

SEARS, HEATHER: London, 1935.

SEBERG, JEAN: Marshalltown, Iowa, Nov. 13, 1938. Iowa U.

SECOMBE, HARRY: Swansea, Wales, Sept. 8, 1921.

SEGAL, GEORGE: NYC, Feb. 13, 1934, Columbia.

SELLERS, PETER: Southsea, Eng., Sept. 8, 1925. Aloysius College.

SELWART, TONIO: Watenberg, Ger., June 9, 1906. Munich U.

SERNAS, JACQUES: Lithuania, July 30, 1925.

SEYLER, ATHENE: (Athene Hannen) London, May 31, 1889.

SEYMOUR, ANNE: NYC, Sept. 11, 1909. American Laboratory Theatre.

SEYMOUR, JANE: Hillingdon, Eng., Feb. 15, 1951.

SHARIF, OMAR: (Michel Shalboub) Alexandria, Egypt, Apr. 10, 1933. Victoria Col.

SHATNER, WILLIAM: Montreal, Can., Mar. 22, 1931. McGill U.

SHAW, ROBERT: Orkney Isles, Scot., Aug. 9, 1927, RADA.

SHAW, SEBASTIAN: Holt, Eng., May 29, 1905. Gresham School.

SHAWLEE, JOAN: Forest Hills, N.Y., Mar. 5, 1929.

SHAWN, DICK: (Richard Shulefand) Buffalo, N.Y., Dec. 1. U. of Miami.

SHEARER, MOIRA: Dunfermline, Scot., Jan. 17, 1926. London Theatre School.

SHEARER, NORMA: Montreal, Can., Aug. 19, 1904.

SHEEN, MARTIN: (Ramon Estevez) Dayton, O., Aug. 3, 1940.

SHEFFIELD, JOHN: Pasadena, Calif., Apr. 11, 1931. UCLA.

SHEPHERD, CYBILL: Memphis, Tenn., 1950. Hunter, NYU.

SHORE, DINAH: (Frances Rose Shore) Winchester, Tenn., Mar. 1, 1917. Vanderbilt U.

SHOWALTER, MAX: (Formerly Casey Adams) Caldwell, Kan., June 2, 1917. Pasadena Playhouse.

SIDNEY, SYLVIA: NYC, Aug. 8, 1910. Theatre Guild School.

SIGNORET, SIMONE: (Simone Kaminker) Wiesbaden, Ger., Mar. 25, 1921. Solange Sicard School.

SILVERS, PHIL: (Philip Silversmith) Brooklyn, May 11, 1912.

SIM, ALASTAIR: Edinburgh, Scot., 1900.

SIMMONS, JEAN: London, Jan. 31, 1929. Aida Foster School.

SIMON, SIMONE: Marseilles, France, Apr. 23, 1914.

SINATRA, FRANK: Hobokan, N.J., Dec. 12, 1917.

SINDEN, DONALD: Plymouth, Eng., Oct. 9, 1923. Webber-Douglas.

SKELTON, RED: (Richard) Vincennes, Ind., July 18, 1913.

SLEZAK, WALTER: Vienna, Austria, May 3, 1902.

SMITH, ALEXIS: Penticton, Can., June 8, 1921. LACC.

SMITH, JOHN: (Robert E. Van Orden) Los Angeles, Mar. 6, 1931. UCLA.

SMITH, KATE: (Kathryn Elizabeth) Greenville, Va., May 1, 1909.

SMITH, KENT: NYC, Mar. 19, 1907. Harvard U.

SMITH, MAGGIE: Ilford, Eng., Dec. 28, 1934.

SMITH, ROGER: South Gate, Calif., Dec. 18, 1932. U. of Ariz.

SNODGRESS, CARRIE: Chicago, Oct. 27, 1946. UNI.

SOMMER, ELKE: Berlin, Nov. 5, 1941.

SONNY: (Salvatore Bono) 1935.

SORDI, ALBERTO: Rome, Italy, 1925.

SORVINO, PAUL: NYC, 1939, AMDA.

SOTHERN, ANN: (Harriet Lake) Valley City, N.D., Jan. 22, 1909. Washington U.

STACK, ROBERT: Los Angeles, Jan. 13, 1919. USC.

STADLEN, LEWIS J.: Brooklyn, Mar. 7, 1947, Neighborhood Playhouse.

STAMP, TERENCE: London, 1940.

STANDER, LIONEL: NYC, Jan. 11, 1908. UNC.

STANG, ARNOLD: Chelsea, Mass., Sept. 28, 1925.

STANLEY, KIM: (Patricia Reid) Tularosa, N.M., Feb. 11, 1921. U. of Tex.

STANWYCK, BARBARA: (Ruby Stevens) Brooklyn, July 16, 1907.

STAPLETON, MAUREEN: Troy, N.Y., June 21, 1925.

STEEL, ANTHONY: London, May 21, 1920. Cambridge.

STEELE, TOMMY: London, Dec. 17, 1936.

STEIGER, ROD: Westhampton, N.Y., Apr. 14, 1925.

STERLING, JAN: (Jane Sterling Adriance) NYC, Apr. 3, 1923. Fay Compton School.

STERLING, ROBERT: (William Sterling Hart) Newcastle, Pa., Nov. 13, 1917. U. of Pittsburgh.

STEVENS, CONNIE: (Concetta Ann Ingolia) Brooklyn, Aug. 8, 1938. Hollywood Professional School.

STEVENS, KAYE: (Catherine) Pittsburgh, July 21, 1933.

STEVENS, MARK: (Richard) Cleveland, Ohio, Dec. 13, 1922.

STEVENS, STELLA: (Estelle Eggleston) Hot Coffee, Miss., Oct. 1, 1936.

STEWART, ALEXANDRA: Montreal, Can., June 10. Louvre.

STEWART, ELAINE: Montclair, N.J., May 31, 1929.

STEWART, JAMES: Indiana, Pa., May 20, 1908. Princeton.

STEWART, MARTHA: (Martha Haworth) Bardwell, Ky., Oct. 7, 1922.

STOCKWELL, DEAN: Hollywood, March 5.

STORM, GALE: (Josephine Cottle) Bloomington, Tex., Apr. 5, 1922.

STRASBERG, SUSAN: NYC, May 22, 1938.

STRAUD, DON: Hawaii, 1943.

Donald Sutherland

Jessica Tandy

Rip Torn

Brenda Vaccaro

Bobby Van

STREISAND, BARBRA: Brooklyn, Apr. 24, 1942.

STRODE, WOODY: Los Angeles, 1914.

STRUDWICK, SHEPPERD: Hillsboro, N.C., Sept. 22, 1907. U. of N.C.

STRUTHERS, SALLY: Portland, Ore., July 28, 1948, Pasadena Playhouse.

SULLIVAN, BARRY: (Patrick Barry) NYC, Aug. 29, 1912. NYU.

SULLY, FRANK: (Frank Sullivan) St. Louis, 1910. St. Teresa's College.

SUTHERLAND, DONALD: St. John, New Brunswick, July 17, 1934. U. Toronto.

SWANSON, GLORIA: (Josephine May Swenson) Chicago, Mar. 27, 1898. Chicago Art Inst.

SWINBURNE, NORA: Bath, Eng., July 24, 1902. RADA.

SWIT, LORETTA: Passaic, NJ, Nov. 4, AADA.

SYLVESTER, WILLIAM: Oakland, Calif., Jan. 31, 1922. RADA.

SYMS, SYLVIA: London, 1934. Convent School.

TABORI, KRISTOFFER: Los Angeles, Aug. 4, 1952.

TALBOT, LYLE: (Lysle Hollywood) Pittsburgh, Feb. 8, 1904.

TALBOT, NITA: NYC, Aug. 8, 1930. Irvine Studio School.

TAMBLYN, RUSS: Los Angeles, Dec. 30.

TANDY, JESSICA: London, June 7, 1909. Dame Owens' School.

TAYLOR, DON: Freeport, Pa., Dec. 13, 1920. Penn State U.

TAYLOR, ELIZABETH: London, Feb. 27, 1932. Byron House School.

TAYLOR, KENT: (Louis Weiss) Nashua, Iowa, May 11, 1907.

TAYLOR, ROD: (Robert) Sydney, Aust., Jan. 11, 1930.

TAYLOR-YOUNG, LEIGH: Wash., D.C., Jan. 25, 1945. Northwestern.

TEAGUE, ANTHONY SKOOTER: Jacksboro, Tex., Jan. 4, 1940.

TEAL, RAY: Grand Rapids, Mich., Jan. 12, 1902. Pasadena Playhouse.

TEMPLE, SHIRLEY: Santa Monica, Calif., Apr. 23, 1928.

TERRY-THOMAS: (Thomas Terry Hoar Stevens) Finchley, London, July 14, 1911. Ardingly College.

TERZIEFF, LAURENT: Paris, 1935.

THACKER, RUSS: Washington, DC, June 23, 1946, Montgomery Col.

THATCHER, TORIN: Bombay, India, Jan. 15, 1905. RADA.

THAXTER, PHYLLIS: Portland, Me., Nov. 20, 1921. St. Genevieve School.

THOMAS, DANNY: (Amos Jacobs) Deerfield, Mich., Jan. 6, 1914.

THOMAS, MARLO: (Margaret) Detroit, Nov. 21, 1938. USC.

THOMAS, PHILIP: Columbus, O., May 26, 1949. Oakwood Col.

THOMAS, RICHARD: NYC, June 13, 1951. Columbia.

THOMPSON, MARSHALL: Peoria, Ill., Nov. 27, 1925. Occidental College.

THOMPSON, REX: NYC, Dec. 14, 1942.

THOMPSON, SADA: Des Moines, Io., Sept. 27, 1929, Carnegie Tech.

THORNDIKE, SYBIL: Gainsborough, Eng., Oct. 24, 1882. Guild Hall School of Music.

THULIN, INGRID: Solleftea, Sweden, Jan. 27, 1929, Royal Drama Theatre.

TIERNEY, GENE: Brooklyn, Nov. 20, 1920. Miss Farmer's School.

TIERNEY, LAWRENCE: Brooklyn, Mar. 15, 1919. Manhattan College.

TIFFIN, PAMELA: (Wonso) Oklahoma City, Oct. 13, 1942.

TODD, RICHARD: Dublin, Ire., June 11, 1919. Shrewsbury School.

TOLO, MARILU': Rome, Italy, 1948.

TOPOL: (Chaim Topol) Tel-Aviv, Israel, Sept. 9, 1935.

TORN, RIP: Temple, Tex., Feb. 6, 1931. U. Tex.

TOTTER, AUDREY: Joliet, Ill., Dec. 20.

TRAVERS, BILL: Newcastle-on-Tyne, Eng., Jan. 3, 1922.

TRAVIS, RICHARD: (William Justice) Carlsbad, N.M., Apr. 17, 1913.

TREACHER, ARTHUR: (Veary) Brighton, Eng., July 2, 1894.

TREMAYNE, LES: London, Apr. 16, 1913. Northwestern Columbia, UCLA.

TRINTIGNANT, JEAN-LOUIS: Pont-St. Esprit, France, Dec. 11, 1930. Dullin-Balachova Drama School.

TRYON, TOM: Hartford, Conn., Jan. 14, 1926. Yale.

TSOPEI, CORINNA: Athens, Greece, June 21, 1944.

TUCKER, FORREST: Plainfield, Ind., Feb. 12, 1919. George Washington U.

TURNER, LANA: (Julia Jean Mildred Frances Turner) Wallace, Idaho, Feb. 8, 1920.

TUSHINGHAM, RITA: Liverpool, Eng., 1942.

TUTTLE, LURENE: Pleasant Lake, Ind., Aug. 20, 1906, USC.

TWIGGY: (Lesley Hornby) London, Sept. 19, 1949.

TYLER, BEVERLY: (Beverly Jean Saul) Scranton, Pa., July 5, 1928.

TYSON, CICELY: NYC, Dec. 19.

UGGAMS, LESLIE: NYC, May 25, 1943.

ULLMAN, LIV: Tokyo, Dec. 16, 1939, Webber-Douglas Acad.

URE, MARY: Glasgow, Scot., 1934. Central School of Drama.

USTINOV, PETER: London Apr. 16, 1921. Westminster School.

VACCARO, BRENDA: Brooklyn, Nov. 18, 1939. Neighborhood Playhouse.

VALLEE, RUDY: (Hubert) Island Pond, Vt., July 28, 1901. Yale.

VALLI, ALIDA: Pola, Italy, May 31, 1921. Rome Academy of Drama.

VAN, BOBBY: (Stein) NYC, Dec. 6, 1930.

VAN CLEEF, LEE: Somerville, N.J., Jan. 9, 1925.

VAN DEVERE, TRISH: (Patricia Dressel) Englewood Cliffs, NJ, Mar. 9, 1945, Ohio Wesleyan.

VAN DOREN, MAMIE: (Joan Lucile Olander) Rowena, S.D., Feb. 6, 1933.

VAN DYKE, DICK: West Plains, Mo., Dec. 13, 1925.

VAN FLEET, JO: Oakland, Cal., 1922.

VAN PATTEN, DICK: NYC, Dec. 9, 1928.

VAN PATTEN, JOYCE: NYC, Mar. 9, 1934.

VAUGHN, ROBERT: NYC, Nov. 22, 1932. USC.

VEGA, ISELA: Mexico 1940.

VENUTA, VENAY: San Francisco, Jan. 27, 1911.

VERA-ELLEN (Rohe): Cincinnati, Feb. 16, 1926.

VERDON, GWEN: Culver City, Calif., Jan. 13, 1925.

VINCENT, JAN-MICHAEL: Denver, Col., July 15, 1944. Ventura Col.

VIOLET, ULTRA: (Isabelle Collin-Dufresne) Grenoble, France.

VITALE, MILLY: Rome, Italy, July 16, 1938. Lycee Chateaubriand.

VOIGHT, JON: Yonkers, N.Y., Dec. 29, 1938. Catholic U.

VOLONTE, GIAN MARIA: Milan, Italy, Apr. 9, 1933.

VON SYDOW, MAX: Lund, Swed., July 10, 1929, Royal Drama Theatre.

VYE, MURVYN: Quincy, Mass., July 15, 1913. Yale.

WAGNER, ROBERT: Detroit, Feb. 10, 1930.

| James Whitmore | Jessica Walter | Demond Wilson | Natalie Wood | Gig Young |

WAITE, GENEVIEVE: South Africa 1949.

WALKEN, CHRISTOPHER: Astoria, NY, Mar. 31, 1943, Hofstra U.

WALKER, CLINT: Hartfold, Ill., May 30, 1927. USC.

WALKER, NANCY: (Ann Myrtle Swoyer) Philadelphia, May 10, 1921.

WALLACH, ELI: Brooklyn, Dec. 7, 1915. CCNY, U. of Tex.

WALLIS, SHANI: London, Apr. 5, 1941.

WALSTON, RAY: New Orleans, Nov. 22, 1918. Cleveland Playhouse.

WALTER, JESSICA: Brooklyn, NY, Jan. 31, 1940. Neighborhood Playhouse.

WANAMAKER, SAM: Chicago, 1919. Drake.

WARD, BURT: (Gervis) Los Angeles, July 6, 1945.

WARDEN, JACK: Newark, N.J., Sept. 18, 1920.

WARREN, LESLEY ANN: NYC, Aug. 16, 1946.

WARRICK, RUTH: St. Joseph, Mo., June 29, UMo.

WASHBOURNE, MONA: Birmingham, Eng., Nov. 27, 1903.

WATERS, ETHEL: Chester, Pa., Oct. 31, 1900.

WATERSTON, SAM: Cambridge, Mass., Nov. 15, 1940. Yale.

WATLING, JACK: London, Jan. 13, 1923. Italia Conti School.

WATSON, DOUGLASS: Jackson, Ga., Feb. 24, 1921. UNC.

WAYNE, DAVID: (Wayne McKeehan) Travers City, Mich., Jan. 30, 1916. Western Michigan State U.

WAYNE, JOHN: (Marion Michael Morrison) Winterset, Iowa, May 26, 1907. USC.

WAYNE, PATRICK: Los Angeles, July 15, 1939. Loyola.

WEAVER, DENNIS: Joplin, Mo., June 4, 1925. U. Okla.

WEAVER, MARJORIE: Crossville, Tenn., Mar. 2, 1913. Indiana U.

WEBB, ALAN: York, Eng., July 2, 1906. Dartmouth.

WEBB, JACK: Santa Monica, Calif. Apr. 2, 1920.

WEBBER, ROBERT: Santa Ana, Cal., Oct. 14, Compton Jr. Col.

WELCH, RAQUEL: (Tejada) Chicago, Sept. 5, 1940.

WELD, TUESDAY: (Susan) NYC, Aug. 27, 1943. Hollywood Professional School.

WELDON, JOAN: San Francisco, Aug. 5, 1933. San Francisco Conservatory.

WELLES, GWEN: NYC, Mar. 4.

WELLES, ORSON: Kenosha, Wisc., May 6, 1915. Todd School.

WERNER, OSKAR: Vienna, Nov. 13, 1922.

WEST, MAE: Brooklyn, Aug. 17, 1892.

WHITAKER, JOHNNY: Van Nuys, Cal., Dec. 13. 1959.

WHITE, CAROL: London, Apr. 1, 1944.

WHITE, CHARLES: Perth Amboy, NJ, Aug. 29, 1920, Rutgers U.

WHITE, JESSE: Buffalo, N.Y., Jan. 3, 1919.

WHITMAN, STUART: San Francisco, Feb. 1, 1929. CCLA.

WHITMORE, JAMES: White Plains, NY, Oct. 1, 1922, Yale.

WIDDOES, KATHLEEN: Wilmington, Del., Mar. 21, 1939.

WIDMARK, RICHARD: Sunrise, Minn., Dec. 26, 1914. Lake Forest U.

WILCOX-HORNE, COLIN: Highlands N.C., Feb. 4, 1937. U. Tenn.

WILCOXON, HENRY: British West Indies, Sept. 8, 1905.

WILDE, CORNEL: NYC, Oct. 13, 1915. CCNY, Columbia.

WILDER, GENE: Milwaukee, Wis., June 11, 1936. U Iowa.

WILDING, MICHAEL: Westcliff, Eng., July 23, 1912. Christ's Hospital.

WILLIAMS, BILLY DEE: NYC, Apr. 6, 1937.

WILLIAMS, CINDY: Van Nuys, Ca., 1948, LACC.

WILLIAMS, EMLYN: Mostyn, Wales, Nov. 26, 1905. Oxford.

WILLIAMS, ESTHER: Los Angeles, Aug. 8, 1923.

WILLIAMS, GRANT: NYC, Aug. 18, 1930. Queens College.

WILLIAMS, JOHN: Chalfont, Eng., Apr. 15, 1903. Lancing College.

WILLIAMSON, FRED: Gary, Ind., 1938, Northwestern.

WILSON, DEMOND: NYC, Oct. 13, 1946, Hunter Col.

WILSON, FLIP: (Clerow Wilson) Jersey City, N.J., Dec. 8, 1933.

WILSON, NANCY: Chillicothe, O., Feb. 20, 1937.

WILSON, SCOTT: Atlanta, Ga., 1942.

WINDOM, WILLIAM: NYC, Sept. 28, 1923, Williams Col.

WINDSOR, MARIE: (Emily Marie Bertelson) Marysvale, Utah, Dec. 11, 1924. Brigham Young U.

WINFIELD, PAUL: Los Angeles, 1940, UCLA.

WINKLER, HENRY: NYC, 1947. Yale.

WINN, KITTY: Wash., D.C., 1944. Boston U.

WINTERS, JONATHAN: Dayton Ohio, Nov. 11, 1925. Kenyon College.

WINTERS, ROLAND: Boston, Nov. 22, 1904.

WINTERS, SHELLEY: (Shirley Schrift) St. Louis, Aug. 18, 1922. Wayne U.

WINWOOD, ESTELLE: Kent, Eng., Jan. 24, 1883. Lyric Stage Academy.

WITHERS, GOOGIE: Karachi, India, Mar. 12, 1917. Italia Conti School.

WOOD, NATALIE: (Natasha Gurdin) San Francisco, July 20, 1938.

WOOD, PEGGY: Brooklyn, Feb. 9, 1894.

WOODLAWN, HOLLY: (Harold Ajzenberg) Juana Diaz, PR, 1947.

WOODS, JAMES: Vernal, U., Apr. 18, 1947, MIT.

WOODWARD, JOANNE: Thomasville, Ga., Feb. 27, 1931. Neighborhood Playhouse.

WOOLAND, NORMAN: Dusseldorf, Ger., Mar. 16, 1910. Edward VI School.

WRAY, FAY: Alberta, Can., Sept. 15, 1907.

WRIGHT, TERESA: NYC, Oct. 27, 1918.

WYATT, JANE: Campgaw, N.J., Aug. 10, 1912. Barnard College.

WYMAN, JANE: (Sarah Jane Fulks) St. Joseph, Mo., Jan. 4, 1914.

WYMORE, PATRICE: Miltonvale, Kan., Dec. 17, 1927.

WYNN, KEENAN: NYC, July 27, 1916. St. John's.

WYNN, MAY: (Donna Lee Hickey) NYC, Jan. 8, 1930.

WYNTER, DANA: London, June 8, Rhodes U.

YORK, DICK: Fort Wayne, Ind., Sept. 4, 1928. De Paul U.

YORK, MICHAEL: Fulmer, Eng., Mar. 27, 1942. Oxford.

YORK, SUSANNAH: London, Jan. 9, 1941. RADA.

YOUNG, ALAN: (Angus) North Shield, Eng., Nov. 19, 1919.

YOUNG, GIG: (Byron Barr) St. Cloud, Minn., Nov. 4, 1913. Pasadena Playhouse.

YOUNG, LORETTA: (Gretchen) Salt Lake City, Jan. 6, 1913. Immaculate Heart College.

YOUNG, ROBERT: Chicago, Feb. 22, 1907.

ZETTERLING, MAI: Sweden, May 27, 1925. Ordtuery Theatre School.

ZIMBALIST, EFREM, JR.: NYC, Nov. 30, 1923. Yale.

"Bud" Abbott (1959)   Jack Benny (1974)   Edna Best (1953)

OBITUARIES

WILLIAM A. "BUD" ABBOTT, 78, "straight man" to Lou Costello, and the taller of the comedy team, died of cancer Apr. 24, 1974 in his Woodland Hills, Ca. home. The team split in 1957 and Mr. Costello died two years later. They had appeared together in burlesque, vaudeville, theatre, radio, tv, and movies where they were among the highest paid performers during the 1940's. Their association began in 1931. After appearing on Broadway in "Streets of Paris," they were signed by Hollywood where they made 30 films, including "Buck Privates," "In the Navy," "Pardon My Sarong," "Who Done It?," "Lost in a Harem," "Abbott and Costello Meet Frankenstein," "Mexican Hayride," "Jack and the Beanstalk," and their last "Dance with Me, Henry." He is survived by his widow, a son and a daughter.

RODOLFO ACOSTA, 54, Mexican-born film and stage actor, died Nov. 7, 1974 in Woodland Hills, Ca. He went to Hollywood in 1951 for "One Way Street," and subsequently appeared in such films as "Pancho Villa Returns," "Bullfighter and the Lady," "Hondo," "Proud Ones," "Rio Conchos," and "The Reward." Five children survive.

FERN ANDRA, 80, who produced and starred in many silent German films, died Feb. 8, 1974 in Aiken, S.C. Born in Watseka, Ill., she began her career as an aerialist with the Millman Trio that toured the U.S. and Europe. She began her film career in Vienna in "Crushed." During WW1 she formed her own company in Berlin and produced over 80 films, and appeared in many of them. She returned to the U.S. during the Nazi regime. She was the widow of Sam Edge Dockrell, commandant of the Putnam Phalanx. No known survivors.

CLIFF ARQUETTE, 68, comic actor, died of a heart attack Sept. 23, 1974 in Los Angeles. He was best known for his rustic, folksy TV character, Charley Weaver. He appeared in the film "Comin' Round the Mountain." Twice married and divorced, he is survived by a son.

OLGA BACLANOVA, 74, Russian-born film and stage actress, died Sept. 6, 1974 in Vevey, Switz. She came to the U.S. in 1926 and appeared in the theatre before going to Hollywood where her films include "Three Sinners," "The Man Who Laughs," "Forgotten Faces," "Docks of New York," "Wolf of Wall Street," "Dangerous Woman," "The Great Lover," "Downstairs," "Billion Dollar Scandal," and her most famous "Freaks." Surviving are her husband, Richard Davis, and a son by a previous marriage, Nicholas Soussanin, Jr.

HARRY BAUM, 58, died of a heart attack Jan. 31, 1974 in his Hollywood home. For 51 years he had been active as actor, dancer, stand-in, and stuntman. Surviving are his mother, and a daughter.

COMPTON BENNETT, 74, British film director, died Aug. 13, 1974 in London. He broke into films in the early 1930's as a film editor for Alexander Korda. His credits include "The Seventh Veil," "The Years Between," "My Own True Love," "Daybreak," "That Forsyte Woman," "King Solomon's Mines," "Glory at Sea," "It Started in Paradise," "So Little Time," and "Desperate Moment." No reported survivors.

JACK BENNY, 80, vaudeville, stage, nightclub, radio, film, and tv comedian, died of cancer of the pancreas in his Beverly Hills, Cal., home on Dec. 26, 1974. Born Benjamin Kubelsky in Waukegan, Ill., he began his career as a violinist, but ultimately became one of the best loved masters of timing and comedy in the world. He portrayed himself as timid, stingy, vain, and never older than 39. In reality he was modest, generous, and raised millions for charitable organizations, and leading orchestras in the U.S. For 47 years he was married to Sadie Marks who appeared with him as Mary Livingston. Beginning in 1931, and for the next 32 years without interruption, he had his own show on radio or tv. His films include "Hollywood Revue of 1929," "Chasing Rainbows," "Transatlantic Merry-Go-Round," "Broadway Melody of 1936," "It's in the Air," "Big Broadcast of 1937," "College Holiday," "Artists and Models," "Artists and Models Abroad," "Man about Town," "Buck Benny Rides Again," "Love Thy Neighbor," "Charley's Aunt," "To Be or not to Be," "George Washington Slept Here," "Meanest Man in the World," "Hollywood Canteen," "The Horn Blows at Midnight," "It's in the Bag," and "Guide for the Married Man." Surviving are his widow, an adopted daughter, and grandchildren.

OUIDA BERGERE, 88, writer for stage and screen, actress, and theatrical agent, died Nov. 29, 1974 in NYC. Her screen credits include "Kick In," "Bella Donna," and screenplays for "Witness for the Defense," "On with the Dance," "Three Live Ghosts," "Man from Home," "To Have and to Hold," "Rustle of Silk," "The Cheat," "Garden of Allah," and "Peter Ibbetson." She was the widow of actor Basil Rathbone. A brother survives.

EDNA BEST, 74, British film and stage actress, died Sept. 18, 1974 in Geneva, Switz. After her screen debut in 1923 she appeared in such films as "Loose Ends," "Escape," "Sleeping Partners," "Michael and Mary," "Faithful Heart," "The Key," "The Man Who Knew Too Much," "Prison without Bars," "Intermezzo," "Swiss Family Robinson," "The Late George Apley," "The Ghost and Mrs. Muir," and "Iron Curtain." Surviving are twin sons by her first husband, actor Seymour Beard, and a daughter, actress Sarah Marshall by her second husband, actor Herbert Marshall. Her third husband, Nat Wolff, predeceased her.

CARLYLE BLACKWELL, JR., 61, photographer, and former actor, died Sept. 20, 1974 in his North Hollywood home after a long illness. He was the son of the silent star, and had appeared in over 30 films, including "The Calling of Dan Matthews," and "Romeo and Juliet." Survivors include his widow, a son, and a daughter.

RALPH BLOCK, 84, film producer, writer, and critic, died Jan. 2, 1974 in Wheaton, Md. Was a founding member of Screen Writers Guild, and served as its president. His film credits include "Massacre," "I Am a Thief," "In Caliente," "It's a Date," "Nancy Goes to Rio," "The Right to Live," and "The Melody Lingers On." A daughter survives.

TRUMAN BRADLEY, 69, radio announcer, tv host, and former film actor, died July 28, 1974 in Los Angeles. He appeared in over 20 films, including "Young Dr. Kildare," "Spring Madness," "The Hardys Ride High," "On Borrowed Time," "Northwest Passage," "Bombay Clipper," "The Horn Blows at Midnight," and "I Wonder Who's Kissing Her Now." No reported survivors.

CHARLES BRASWELL, 49, screen and stage actor, died of cancer May 17, 1974 in NYC. His film credits include "The Only Game in Town," "Bail Out at 43,000," and "Pretty Boy Floyd." Surviving are his widow, and two daughters.

WALTER BRENNAN, 80, winner of three Academy Awards, died of emphysema Sept. 21, 1974 in Oxnard, Ca. Included among the more than 100 films in which he appeared are "Law and Order," "Wedding Night," "Man on the Flying Trapeze," "Seven Keys to Baldpate," "Three Godfathers," "Fury," "Buccaneer," "Tom Sawyer," "Texans," "Cowboy and the Lady," "They Shall Have Music," "Vernon and Irene Castle," "Stanley and Livingstone," "Sgt. York," "North Star," "Stolen Life," "Red River," "My Darling Clementine," "Along the Great Divide," "Bad Day at Black Rock," "Rio

Walter Brennan (1971)   Pamela Britton (1950)   Clive Brook (1938)   Johnny Mack Brown   Donald Crisp (1964)
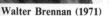   (1935)

Bravo," "The Oscar," "Gnome-mobile," and the three for which he received "Oscars" as best supporting actor, "Come and Get It," "Kentucky," and "The Westerner."

PAMELA BRITTON, 51, screen, stage, and tv actress, died of a brain tumor June 17, 1974 in Chicago. She was appearing at the Arlington Park Theatre. After appearing on Broadway, she was signed by MGM, and subsequently appeared in "Anchors Aweigh," "A Letter from Evie," "Key to the City," "Dead on Arrival," and "Watch the Birdie." She was a regular on the tv series "My Favorite Martian," and "Blondie." She is survived by her husband, hotel executive Arthur Steel, and a daughter.

CLIVE BROOK, 87, English film and stage actor, died Nov. 17, 1974 in his London home. After stage successes, he left London for Hollywood in 1924 and stayed for 11 years. He appeared in over 100 films, including "Woman to Woman," "Declassee," "Home Maker," "Seven Sinners," "Barbed Wire," "French Dressing," "Yellow Lily," "Dangerous Woman," "Four Feathers," "Return of Sherlock Holmes," "Paramount on Parade," "East Lynne," "Tarnished Lady," "Slightly Scarlet," "Shanghai Express," "Cavalcade," "Gallant Lady," "Convoy," "On Approval," "The List of Adrian Messenger." Surviving are a daughter, actress Faith Brook, and a son, playwright Lyndon Brook.

JOHNNY MACK BROWN, 70, cowboy star, died of kidney failure Nov. 14, 1974 in Woodland Hills, Ca. All America football star for U. Ala., he made his first western in 1930, and subsequently appeared in over 300 films, including "Our Dancing Daughters," "Coquette," "Billy the Kid," "Woman of Affairs," "The Valiant," "Undertow," "Saturday's Millions," "Female," "Son of a Sailor," "Belle of the '90's," "Wells Fargo," "West of Carson City," "Stampede," and "Short Grass." He retired in the '60's and was host and manager of a restaurant. He is survived by his widow and four children.

JULIEN H. BRYAN, 75, well known for his documentaries and lectures, died Oct. 20, 1974 in Bronxville, NY. Since 1945 he had been executive director of the International Film Foundation. He filmed documentaries all over the world, including 30 for the State Department for use in foreign countries. Surviving are his widow, and a son.

PAULINE CARTON, 89, French screen and stage actress, died June 17, 1974 in Paris. She appeared in most of the films by Sacha Guitry, and included in her credits are "The Parisian," "Meet Miss Mozart," "Story of a Cheat," "Indiscretions," "Louise," "Private Life of an Actor," "The Prize," "Miquette," "Fruits of Summer," and "Virtuous Scoundrel." No reported survivors.

GINO CERVI, 72, Italy's most popular film and stage actor, died of a pulmonary stroke in his home in Punta, Ala. on Jan. 3, 1974. He was best known as the mayor in the "Don Camillo" series. He also appeared in such films as "Les Miserables," "Fabiola," "William Tell," "Anna Karenina," "Queen of Sheba," "Indiscretion of an American Wife," "Naked Maja," "Revolt of the Slaves," and "Becket." He was also Inspector Maigret in a popular tv series. Surviving is a son, film producer Tonino Cervi.

ERIK CHARREL, 80, German-born stage and film producer-director, died July 15, 1974 in his home in Munich, W. Ger. He was best known for his musical comedies and operettas, including "Congress Dances." No reported survivors.

ANDREA CHECCHI, 57, film, stage, and tv actor, died of a rare virus infection in Rome on Mar. 31, 1974. He began his career in films at 10, and among his credits are "Schoolgirl Diary," "The Earth Cries Out," "Walls of Malapaga," "Paolo and Francesca," "House of Ricordi," "Black Sunday," and

"Italiano Brava Gente." During his last years, he had been active on tv, and displaying his paintings in art shows. His widow and son survive.

EDMUND COBB, 82, former western star, died of a congestive heart attack Aug. 15, 1974 in Woodland Hills, Ca. He began his career in 1910 as a heavy before becoming a cowboy star for Universal. He was active for 52 years until his retirement in 1962. Some of his later credits are "I'm from the City," "I Was a Prisoner on Devil's Island," "Texas," and "River of No Return." His wife predeceased him by a month.

SAMUEL M. COMER, 81, a four-time Academy Award winner for set decorations, died Dec. 27, 1974 in La Jolla, Ca. He received "Oscars" for "Frenchman's Creek," "Samson and Delilah," "Sunset Boulevard," and "The Rose Tattoo." No reported survivors.

BETTY COMPSON, 77, blonde star of silent films, died Apr. 18, 1974 in Glendale, Ca. She began her career as a vaudeville violinist at 15, and in 1915 was signed for Christie comedies, subsequently appearing in 78 two-reelers, and 35 feature films. She was successful in the transition to talkies, and her credits include "Street Girl," "Docks of New York," "The Spoilers," "The Little Minister," "The Miracle Man," "To Have and to Hold," "Prisoners of Love," "Woman to Woman," "Silver Lining," "She Got What She Wanted," "Blaze of Glory," "The Great Gabbo," "Female," "Scarlet Seas," "The Barker," "Hollywood Boulevard," "Port of Missing Girls," "Mr. and Mrs. Smith," "News Is Made at Night," "Second Chance," "and "Here Comes Trouble." She was married three times. No reported survivors.

CURT CONWAY, 58, stage and screen actor, and teacher, died of a heart attack Apr. 11, 1974 in Los Angeles. After appearing on Broadway, he moved to Los Angeles where he was on the faculty of the Calif. Institute of Arts, and Civic Light Opera Workshop. His film credits include "Singapore," "Gentlemen's Agreement," "Casbah," "Raw Deal," "The Lady Gambles," "The Goddess," "Wind across the Everglades," and "Hud." Surviving are his widow and three children.

ROBERT COX, 79, last surviving member of the original Keystone Kops, died Sept. 8, 1974, in Phoenix, Ariz. where he had lived since 1951. During the four years he worked for Mack Sennett, he appeared in over 300 one-reelers, as the smallest of the cops. No reported survivors.

DONALD CRISP, 93, English-born character actor, died May 25, 1974 in Van Nuys, Ca. He came to the U.S. in 1906, made his debut in one-reelers with the Biograph Studios, and eventually became one of the busiest supporting actors in Hollywood. In 1941 he received an "Oscar" for his performance in "How Green Was My Valley." Among his many credits are "White Angel," "Woman Rebel," "Charge of the Light Brigade," "Lassie Come Home," "National Velvet," "Broken Blossoms," "Don Q," "The Viking," "Pagan," "Return of Sherlock Holmes," "Birth of a Nation," "Svengali," "Red Dust," "What Every Woman Knows," "Little Minister," "Mutiny on the Bounty," "Mary of Scotland," "Parnell," "Life of Emile Zola," "Jezebel," "Valley of the Giants," "The Sisters," "Dawn Patrol," "Wuthering Heights," "Juarez," "The Old Maid," "Private Lives of Elizabeth and Essex," "Dr. Ehrlich's Magic Bullet," "Brother Orchid," "Sea Hawk," "Knute Rockne," "Dr. Jekyll and Mr. Hyde," "Forever and a Day," "Valley of Decision," "Son of Lassie," "Bright Leaf," "Long Gray Line," "Saddle the Wind," "The Last Hurrah," "Pollyanna," and "Spencer's Mountain." No reported survivors.

PATRICIA CUTTS, 47, British screen, stage, and tv actress, committed suicide in her London home Sept. 11, 1974. Her

Candy Darling (1971)   **Vittorio De Sica (1966)**   **Billy De Wolfe (1951)**   **Douglass Dumbrille (1945)**   **Joe Flynn (1969)**

film credits include "The Man Who Loved Redheads," "Merry Andrew," and "The Tingler." No reported survivors.

CANDY DARLING, (nee James Slattery) 26, female impersonator on stage and screen, died of cancer and pneumonia Mar. 21, 1974 in NYC. The performer was discovered by Andy Warhol and appeared in several of his productions. Film credits include "Flesh," "Brand X," "Some of My Best Friends Are," "Women in Revolt," "Lady Liberty," and "Silent Night, Bloody Night." Mother and father survive.

LILI DARVAS, 72, Hungarian-born film and stage actress, died July 22, 1974 in her NYC home. Primarily a stage actress, she appeared in such films as "Affairs of Maupassant," "Meet Me in Las Vegas," "Cimarron," and "Love." She left no immediate survivors.

RUFUS DAVIS, 66, character actor of stage, screen, and tv, died Dec. 13, 1974 in Torrance, Ca. His films include "Mountain Music," "This Way Please," "Blossoms on Broadway," "Big Broadcast of 1938," "Dr. Rhythm," "Cocoanut Grove," "Ambush," "Some Like It Hot," "Radio Stars on Parade," and twelve pictures in the "Three Mesquiteers" series. He was a regular on the "Petticoat Junction" tv series. No reported survivors.

IVOR DEAN, 57, British film and tv actor, died of heart failure Aug. 10, 1974 in Truro, Cornwall, Eng. Among his films were "Where Eagles Dare," "The Oblong Box," "The Sorcerers," "Theatre of Death," and "Stranger in the House." He also appeared in the tv "Saint" series. Surviving are his actress wife, Patricia Hamilton, and three daughters.

DORIS DEANE, 73, former actress in "Fatty" Arbuckle comedies, died of a heart attack Mar. 24, 1974 in her Hollywood home. She was divorced from Mr. Arbuckle, and left no known survivors.

NED E. DEPINET, 84, retired president of RKO-Radio Pictures, died Dec. 29, 1974 in NYC. He had worked with Universal and First National before joining RKO in 1931. He retired in 1952. No reported survivors.

EDGAR DEARING, age not reported, died of cancer Aug. 17, 1974 in Woodland Hills, Ca. His many film credits include: "Jazz Age," "Free and Easy," "Abraham Lincoln," "Rainmakers," "Swing Time," "Big City," "Nick Carter," "No Time for Comedy," "Star Spangled Rhythm," "It Came from Outer Space," and "Pollyanna." His wife survives.

VITTORIO DE SICA, 73, Italian-born, internationally recognized actor, film director, producer, and screenwriter, died Nov. 13, 1974 in Paris. He began his career as an actor in 1923 and appeared in over 200 roles. As a director he became a leader in the "new realism" movement, and had just completed his 30th film. He had received "Oscars" for "The Bicycle Thief," "Shoe Shine," "Yesterday, Today, and Tomorrow," and "The Garden of the Finzi-Continis." Other films include "Indiscretion of an American Wife," "Umberto D," "Two Women," "Miracle in Milan," "Marriage Italian Style," and "After the Fox." Surviving are his second wife, Spanish actress Maria Mercader, and three children.

BILLY DE WOLFE, 67, screen and stage comedian-actor, born William Jones, died of lung cancer Mar. 5, 1974 in Los Angeles. He started his career as a dancer on Broadway, and made his first film "Dixie" in 1943. Other screen roles were in "Duffy's Tavern," "Miss Susie Slagle's," "Our Hearts Were Growing Up," "Blue Skies," "Dear Ruth," "Perils of Pauline," "Dear Wife," "Lullaby of Broadway," "Call Me Madam," and "Billie." No reported survivors.

DOUGLASS DUMBRILLE, 84, Canadian-born film, stage, and tv actor died of a heart attack Apr. 2, 1974 in Woodland Hills, Ca. After successful Broadway roles, he made his first

movie in 1932, and subsequently appeared in over 250 films, including "Blondie of the Follies," "Elmer the Great," "Female," "Lady Killer," "Lives of a Bengal Lancer," "Naughty Marietta," "Peter Ibbetson," "Three Musketeers," "I Married an Angel," "Lost in a Harem," "Dishonored Lady," "10 Commandments," and "Buccaneer." He was a regular on the tv series "You'll Never Get Rich," "Sgt. Bilko," and "China Smith." He is survived by his second wife, actress Patricia Mowbray, and two sons.

CHARLES EINFELD, 73, a promotional executive, and retired vice president of 20th Century-Fox, died in Ascona, Switz., Dec. 27, 1974. He was a co-founder of Enterprise Productions that presented "Arch of Triumph," "Body and Soul," and "Force of Evil," among others. Surviving are his widow, a son, and two daughters.

DUKE ELLINGTON, 75, internationally acclaimed musician and composer, died of pneumonia May 24, 1974 in NYC. Among other films, he appeared in "The Hit Parade," "Reveille with Beverly," "Anatomy of a Murder," and composed the score for "The Hit Parade" and "New Faces of 1937." Surviving are his son Mercer, and a sister.

DOROTHY FIELDS, 69, Academy-Award-winning lyricist, died of a heart attack Mar. 28, 1974 in her NYC home. She was the only female among 10 songwriters named to the Songwriters Hall of Fame. With Jerome Kern, she won an "Oscar" in 1936 for "The Way You Look Tonight." She had contributed lyrics to over 400 songs in collaboration with Jimmy McHugh, Jerome Kern, Harold Arlen, Cy Coleman, and her brother Herbert Fields. No reported survivors.

HAROLD A. FIMBERG, 67, screenwriter, died of cancer Apr. 6, 1974 in Los Angeles. His credits include "Who Killed Aunt Maggie," "The Gib Store," "You Can't Ration Love," "In Society," "A Wave, A Wac, and A Marine," "Naughty Nineties," and "Our Man Flint." He also wrote many tv scripts. Surviving are his widow, a son, and a daughter.

JOE FLYNN, 49, Ohio-born film and tv comedian, died of a heart attack July 18, 1974 while swimming in the pool of his Beverly Hills, Ca. home. Film credits include "Seven Little Foys," "Love Bug," "Divorce American Style," "Million Dollar Duck," "Superdad," "Lover Come Back," "Big Chase," "That Happy Feeling," "The Boss," "Ten Commandments," "Panama Sal," and "The Last Time I Saw Paris." He was probably best known for his role in tv's "McHale's Navy." He leaves his widow and two sons.

MARY FORBES, 91, British-born stage and film actress, died July 23, 1974 in Beaumont, Ca. Among her many film credits are "Sunny Side Up," "East Is West," "The Brat," "Farewell to Arms," "Cavalcade," "Les Miserables," "Laddie," "Anna Karenina," "Awful Truth," "You Can't Take It with You," "South of Suez," "Picture of Dorian Gray," "Earl Carroll Vanities," "Ivy," and "You Gotta Stay Happy." Surviving are her second husband, Wesley Wall, and a daughter, actress Brenda Forbes.

HARRY FRASER, 85, director of over 250 films, died Apr. 8, 1974 in Pomona, Ca. He was a pioneer of western films with such stars as Hoot Gibson, Rex Bell, Ken Maynard, Bob Steele, Tex Ritter, and John Wayne. His credits include "Whispering Skull," "Dead or Alive," "Montana Kid," "Oklahoma Jim," "Rustler's Paradise," "Fighting Pioneers," "Wagon Trail," "Pecos Kid," "Spirit of Youth," and "Heroes of the Alamo." No reported survivors.

CLIFF FRIEND, 80, songwriter and pianist, died June 27, 1974 in Las Vegas, Nev. He wrote scores for Broadway, and his film credits include "New Movietone Follies," "Down to Their Last Yacht," "George White's 1935 Scandals," "The Hit Parade," and "Shine on Harvest Moon." His best known

Pietro Germi (1968)   Allen Jenkins (1937)   Arline Judge (1937)   Otto Kruger (1952)

songs were "The Merry-go-round Broke Down," and "When My Dream Boat Comes Home." No reported survivors.

MARGARET FURSE, 63, costume designer, died of cancer July 8, 1974 in her London home. She received an "Oscar" for "Anne of the Thousand Days," and among her other credits are "Love among the Ruins," "Mary Queen of Scots," "The Nelson Affair," "Scrooge," "A Lion in Winter," "Oliver Twist," "The Mudlark," "Kidnapped," "Becket," "A Shot in the Dark," and "Cast a Giant Shadow." Surviving is her second husband, editor-critic Stephen Watts.

LORRAINE GAUGUIN, 50, writer, and former film actress, died Dec. 22, 1974 when fire destroyed her Los Angeles home. Among the films in which she appeared are "One Million B. C.," "The Falcon" series, and several musicals. She later wrote a column for "Hollywood Callboard," and several fan magazines. She is survived by her father, and a daughter.

PIETRO GERMI, 60, actor, producer, screenwriter, and Academy Award winning director, died of hepatitis, Dec. 5, 1974 in Rome. His career began after WWII with films dealing with problems in post-war Italy. He achieved international recognition in 1962 with "Divorce Italian Style" that won an "Oscar" for him. His other credits include "Flight into France," "Lost Youth," "Mafia," "Path of Hope," "Seduced and Abandoned," "The City Defends Itself," "The Climax," "The Birds, the Bees and the Italians," "Railroad Man," and "Alfredo, Alfredo." Surviving are his widow and a daughter.

FOSCO GIACHETTI, 70, popular Italian screen and stage actor, died of a heart ailment Dec. 22, 1974 in Rome. Among his many film credits are "White Squadron," "Naples That Never Dies," "Life of Giuseppe Verdi," "Last Enemy," "Life Begins Anew," "The Damned," "Fear No Evil," and "Love and Larceny." No reported survivors.

RAYMOND GLENN, 76, actor, died of natural causes Dec. 27, 1974 in his home in Torrance, Ca. As Bob Custer, he appeared as a cowboy in over 100 silent films, and later made several sound pictures. Among his other credits are "Law of the Mounted," "Texas Bearcat," "Last Roundup," "Riders of the Rio Grande," "Code of the West," and "Ladies at Ease." Surviving are his widow, and a son.

ROBERT GOLDSTEIN, 70, producer and former production chief at 20th Century-Fox, died of a cerebral hemorrhage in his London home on Apr. 8, 1974. He had also been a producer for Universal-International, and Warner Bros. No reported survivors.

SAMUEL GOLDWYN, 91, distinguished pioneer film producer, died Jan. 31, 1974 in his Los Angeles home. Among the more than 70 films he produced were "The Best Years of Our Lives," "Wuthering Heights," "Pride of the Yankees," "Dodsworth," "Arrowsmith," "Stella Dallas," "Dead End," "The Westerner," "The Little Foxes," "Street Scene," "Hans Christian Andersen," "Guys and Dolls," "North Star," "Up in Arms," "Porgy and Bess," and "The Adventures of Marco Polo." Many were nominated for Academy Awards but only "The Best Years of Our Lives" received the "Oscar." Surviving are his second wife, actress Frances Howard, and their son Samuel, Jr.

BERT GORDON, 76, vaudeville, radio, and screen comedian, died of cancer Nov. 30, 1974 in Duarte, Ca. Known as "The Mad Russian," he appeared regularly on radio shows with Eddie Cantor, Milton Berle, and Jack Benny. His film credits include "She Gets Her Man," "New Faces of 1937," "Outside of Paradise," and "Sing for Your Supper." Two brothers, and two sisters survive.

KITTY GORDON, 96, English-born beauty of stage and films, died May 26, 1974 in Brentwood, NY. She was one of the first stars to appear in silent films, her most notable being

"No Man's Land," and "The Interloper." No reported survivors.

HOWARD GREER, 78, Nebraska-born costume designer, died Apr. 17, 1974 in Culver City, Ca. Before his retirement in 1962 he was one of the most popular designers for films, and its stars. No reported survivors.

REED HADLEY, 63, radio, tv, and film actor, died of a heart attack Dec. 11, 1974 in Los Angeles. He was Red Ryder on the radio series, Capt. Braddock in tv's "Racket Squad," and a regular on "Public Defender." His movies include "Female Fugitive," "Calling Dr. Kildare," "I Take This Woman," "Bank Dick," "Whistling in the Dark," "Guadalcanal Diary," "Wing and a Prayer," "Dark Corner," "I Shot Jesse James," "Dallas," "Half Breed," "Big House U.S.A.," "House on 92 St.," "Captain from Castile," "Walk a Crooked Mile," and "St. Valentine's Day Massacre." Surviving are his widow, and a son.

RALF HAROLDE, 75, actor, died of pneumonia Nov. 1, 1974 in Santa Monica, Ca. His career began in 1930 with "Officer O'Brien," "Framed," "Dixiana," "Hook, Line and Sinker," followed by, among others, "Night Nurse," "Alexander Hamilton," "Winner Take All," "Night Flight," "I'm No Angel," "Jimmy the Gent," "Perfect Clue," "Million Dollar Baby," "Tale of Two Cities," "Song and Dance Man," "Conquest," "Sea Wolf," "Broadway," "Murder, My Sweet," and "Sin Town." His widow survives.

JUNE HARRISON, 48, former child actress, died of cirrhosis of the liver Mar. 10, 1974 in Hollywood. Born in Chicago, she went to Hollywood in 1937 and appeared in such films as "Girl of the Golden West," "Sun Valley Serenade," "Bringing Up Father," and "Citizen Saint." Surviving are her husband, George Campeau, and four children.

MAURITZ HUGO, 65, actor, died June 16, 1974 in Woodland Hills, Ca. During his 36 years in Hollywood, he appeared in over 300 films, including "Wanted by the Police," "The Iron Curtain," "Ticket to Tomahawk," and "No Questions Asked." A son survives.

WARREN HULL, 71, film actor, and radio-tv master of ceremonies, died Sept. 14, 1974 in Southbury Conn. After great popularity on radio, he went to Hollywood where he appeared in over 36 movies, including "The Big Noise," "Bengal Tiger," "Bowery Blitzkreig," the "Green Hornet" and "Spider" series, "Miss Pacific Fleet," "The Walking Dead," "Fugitive in the Sky," "Night Key," "Hawaii Calls," and "Wagons Westward." He was best known as mc for the radio-tv show "Strike It Rich." He is survived by his widow, three sons, a step-son, and two step-daughters.

DAVID C. IMBODEN, 87, silent film actor, died Mar. 18, 1974 in Kansas City, Mo. He appeared in over 100 films, including "The King of Kings." He retired to Kansas City and was a former director of its civic theatre. No reported survivors.

CARL JAFFE, 72, German-born film actor and producer, died Apr. 12, 1974 in London. Among the many films in which he appeared are "The Saint in London," "Life and Death of Colonel Blimp," "Lilli Marlene," "Ivanhoe," "Desperate Moment," "Mad Little Island," "Operation Crossbow," and "The Roman Spring of Mrs. Stone." No reported survivors.

ALLEN JENKINS, 74, character actor, died following lung surgery July 20, 1974 in Santa Monica, Ca. A film actor since 1933, he had appeared in over 175 pictures, including "Blessed Event," "Fugitive from a Chain Gang," "42nd Street," "Big Shakedown," "Page Miss Glory," "Cain and Mabel," "Three Men on a Horse," "Dead End," "Slight Case of Murder," "Gold Diggers in Paris," "Amazing Dr. Clitterhouse," "Destry Rides Again," "Brother Orchid," "Ball of

Rosemary Lane   Richard Long (1956)   Ilona Massey (1948)   Agnes Moorehead (1972)

Fire," "Tortilla Flat," "Stage Door Canteen," "Wonder Man," "Lady on a Train," "Pillow Talk," and "Doctor, You've Got to Be Kidding." Surviving are a son and two daughters.

ARLINE JUDGE, 61, film actress, died Feb. 7, 1974 in her Hollywood apartment. She began her career as a dancer on Broadway, and made her first film in 1931, rapidly rising to stardom. Her credits include "Bachelor Apartment," "American Tragedy," "Are These Our Children," "Girl Crazy," "Age of Consent," "George White's Scandals," "Million Dollar Baby," "King of Burlesque," "Pigskin Parade," "The Lady Is Willing," and "Mad Wednesday." She was married and divorced seven times. No reported survivors.

LEE KINSOLVING, 36, screen and stage actor, died Dec. 4, 1974 in Palm Beach, Fla. where he was managing an art gallery. His film credits include "All the Young Men," "Khovanshina," "The Dark at the Top of The Stairs," and "The Explosive Generation." Surviving are his parents, Rev. and Mrs. Arthur L. Kinsolving, a sister and two brothers.

OTTO KRUGER, 89, Ohio-born film, stage and tv actor, died of a stroke Sept. 6, 1974 in Woodland Hills, Ca. After successful stage career, he turned to films in 1933, and subsequently appeared in over 100, including "Chained," "Vanessa, Her Love Story," "Prizefighter and the Lady," "Men in White," "Treasure Island," "Thanks for the Memory," "Zero Hour," "Dr. Ehrlich's Magic Bullet," "Seventeen," "Saboteur," "Hitler's Children," "Stage Door Canteen," "Cover Girl," "Knickerbocker Holiday," "Duel in the Sun," "Payment on Demand," "High Noon," "Magnificent Obsession," and "Wonderful World of the Brothers Grimm." He was also host of the Lux Radio Theatre and Lux Video Theatre. Surviving are his widow, former actress Sue MacManamy, and a daughter, former actress Ottilie Kruger.

ROSEMARY LANE, 61, singer and actress, died from pulmonary obstruction and diabetes Nov. 25, 1974 in Woodland Hills, Ca. She began her career with her three sisters (Leota, Priscilla, Lola) singing with Fred Waring's band. Her first film, in 1937, "Varsity Show," was followed by, among others, "Hollywood Hotel," "Gold Diggers in Paris," "Four Daughters," "Daughters Courageous," "Boys from Syracuse," "Time out for Rhythm," "Chatterbox," and "All by Myself." She is survived by a daughter, and sisters Lola and Priscilla.

RAYMOND LARGAY, 88, retired character actor, died of a stroke Sept. 28, 1974 in Woodland Hills, Ca. After appearing in vaudeville and on Broadway, made his film debut in 1930. His credits include "Soldiers and Women," "The Shocking Miss Pilgrim," "Are You with It?," "Four Faces West," "Force of Evil," "Johnny One-Eye," "Second Woman," "Gentleman's Agreement," and "April in Paris." Surviving are his second wife, and step-daughter.

ANATOLE LITVAK, 72, Russian-born director-producer, died Dec. 15, 1974 in Neuilly, France. His work in Europe, notably "Mayerling," brought him to Hollywood where he directed such films as "Woman I Love," "Tovarich," "Confessions of a Nazi Spy," "City for Conquest," "Blues in the Night," "The Long Night," "Sorry, Wrong Number," "Snake Pit," "Decision before Dawn," "Anastasia," "Deep Blue Sea," and "Night of the Generals." He had been living in Paris for many years where he made his last film "Lady in a Car." After divorcing star Miriam Hopkins, he married Sophie Steur who survives.

RICHARD LONG, 47, film and tv actor, died of a heart ailment Dec. 21, 1974 in Los Angeles. His screen credits include "Tomorrow Is Forever," "The Stranger," "Dark Mirror," "Egg and I," "Tap Roots," "Life of Riley," "Ma and Pa Kettle," "Air Cadet," "Follow the Boys," "Make Like a Thief," and "Fury at Gunsight Pass." On TV he appeared in

"Maverick," "Bourbon St. Beat," "77 Sunset Strip," "Nanny and the Professor," and "Big Valley." Surviving are his widow, actress Mara Corday, and three children.

WILLIAM A. LYON, 71, film editor, died after a stroke Mar. 18, 1974 in his Hollywood home. He received "Oscars" for best film editing on "From Here to Eternity" and "Picnic." His wife and daughter survive.

EVE MARCH, age unreported, film and stage actress, died of cancer Sept. 19, 1974 in Hollywood. Her screen credits include "How Green Was My Valley," "Curse of the Cat People," "Killer McCoy," "Adam's Rib," and "The Sun Shines Bright." Surviving are a son and a daughter.

ILONA MASSEY, 62, Hungarian-born screen, stage, radio, and tv actress, died Aug. 20, 1974 in Bethesda, Md. After her film debut in 1937 in "Rosalie," she appeared in "Balalaika," "International Lady," "New Wine," "Invisible Agent," "Frankenstein Meets the Wolf Man," "Holiday in Mexico," "Northwest Outpost," "The Plunderers," "Love Happy," and "Jet over the Atlantic." She became a U.S. citizen in 1946. Surviving is her fourth husband, Donald S. Dawson, a retired air force general.

JOHN McCARTEN, 63, Philadelphia-born film and drama critic for the New Yorker magazine, died Sept. 25, 1974 in Dublin, Ire., where he had lived for six years. He is survived by his second wife, and two sons by his first marriage.

LOTHAR MENDES, 79, German-born director, producer, and screenwriter, died Feb. 25, 1974 in London. His film credits include "Man Who Could Work Miracles," "Jew Suss," "Dangerous Curves," "Payment Deferred," "Convoy," "Prince of Tempters," "Moonlight Sonata," "International Squadron," "Flight for Freedom," "Tampico," and "The Walls Came Tumbling Down." No reported survivors.

SETON I. MILLER, 71, retired actor, producer, and screenwriter, died Mar. 29, 1974 in Woodland Hills, Ca. His credits include "The St. Louis Kid," "Murder on a Honeymoon," "It Happened in New York," "G Man," "Frisco Kid," "Two in the Dark," "Leathernecks Have Landed," "Bullets or Ballots," "Kid Galahad," "Adventures of Robin Hood," "Valley of the Giants," "Dawn Patrol," "Sea Hawk," "Here Comes Mr. Jordan," "My Gal Sal," "Black Swan," "Two Years before the Mast," "Calcutta," "Fighter Squadron," "Mississippi Gambler," "Shanghai Story," and "The Last Mile." Surviving are his widow, former actress Ann Evers, a daughter, a son, and another daughter by a previous marriage.

HAL MOHR, 79, Academy Award winning cinematographer, died May 10, 1974 in Santa Monica, Ca. He received two "Oscars": one for "A Midsummer Night's Dream," and a second for "Phantom of the Opera." He was also a photographer for several tv series, including "I Married Joan," "Bob Cummings Show," "Life with Father," and "Father of the Bride." He leaves his widow, former actress Evelyn Venable, a son, and four daughters.

AGNES MOOREHEAD, 67, screen, stage, radio and tv star, died of lung cancer Apr. 30, 1974 in Rochester, Minn. She began her career at ten, but went on to earn an M.A. degree at the Univ. of Wisc. Her movie debut was in 1941 in "Citizen Kane," and she subsequently appeared in over 100 films, including "Magnificent Ambersons," "Big Street," "Journey into Fear," "Jane Eyre," "Since You Went Away," "Dragon Seed," "Mrs. Parkington," "Tomorrow the World," "Our Vines Have Tender Grapes," "Dark Passage," "Johnny Belinda," "Caged," "Show Boat," "Magnificent Obsession," "The Swan," "Pollyanna," "How the West Was Won," "Hush, Hush, Sweet Charlotte," and "The Singing Nun." She was probably best known for the TV series "Bewitched." Surviving are her mother, and an adopted son.

Edward Platt (1958)

Florence Rice (1936)

Francoise Rosay (1961)

Barbara Ruick (1956)

Howard St. John (1963)

GLENN MORRIS, 62, Olympics champion and former movie Tarzan, died Jan. 31, 1974 after a long illness in Palo Alto, Ca. He succeeded Johnny Weissmuller as Tarzan for several films before joining the Detroit Lions as a professional football player. Surviving are two brothers and three sisters.

JAMES W. MORRISON, 86, silent screen actor, died Nov. 15, 1974 in NYC. After appearances on Broadway, he made such films as "Black Beauty," "Dangerous Age," "Nth Commandment," "The Man Next Door," "On the Banks of the Wabash," "Wine of Youth," and "Captain Blood." He had taught speech and drama at Packer Collegiate Institute in Brooklyn for 17 years. No reported survivors.

MICHAEL MYERBERG, 67, stage and film producer, died Jan. 6, 1974 in Baltimore, Md. His screen credits include "100 Men and a Girl," "Hansel and Gretel," and "Patterns." Two sons survive.

ANNA Q. NILSSON, 85, Swedish-born film star, died Feb. 11, 1947 in Hemet, Ca. She made her debut in 1919 in "The Love Burglar," and her last film in 1950, "Sunset Boulevard." Other credits include "Soldiers of Fortune," "Three Live Ghosts," "Rustle of Silk," "Hollywood," "The World Changes," "The Spoilers," "Toll Gate," "Inez of Hollywood," "Top of the World," "Sorrell and Son," "Thirteenth Juror," "Farmer's Daughter," and "Fighting Father Dunne." No reported survivors.

CARROLL NYE, 72, film and radio actor, died of a heart attack and kidney failure Mar. 17, 1974 in his North Hollywood home. After his first picture in 1925 he appeared in such films as "Kosher Kitty Kelly," "The Brute," "Death Valley," "While the City Sleeps," "Craig's Wife," "Madame X," "The Squall," "The Bishop Murder Case," "Traveling Saleslady," "Rebecca of Sunnybrook Farm," and "Gone with the Wind." He is survived by his widow.

PAUL PAGE, 70, early leading man of films, died of a heart attack Apr. 28, 1974 in his home in Hermosa Beach, Ca. His movie career began in 1929 with "Speakeasy," followed by, among others, "Girl from Havana," "Happy Days," "Born Reckless," "Palmy Days," "Phantom Broadcast," "Road to Ruin," "Countess of Monte Cristo," "Have a Heart," and "Kentucky Kernels." He retired in 1940. A daughter survives.

MARCEL PAGNOL, 79, French director and playwright, died Apr. 18, 1974 after a long illness in his Paris home. Among his many credits are "Heartbeat," "Harvest," "The Baker's Wife," "The Well-Digger's Daughter," "Cesar," "Ways of Love," "Topaze," and "Letters from My Windmill." Surviving are his widow, former actress Jacqueline Bouvier, a son, and three children by a previous marriage.

ALBERT PARKER, 87, director, and actors' representative, died Aug. 10, 1974 in his home in London. Among the pictures he directed are "Sherlock Holmes," "Black Pirate," "Love's Redemption," "Rejected Woman," and "Loves of Sunya." He is survived by his widow, actress Margaret Johnson, and a daughter by his first marriage.

EDWARD PLATT, 58, screen, stage, and TV actor, died Mar. 19, 1974 in his Santa Monica, Ca. home. Among his film credits are "The Shrike," "Rebel without a Cause," "Illegal," "Serenade," "Backlash," "Written on the Wind," "Designing Woman," "Helen Morgan Story," "Gift of Love," "North by Northwest," "Pollyanna," and "A Ticklish Affair." Surviving are his widow, a daughter, and two sons.

ROGER PRYOR, 72, former band leader, stage and film star, died Jan. 31, 1974 of a heart attack on a trip to Puerta Vallarta, Mex. His screen credits include "Belle of the Nineties," "Wake up and Dream," "To Beat the Band," "Ticket to Paradise," "Sued for Libel," "Man with Nine Lives," "She Couldn't Say No," "Power Dive," "The Officer and the Lady," and "I Live for Danger." Survivors include his widow and a daughter.

CHARLES QUINLIVAN, 50, stage and film actor, died Nov. 12, 1974 of a coronary while playing tennis near his home in Fountain Valley, Ca. Among his credits are "All the Young Men," and "Airport 75." He is survived by his widow, a son, and three daughters.

PEDRO REGAS, 82, Greek-born stage and film actor, died in his sleep Aug. 10, 1974 in his Hollywood home. While appearing on Broadway in 1920, Mary Pickford persuaded him to try films, and he remained in Hollywood. His many credits include "Black Fury," "Only Angels Have Wings," "Perilous Holiday," "Unchained," "Pocket Full of Money," and "High Plain Drifter." He also appeared on several tv series. Surviving are his widow, a son and a daughter.

STAFFORD REPP, 56, film and tv actor, died Nov. 5, 1974 in Inglewood, Ca. He had appeared in over 30 films and 600 TV episodes. His film credits include "I Want to Live," "Not as a Stranger," "Hot Spell," "Very Special Favor," and "The Other Side of the Wind." He had appeared as Chief O'Hara in the TV series "Batman." His widow and five children survive.

FLORENCE RICE, 67, stage and screen actress, died of lung cancer; Feb. 23, 1974 in Honolulu, Ha. She appeared in over 25 films, including "Best Man Wins," "Carnival," "Escape from Devil's Island," "Pride of the Marines," "Longest Night," "Double Wedding," "Navy Blue and Gold," "Fast Company," "Sweethearts," "Broadway Melody of 1940," "Secret Seven," "Mr. District Attorney," "Father Takes a Wife," and with William Powell in the "Thin Man" series. She leaves her husband, Fred Butler.

PAUL RICHARDS, 50, screen, stage, and tv actor, died of cancer Dec. 10, 1974 in Los Angeles. His film credits include "Fixed Bayonets," "Phantom of the Rue Morgue," "The Strange One," "Monkey on My Back," "All the Young Men," and "Beneath the Planet of the Apes." His widow survives.

TEX RITTER, 67, guitar-playing singer, actor, and politician, died of a heart attack Jan. 2, 1974 in Nashville, Tenn. He had appeared in over 78 western films, including "Mystery of the Hooded Horsemen," "Frontier Town," and "Frontier Badmen." No reported survivors.

FRANCOISE ROSAY, 82, French stage and screen actress, died Mar. 28, 1974 in Paris. She began her film career in 1913 and appeared in over 100 pictures, including "Falstaff," "Carnet de Bal," "Jenny," "Drole de Drame," "Carnival in Flanders," "13th Letter," "Halfway House," "Johnny Frenchman," "September Affair," "Seven Deadly Sins," "Father Fights Back," and "The Longest Day." She was the widow of Belgian director Jacques Feyder. Three sons survive.

HARRY RUBY, 79, composer and writer, died Feb. 23, 1974 in Woodland Hills, Ca. His career and that of his chief collaborator, lyricist Bert Kalmar, were portrayed in the film "Three Little Words," title of their best known song. They were an outstanding team for more than 30 years. Film credits include "Horse Feathers," "Kid from Spain," "Wake up and Dream," "Life of the Party," and "Lovely to Look at." Surviv-

BARBARA RUICK, 42, film, radio, and tv actress-singer, died Mar, 3 1974 in Reno, Nev. while on location for "California Split." Other screen credits include "Invitation," "You for Me," "Above and Beyond," "I Love Melvin," and "Carousel." She is survived by her second husband, composer John Williams, two sons, a daughter, and her mother, actress Lurene Tuttle.

HOWARD ST. JOHN, 68, screen, stage, and tv actor, died of a heart attack Mar. 13, 1974 in his NYC home. After

Stanley Smith (1933)   Henry Wadsworth (1935)   Michael Whalen (1940)   Blanche Yurka (1950)

several Broadway successes, he appeared in over 30 films, including "711 Ocean Drive," "The Men," "Born Yesterday," "Goodbye, My Fancy," "Strangers on a Train," "Three Coins in the Fountain," "The Tender Trap," "Lafayette," "Strange Bedfellows," and "Fate Is the Hunter." Surviving is his widow.

ALMIRA SESSIONS, 85, stage, screen and tv actress, died Aug. 3, 1974 in Los Angeles. Before a fall in 1973 made her a semi-invalid, she had been acting for 65 years. Among her more than 500 films, are "Little Nelly Kelly," "Diary of a Chambermaid," "Chad Hanna," "Sullivan's Travels," "Miracle of Morgan's Creek," "Apartment for Peggy," "Roseanna McCoy," "The Fountainhead," "A Family Affair," "Boston Strangler," "Rosemary's Baby," and "Everything You Wanted to Know about Sex. . . ." No reported survivors.

LEON SHAMROY, 72, Academy-Award-winning cinematographer, died July 7, 1974 in Hollywood after a long illness. He won "Oscars" for "The Black Swan," "Wilson," "Leave Her to Heaven," and "Cleopatra." Other credits include "Twelve O'Clock High," "Young at Heart," "The Robe," "South Pacific," "The King and I," "Love Is a Many Splendored Thing," "Snows of Kilimanjaro," "A Tree Grows in Brooklyn," "Porgy and Bess," "The Cardinal," "David and Bathsheba," and "The Agony and the Ecstacy." Surviving are his widow, actress Mary Anderson, a son and a daughter.

STANLEY SMITH, 69, former screen and stage leading man, died Apr. 13, 1974 after a lengthy illness in his Pasadena, Ca., home. His film career began in 1929, and his credits include "The Sophomore," "Sweetie," "Honey," "King of Jazz," "Love among the Millionaires," "Queen High," "Good News," "Follow the Leader," "Stepping Sisters," "Flight Command," and "Reform Girl." He is survived by his widow and daughter.

ELLIOTT SULLIVAN, 66, stage, tv, and screen actor, died June 2, 1974 in Los Angeles. His film credits of over 80 pictures, include "They Won't Forget," "Accidents Will Happen," "Gangs of New York," "Racket Busters," "The Saint's Double Trouble," "Millionaires in Prison," "The Lady Gambles," "Winged Victory," "Guilty Bystander," "Yankee Doodle Dandy," and "The Great Gatsby." He leaves his widow, a son, and a daughter.

FRANK SUTTON, 51, screen, stage, and tv actor, died of a heart attack just before a stage performance in Shreveport, La., June 28, 1974. His film credits include "Marty," "Town without Pity," and "The Satan Bug." He was best known as the tough Marine sergeant on the "Gomer Pyle" tv series. Survivors include his widow, a son, and daughter.

VERA VAGUE, nee Barbara Jo Allen, age unreported, film, radio, and tv comedienne, died Sept. 14, 1974 in Santa Barbara, Ca., where she had retired. She began her career as a serious actress on Broadway, then took the name of Vera Vague when she became associated with Bob Hope's radio shows as a comedienne. Her film credits include "Priorities on Parade," "Lake Placid Serenade," "Snafu," "Earl Carroll Sketchbook," "Kiss the Boys Goodbye," "The Mad Doctor," "Ice-Capades," "Design for Scandal," and "Melody Ranch." She is survived by her husband, tv producer Norman Morell, and a daughter.

HENRY WADSWORTH, 72, stage and screen actor, died Dec. 5, 1974 in NYC. After his film debut in 1929 he appeared as the juvenile in over 30 pictures, including "Applause," "Slightly Scarlet," "Fast and Loose," "Luxury Liner," "Soldiers of the Storm," "This Side of Heaven," "The Show-Off," "The Thin Man," "West Point of the Air," "Big Broadcast of 1936," "Ceiling Zero," "Doctor Rhythm," and "Silver Skates." He was a past president of the AF of L Film Council,

and administrator of the Motion Picture Health and Welfare Plan. No reported survivors.

OTTO WALDIS, 68, German-born actor, died of a heart attack Mar. 25, 1974 in Hollywood where he had lived since 1947. His film credits include "The Exile," "Letters from an Unknown Wife," "Berlin Express," "Fighting O'Flynn," "Border Incident," "Bagdad," "Bird of Paradise," "Anything Can Happen," "Knock on Wood," "Sincerely Yours," "Desert Sands," and "Nuremberg Trials." His widow survives.

JAMES R. WEBB, 64, Academy-Award-winning screenwriter, died Sept. 27, 1974 in his sleep in Hollywood. His screenplays include "Trapeze," "Apache," "Big Country," "Pork Chop Hill," "Cape Fear," "Cheyenne Autumn," "The Hawaiians," "The Organization," "Phantom of the Rue Morgue," "They Call Me Mr. Tibbs," "Guns for San Sebastian," and his Oscar-winning "How the West Was Won." He leaves his widow, a son and a daughter.

JOHN E. WENGRAF, 77, actor and director, died May 4, 1974 in his Santa Barbara, Ca., home. He was leading man and director of the Vienna State Theatre before coming to the U.S. in 1939. He appeared on Broadway, and his film credits include "Convoy," "Seventh Cross," "Tomorrow Is Forever," "Razor's Edge," "Five Fingers," "Desert Rats," "Oh Men! Oh! Women!," "Judgment at Nuremberg," "The Prize," "Mission to Moscow," and "Ship of Fools." Surviving is his daughter.

MICHAEL WHALEN, 72, singer and actor, died of bronchial pneumonia Apr. 14, 1974 in Woodland Hills, Ca. His film credits include "Song and Dance Man," "Poor Little Rich Girl," "Sing, Baby, Sing," "The Man I Marry," "Time out for Romance," "Island in the Sky," "Time out for Murder," "Ellery Queen," and "Elmer Gantry." Two sisters survive.

CRANE WILBUR, 86, a leading man on Broadway and in silent films, director, and writer, died following a stroke on October 18, 1973 in his home in Toluca Lake, Ca. After his screen debut in 1912, he directed 31 films, and wrote 43, including "The Monster," "Alcatraz Island," "West of Shanghai," "Hell's Kitchen," "Red Stallion," "Adventures of Casanova," "He Walked by Night," "I Was a Communist for the F.B.I.," "House of Wax," "Phenix City Story," "The Bat," "House of Women," and "Yellow Cargo." He played Handsome Harry in the "Perils of Pauline" serial, and became one of the first matinee idols. Surviving is his fourth wife, former actress Lenita Lane.

FRANK WILCOX, 66, stage and screen actor, died Mar. 3, 1974 in his Granada Hills, Ca., home. He divided his time between Hollywood and Broadway, and appeared in over 50 films, including "Fighting 69th," "'Til We Meet Again," "Wagons Roll at Night," "They Died with Their Boots on," "Conflict," "Gentlemen's Agreement," "Miracle of the Bells," "Greatest Show on Earth," "Ruby Gentry," and "A Majority of One." He was also on tv as Mr. Brewster in "Beverly Hillbillies," and Elliot Ness' boss in "The Untouchables." Surviving are his widow and three daughters.

BLANCHE YURKA, 86, Broadway and film actress, died of arteriosclerosis in NYC on June 6, 1974. She was born in Czechoslovakia and was brought to the U.S. as an infant. After singing at the Metropolitan Opera, she became a Broadway star, and made her film debut in 1935 as Mme. DeFarge in "A Tale of Two Cities." Other screen credits include "Queen of the Mob," "City for Conquest," "Escape," "Lady for a Night," "A Night to Remember," "Tonight We Raid Calais," "Song of Bernadette," "Bridge of San Luis Rey," "The Southerner," "13 Rue Madeleine," "The Furies," and "Thunder in the Sun." She married and divorced deceased actor Ian Keith. No reported survivors.

INDEX

239

241

243

249

252

256